A HISTORY OF THE FUTURE

A HISTORY OF THE FUTURE

Donna Goodman

THE MONACELLI PRESS

Copyright © 2008 by Donna Goodman and The Monacelli Press,
a division of Random House, Inc.

Published in the United States by The Monacelli Press,
a division of Random House, Inc., New York.

The Monacelli Press and colophon are trademarks of Random House, Inc.

Library of Congress Cataloging-in-Publication Data
Goodman, Donna.
  A history of the future / Donna Goodman. -- 1st ed.
     p. cm.
  Includes bibliographical references and index.
  ISBN 978-1-58093-207-3 (alk. paper)
  1. Architectural design--Forecasting--History. 2. Architectural design--
Technological innovations--History. 3. CIty planning--Forecasting--History.
I. Title.

  NA2750.G626 2008
  709.03--dc22
                              2008035972

Printed in China

10 9 8 7 6 5 4 3 2 1
First edition

Design by Design Per Se

www.monacellipress.com

CONTENTS

INTRODUCTION

In 1927, film director Fritz Lang dazzled audiences with his extraordinary production of *Metropolis*. This dramatic film portrays a complex vision of a future society burdened by the problems of industrialization. It explores such themes as the impact of mass production on labor, the inhumane environments of the poor, and the chaotic quality of modern cities.

On the night of the premiere in Berlin, art director Rudi Feld transformed the facade of the theater into an "extension of the movie set." Large props and intriguing posters were placed near the entrance of the building. The walls were sprayed silver so they would glow in the dark. A great crowd gathered to witness the spectacular event. It was such a special occasion that the president of the Weimar Republic attended with a group of celebrities.

The production of *Metropolis* was a cinematic landmark, one of the most complex films ever made. Despite its importance, the film received mixed reviews. Some critics objected to its religious references and sentimental ending. Others felt its message was ambiguous. Although the story was critical of mechanization, the breathtaking designs of the city seemed to glorify technology.

The images of the visionary city are indeed inspiring. Designers Erich Kettelhut, Otto Hunte, and Karl Vollbrecht used the newest in architectural ideas to portray the future. Huge glass skyscrapers tower over the urban center, based on the concepts of Mies van der Rohe. Traffic fills the streets as in Le Corbusier's projects. Airplanes fly overhead as shown in *King's Views of New York*. There are also expressionist, constructivist, and art nouveau designs. But the most memorable images in the film are the pulsating machines in the underground realm of the city. Their hypnotic quality demonstrates the remarkable power of industrial forms.

The film also portrayed the social problems of modern cities. Metropolis is depicted as a divided community, separated by class structure. The upper classes live in an exciting environment of modern skyscrapers, lavish apartments, and glamorous nightclubs. They lead decadent, carefree lives, filled with sports, entertainment, and sensual pleasures. The lower classes dwell in gloomy underground structures and work as slaves to the demands of relentless machines. Most aspects of their lives are dominated by standardized systems. They walk in unison, wear identical uniforms, and live in repetitive housing projects. They have no individuality or freedom; they do not even have faces. Their personal expressions only appear at spiritual meetings, where their individual identities are briefly restored.

The giant steam engine
in the film *Metropolis*, 1926.
Director: Fritz Lang.

The film also conveys the chaotic environment of modern cities—the noisy traffic, smoke-filled chimneys, and layer of coal dust on the streets—and expresses the ambivalence that many Europeans felt toward mechanization. The technology debate had begun during the first Industrial Revolution, when cities expanded at an incredible rate. From 1830 to 1900, the population of London grew from two million to four million people. Paris also doubled, expanding from one million to two million residents.

Nineteenth-century architects were challenged by the problems of air pollution, water pollution, traffic congestion, and slum housing. Some became environmentalists or social reformers who tried to improve conditions for the working class. They advocated better housing and safer factories, as well as the development of parks, infrastructure, and cultural facilities. There were also a few utopian designers, who imagined concepts of ideal cities. Although none of the early visionaries could design complete road maps for the future, they laid the foundations for twentieth-century design.

In the twentieth century, the second Industrial Revolution emerged. Powered by electricity, it was a cleaner, more flexible system that supported a series of technological transitions that manifested themselves in what are designated in this book as the automobile age, the space age, the media age, and the information age. Each era revitalized economic conditions, altered cultural patterns, and introduced new cognitive skills. Throughout these innovative years, architecture and planning were also transformed, as powerful new technologies generated controversial new environments.

The most intriguing issue was the design of the "ideal city." In each technological era, there were new urban visions—garden cities, industrial cities, floating cities, walking cities, streamlined cities, cyber-cities, cities in space, and cities under glass. The concepts varied from the mechanized visions of the futurists, modernists, and

The workers' underground city in the film *Metropolis*.

constructivists in the early decades to the critical comments of pop architects, post-modernists, and environmentalists in the closing years of the century.

In the twentieth century, architects and planners also faced profound cultural conflicts. Within the first fifty years, there were the two world wars, revolution in Russia, inflation in Europe, and depression in the United States. After each major struggle, there were shortages in housing, resources, and infrastructure. In most cases, the old design solutions could no longer be utilized—the physical and emotional landscapes had changed too much. New concepts were needed for cultures emerging from difficult circumstances, but even in those difficult periods, technology was a key issue.

In the late twentieth century, the need for a third Industrial Revolution became apparent. The world population had tripled in only sixty years with most of the growth occurring in emerging cities with few resources. For architects and planners, the objective had changed from the goal of creating an ideal city to the challenge of designing a sustainable environment, capable of evolving in an era of constant growth. In response to these issues, architects and designers developed new light-weight structures, recycled products, and renewable energy systems. They also defined the principles of green architecture and planning theory.

Although design history has usually been presented as an evolution of aesthetic theories, in the twentieth century, the dialogue on technology was the driving force. Some designers embraced technology as a major aspect of their work; others were critical of machines and their impact on culture and environment. The debate on technology began during the Renaissance with the invention of the printing press and other basic machines. Prior to that time, the future simply meant the time that came after the present. It did not conjure up images of invention as it does now. After the Renaissance, the idea of "the future" acquired new meaning. It hung in the air like a challenge, waiting to be defined.

9

1.1   The Renaissance

In the country of the blind, the one-eyed man is king.
—Desiderius Erasmus [1]

The Renaissance emerged from one of the darkest periods in history, the fourteenth century, when more than a third of Europe's population died from the Black Plague. This devastating disease, which was spread by soldiers returning from the Crusades, decimated many medieval towns, and was finally conquered through strict rules of quarantine and environmental control.

In the fifteenth century, Europeans had to rebuild their economy, redesign their environment, and revitalize their culture. In addition to the great art and architecture of this innovative era, there were several other developments that helped transform Europe from a medieval culture in decline into a dynamic civilization focused on the future.

The first was the printing press, or the technology of movable type, which was invented in the 1440s by Johann Gutenberg. Prior to the printing press, European society had been dominated by religion with whole towns absorbed in building castles and cathedrals. The average person was illiterate, governed by fear and superstition rather than by logic and analysis. The printing press led to a new period of literacy, in which verbal and analytical skills became more widespread. It also increased trade and commerce through the new availability of printed money, stimulated science and technology as knowledge became accessible to more people and across greater distances, and expanded public education, which helped to establish a larger middle class.

By the sixteenth century, books were being published in numerous fields. Italian cartographers created the first atlas, which included about two hundred maps, and the first books on botany, anatomy, and medicine were produced, as well as volumes on mathematics and technical systems. Important cultural issues were also addressed: the multitalented Vasari wrote the first book on art history, and Alberti and Palladio published books on classical design principles.

The printing press established several basic concepts of modern industrial systems. The design of the press included the use of a system of standardized parts and flexible elements. It also led to the forging of stronger metal alloys to create more durable machines.

Although the benefits of the printing press were obvious from the outset, the invention encountered resistance in its early years. Church authorities feared it would be used to spread scientific theory; aristocrats worried about the danger of political rebellion. Despite efforts at censorship and suppression, this powerful innovation could not be denied.

The second development was the concept of humanism. In the fifteenth century, Italian scholars who were struggling to conceive a new philosophy that would lift Europe out of the Dark Ages found inspiration in the achievements of ancient Greece and Rome. The remarkable accomplishments of classical culture in art, architecture, literature, philosophy, and engineering led them to the idea of a rebirth of classical culture and a new vision of society based on logic, science, and rational principles.

Pieter Breugel the Elder,
*The Building of the Tower of
Babel*, 1563.

The humanists shifted cultural emphasis from a God-centered universe to a society
focused on human achievement. In Italy the Medici circle undertook humanist projects in diverse fields. They collected and restored ancient manuscripts, built an
academy to study Plato, and expanded university courses in science and the humanities. They also introduced classical themes in art and architecture by patronizing
artists like Botticelli and Michelangelo, who worked with accurate perspectives and
proportional systems, and architects such as Alberti and Brunelleschi. The Medici
were in constant conflict with the Church because they encouraged intellectual dialogue over meek acceptance of authority and opposed the ruthless efforts of the
Inquisition to limit scientific research.

A third major development was the discovery of the New World. The daring voy-
ages of Ferdinand Magellan, Amerigo Vespucci, and Christopher Columbus
opened doors to new wealth, new opportunities for growth, and new visions of
government. The explorers of this era traveled to India, China, Africa, and the
Americas and brought back novel products that increased trade and stimulated the
economy. As trade expanded, major cities began to prosper again. Port facilities
throughout Europe were enlarged to handle the growing traffic, and new canals
were created to bring ships to inland cities. Irrigation systems were also constructed to improve the productivity of farms, and industrial production increased with
the development of more efficient manufacturing systems.

The exploration of the New World also led to technical improvements in the meas-
urement of time, space, and geological phenomena. More accurate maps, calendars,
and clocks were developed, which led to a better understanding of astronomy,
mathematics, and geography. The expanding technologies and systems of this era
would lay the foundation for the Industrial Revolution.

Aerial view of Palmanova,
Italy, built 1593–1623.

The leading innovators of the Renaissance were recognized for their achievements, but they also paid a high price for their unconventional ideas. Johann Gutenberg had financial problems throughout his career. The costly process of refining the printing press left him bankrupt, and he sold the press to his lawyer, Johann Fust, who implemented the technology. The Medici faced a series of political reversals. After Lorenzo de' Medici's death, most members of the family were banished from Florence, but they eventually returned and reestablished their power.

Columbus had an even bleaker experience. He was named governor of a Spanish colony as a reward for the wealth he had generated, but while he was exploring an adjacent territory, corruption spread throughout the colony and a new governor was sent to replace him. When Columbus finally returned from his venture, he was arrested and sent back to Europe in chains. The Spanish monarchs later pardoned him, but he died in poverty—alone, and unappreciated by his contemporaries.

These three developments—an important new technology, an invigorating philosophical theory, and a concept of frontier—transformed medieval society into a more progressive culture. These discoveries also inspired several artists, architects, and philosophers to create visionary concepts: the architects Filarete, Francesco di Georgio Martini, and Vincenzo Scamozzi rendered ideal city plans based on logical geometrical arrangements. Several military towns, such as Palmanova, Italy, were established on rational planning concepts, which would later become part of the basic principles of modern town planning.

The most influential visionaries of this era were Sir Thomas More and Leonardo da Vinci. The abstract models introduced in their work defined two major directions in conceptual design. Sir Thomas More's novel *Utopia* introduced a social/ environmental philosophy and established the theme of the creation of an ideal society. His communal theory inspired the socialist utopian movement and the work of Marx and Engels. More's novel also served as a basis for the literary genre of utopian/dystopian fiction.

Leonardo da Vinci's notebooks introduced a scientific/technological approach to visionary design. His remarkable sketches expanded the boundaries of artistic theory to include conceptual proposals and inventions and helped to establish the genre of visionary design and the practice of developing new ideas, whether or not they could be realized. In subsequent centuries, science and technology became a driving force in avant-garde architecture and planning theory.

1.2 Leonardo da Vinci	Leonardo da Vinci is known as a great painter, but he completed only about twenty-five works. Most of his life was spent creating conceptual designs. Some historians claim he filled over 13,000 pages of notebooks, although only about 7,000 pages have been preserved. His theoretical inventions include the first bicycle, helicopter, and automated car, as well as important insights in physics, medicine, geology, and dozens of other subjects. He also developed new concepts for industry, infrastructure, and urban planning, addressing some of the problems of his age.[2]

Leonardo was born in the town of Vinci, about fifty miles from Florence. He was the illegitimate son of a prominent notary, who adopted him, and he was raised on the family farm, which probably inspired his interest in nature and basic machines. The circumstances of his birth made it impossible for him to attend a university or join a prestigious guild, but the profession of artist was open to him. Art was considered a lower-class trade, since artists worked with their hands.

Around 1465, his father apprenticed him to Andrea del Verrocchio, the leading artist in Florence, who taught him drawing, painting, sculpture, and related skills. Since Verrocchio was part of the Medici circle, the boy was also exposed to theories of perspective, mathematics, and humanism. He was particularly inspired by the Renaissance idea of *uomo universale*, the universal man, which was first personified by the architect Alberti.[3]

In 1481, Leonardo wrote a letter to the Duke of Milan, whom he knew was looking for artists, architects, and engineers. He presented himself as an expert in all these fields, especially military engineering, creating a list of conceptual war machines that he knew would interest the duke. In conclusion, he mentioned that he could also create paintings, sculpture, and architecture, "as well as any man, whoever he may be." The duke probably recognized that he had no experience in weapons design, but he still invited him to come to Milan to work as a court artist. In the first years, he arranged for Leonardo to plan banquets, paint portraits, and assist other artists. Finally, through the success of his fresco *The Last Supper*, Leonardo achieved recognition and was able to move on to other projects. He began with water systems. He created a plumbing system for the castle, supervised improvements of Milan's canals and waterways, and proposed methods for upgrading the irrigation systems and draining the swamps. He studied urban planning and created a concept for building service roads below the main streets, which was similar to the idea of modern subways.

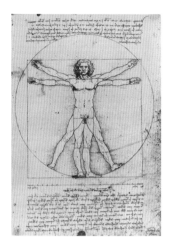

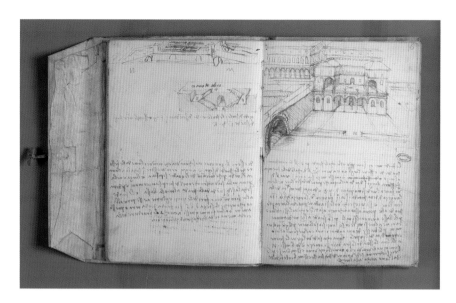

Leonardo da Vinci, *Study of the Proportions of the Human Figure*, after Vitruvius, c.1490.

Leonardo da Vinci, Design of a multi-leveled town, including a nobleman's house, 1488.

14

In 1499, when the French conquered Milan, Leonardo was forced to seek another patron. For several years, he worked for the notorious Cesare Borgia, creating maps and designing weapons and fortification systems, but none of his concepts were ever implemented and he subsequently worked for Giuliano de' Medici on architecture and engineering projects. Eventually he moved to France, where François I named him official painter, engineer, and architect of France. The young king also bought several of his best paintings, which still hang in the Louvre. Leonardo died four years later and bequeathed his notebooks to his assistant, Francesco Melzi, hoping they would be published.

Leonardo was often criticized for his unpredictable work process and for leaving so many projects unrealized. His great horse sculpture was never finished, none of his major inventions were ever built, and his notebooks remained unpublished for several hundred years. But there were two things he did complete within his life-time: a portrait of a universal man and a modern process for exploring ideas through conceptual designs and inventions.

Leonardo was modern in many ways. His willingness to tackle problems without a sponsor helped establish the idea that artists could propose their own work or do "art for its own sake," a twentieth-century notion. His collaborations with doctors and scientists created new roles for artists. Even his drawing style provided new techniques. His images show multiple views of objects, explore relationships of parts and whole, and integrate plans with three-dimensional sketches. He also combined text and images, which give his notebooks a modern graphic quality.

1.3   Sir Thomas More

Sir Thomas More's early education focused on religion. As a boy, he served as a page to an archbishop and studied at St. Anthony's School. He then went to Oxford and read philosophy with the Dutch scholar and humanist Erasmus. Inspired by these rational theories, he considered a career in academia or the Church, but his father, who was a prominent judge, wanted him to study law. He became a lawyer and entered Parliament, rising to high office through a relationship with Henry VIII

The Island of Utopia, woodcut on the title page of the first edition of Sir Thomas More's book *Libellus vere aurens nec minus salutaris quam festivus de optimo reipublicae statu, deque nova insula utopia*, Leuven, 1516.

COLOR BY KATRIN IDRIS 2003

and eventually becoming Lord Chancellor of England. He was known for his high moral character and passion for the truth.

Throughout his political career, More wrote numerous essays on philosophy and religion. In 1516, he published the novel *Utopia*, the first major concept of an ideal society since Plato's *Republic*. *Utopia* was presented through a fictional story, arranged in two parts. The first part contained a critique of British culture; the second part, an introduction to his philosophical theories.

His conceptual community is located on a fictional island somewhere in the New World. It is divided into fifty-four identical city-states, each surrounded by a twelve-mile zone of farmland. The plans of the city-states are similar to medieval town plans, each protected by a wall and moat. Within the community, there are logical subdivisions for various sections of the city. Each family is given a three-story building with a garden for growing vegetables.

More was adamantly opposed to the inequities of feudalism and the extreme poverty of the lower classes. His ideal society is a communist community, enhanced by Christian values. *Utopia* does not allow ownership of private property or any kind of accumulated wealth. In fact, the exchange of money is illegal there. Gold is used to make chamber pots. [4]

15

The governmental system is a highly organized, representative democracy. Each group of families elect a *phylarch*, or a representative, who serves in a national council. The national council is responsible for maintaining urban systems, such as water and sanitation. They also arrange programs for education and scientific research, and elect the prince or the ruler.

The Utopian lifestyle differs from British society of More's time. Women are given the same education as men and have similar occupations. No one works more than six hours a day, and the remaining hours are devoted to gardening and intellectual pursuits. The main weakness in the scheme is its authoritarian quality. Utopia is a homogenous culture, controlled by strict rules. All the citizens wear uniforms, have similar educations, and work at a craft or a trade.

Although More's vision provided little individual freedom, it was far more humane than the existing system under Henry VIII. The book probably survived censorship only because it was originally published in Latin and may not have been read by the authorities. More's strict moral character eventually led to trouble. He was executed in 1535 for refusing to sign the Act of Succession, which endorsed the Church of England and the king's marriage to Anne Boleyn. After his execution, many considered him a martyr. In 1935, four hundred years later, he was canonized a saint in the Catholic Church for refusing to compromise his values.

1.4   The Enlightenment

I have a violent aversion to the social classes that dominate others . . . I hate the great . . . I hate their position, their harshness, their prejudices, their vices.
—Jean-Jacques Rousseau [5]

In the seventeenth century, the seeds planted in the Renaissance began to bear fruit with the publication of *Principia*, Sir Isaac Newton's groundbreaking book that introduced important insights in physics and mathematics and inspired a new philosophical movement now known as the Age of Enlightenment or the Age of Reason. The philosophers of this era posited rational visions of the future based on humanist theories. Their concepts were optimistic, as they believed in the idea of "progress" through a universal code of morality.

But progress did not come easily. The seventeenth and eighteenth centuries were also an era of absolute monarchs who maintained luxurious courts at the expense of the lower classes. This exploitation was especially cruel in France, where the peasants lived in mud huts and often went barefoot in the summer. A traveler, passing through a French town, wrote in a letter, "while the post-horses are changed, the whole town comes out to beg, with such miserable starved faces, and thin tattered clothes, they need no other eloquence to describe the wretchedness of their condition." [6]

While the noblemen were enjoying the lavish life at Fontainebleau and Versailles, the peasants were overwhelmed. They were drafted for unjustified wars, tortured for petty violations, and left to starve in times of famine. They were even exploited by the system of taxation. The aristocrats paid only 5 percent of their income to the government, while the poor had to hand over a third of their meager earnings to the combined coffers of the church, landlord, and political authorities. [7]

The philosophers of this era held fierce debates on government, economic, and political reform. In 1690, the English philosopher John Locke introduced the concept of natural laws. He claimed that all individuals were by nature equal, independent, and entitled to no harm in their "life, health, liberty, or possessions." He also believed that human nature was inherently good, and if society were able to develop naturally, it would create a culture of cooperation rather than corruption.

Locke's theories inspired the American humanists, among them Thomas Jefferson and John Adams, who would later apply his principles in the United States Constitution. His positive view of human nature also influenced French philosophers, such as Morelly, Diderot, and Montesquieu, who wrote on eighteenth-century utopian visions. They all located their imaginary societies in the New World, which was virgin territory, untainted by European traditions.

Morelly's novel *Code de la Nature* was based on More's *Utopia*. It presents a conceptual tribe of Native Americans who maintain a communal way of life. Their ruler is, ironically, a communist king. Diderot's vision is set in a lush island in Tahiti, but his natives are not communists. They own private property and accumulate personal wealth. Montesquieu's utopia presents a group of families who are so civilized that they no longer need laws.

In the 1760s, Jean-Jacques Rousseau also wrote essays on political reform. He advocated a return to nature and a rejection of the materialistic world. In *The Social Contract*, he claims that government requires the "consent of the people." In *Emile*, he created a new educational theory that contrasted the innocence of the state of nature with the corruption of the "civilized world."

Rousseau's love of nature and respect for rural values became a powerful theme in art and culture. It inspired Romantic poets like Ralph Waldo Emerson and Johann Wolfgang von Goethe, as well as political revolutionaries like Jefferson and Maximilien Robespierre. His vision also engendered a popular trend of aristocrats giving picnics dressed like peasants and cultivating romantic gardens, which lasted for over a century. They seemed oblivious to the political ideals beneath the fashion. Rousseau was later exiled from France, but his concept of nature inspired many generations of designers and planners.

Throughout this complex era, architects participated in the debate. Some developed critical images of the injustices of feudalism and the oppressive systems of the Industrial Revolution. Others were influenced by Rousseau's belief in nature and envisioned conceptual towns in rural areas. A few were inspired by the philosophy of the Enlightenment and created visual symbols of an ideal society or drew images that expressed the goals of the French Revolution.

1.5 Giovanni Battista Piranesi

Giovanni Battista Piranesi was a gifted draftsman and artist, who produced many conceptual drawings. He came from a family of builders: his father was a stonemason, who became a master builder; his uncle was an engineer, who worked on the water systems of Venice. Giovanni chose to study printmaking and architectural rendering. He was briefly apprenticed to Giuseppe Vasi in Rome, where he learned the techniques of etching and architectural rendering.

Giovanni Battista Piranesi,
Le Carceri. Eighth Plate,
1760.

After completing his apprenticeship, Piranesi earned a living by making printed images of Rome, which he sold to tourists. In his series *Antichità Romane*, he created powerful drawings of imaginary Roman ruins filled with objects of antiquity arranged in dramatic compositions that convey the chaos and complexity of ancient Rome. Another series, *Gruppo di Scale*, portrays the elegance of uncluttered classical space.

Piranesi was also a humanist scholar who advocated a Roman view of history. In an early essay, he tried to prove that Roman architecture and engineering were based on Etruscan rather than Greek structures. His later work was more eclectic. In another essay, he insisted that artists should be free to mix references from all cultures, and his own work included both Greek and Egyptian concepts. In the twentieth century, his philosophy inspired the eclectic drawings of several postmodernist architects.

Piranesi was very conscious of political issues. In 1745, he began a twenty-year experimental project called *Le Carceri*, a disturbing set of drawings of prisonlike environments that evoked the contemporary sense of cultural anxiety. He called to life fortresslike structures with complex stairways leading nowhere; dangerous machines, which may have been torture devices; and ragged workers, who are trapped inside. The images are enhanced by a dramatic use of light and shadow, distorted perspectives, and mazelike arrangements of space.

Here Piranesi boldly ignored the polite, formal style of the baroque era, creating instead statements of the cruelty that lurked beneath the surface of the still-feudal culture. The public did not appreciate *Le Carceri* when it first appeared, but the drawings later influenced many artists and writers, ranging from Gothic novelists to Romantic poets.[8]

Etienne-Louis Boullée,
Newton's Cenotaph, 1784.

1.6   Etienne-Louis
       Boullée

Throughout these years, two French architects, Etienne-Louis Boullée and Claude-Nicolas Ledoux, also created conceptual projects, but unlike Piranesi's, their work expressed a positive view of society. Boullée's drawings, in particular, had an idealistic quality inspired by the scientific accomplishments of Sir Isaac Newton and the rational philosophy of the Enlightenment.

In his youth, Boullée had wanted to be a painter, but his father had insisted that he study architecture instead. He received classical training from Jacques-François Blondel, a design theorist who focused on mathematics and pure geometrical forms. When he was nineteen years old, Boullée opened his own office and worked as a practicing architect for a few years. He built several mansions, or *hôtels*, for wealthy Parisians but soon found a more compelling direction for his designs.

Boullée joined the architecture faculty of Ecole Nationale des Ponts et Chaussées and began pursuing conceptual projects. His elegant architectural drawings portrayed ideal spaces based on neoclassical principles. He later taught at the Académie d'Architecture and wrote a few essays on design theory. He believed that buildings should speak to emotion as well as reason, and in *Essai sur l'Art*, he expressed the idea that architecture should inspire the "sublime attraction of poetry."

In 1784, he published a series of engravings of conceptual buildings. The most celebrated image is Newton's Cenotaph. The structure is a plain sphere, set against a dramatic sky. His simple Platonic form contains no embellishment; it is free from the baroque details that cluttered most of the buildings of that era. The interior space introduces a subtle consciousness of light within the hollow curves of the sphere. He later worked on other engravings of cenotaphs, one of which he dedicated to Hercules, another to Sparta. These dramatic drawings became symbols of the Age of Reason and the new scientific era. Boullée did not actively participate in the French Revolution since he was over sixty years old when it began, but he supported it through his work. A few of his engravings, such as *The Tower of Babel*, became visual symbols of the newly formed Republic.[9]

Claude-Nicolas Ledoux,
*Perspective View of the Town
of Chaux*, 1804.

Vue perspective de la Ville de Chaux

1.7   Claude-Nicolas
Ledoux

Unlike most conceptualists Ledoux began his career as a practicing architect. He excelled at developing authoritarian plans that appealed to the aristocracy and created several structures for Louis XV and his mistress, Madame du Barry, whose patronage provided him with the wealth and status of the royal circle. In 1771, the king asked him to develop a plan for the salt manufacturing town of Chaux. Ledoux designed several versions of the town plan—one was based on a grid and another on a radial organization—but both are arranged like a modern prison with the director's office in the center of a symmetrical form.

Although his designs favor traditional concepts of authority, they also contain some new ideas. Ledoux proposed neoclassical buildings for the industrial town, which must have surprised the nobility. He also tried to create community facilities for the workers. Both concepts were rejected. The built plan featured elegant stone buildings with no amenities for the workers and their families.

In the 1780s, Ledoux received a large royal commission to build tollgates around the perimeter of Paris. His extensive master plan included a city wall, tollgates, and additional facilities, such as taverns for incoming visitors and new systems for the trade regulation and security. The master plan was rejected, but the government constructed forty-five tollgates based on his designs. During the Revolution, these were regarded as symbols of the monarchy. Some were torn down; others were manned with the revolutionaries who took control of the city. In 1793, Ledoux was imprisoned in the Bastille because of his association with the royal family. He was released a year later, but his career as an architect had ended. His final years were spent developing a book of his projects.[10]

In the last years of his life, Ledoux revised the plans of the town of Chaux and added community spaces for the workers. They include a House of Union, a House of Passion, and a House of Education. The final version also presents a utopian concept of a unified culture that embodies a unique social and economic system. His conceptual design was eventually published and became a valuable historical document. It provided a clear concept of an eighteenth-century town plan and showed how planning could become an important new direction in visionary design.

1.8 Thomas Jefferson

Throughout this era, the principles of the Enlightenment became increasingly influential in America. In 1745, an American Philosophical Society was established in Philadelphia, which included Benjamin Franklin, Dr. Benjamin Rush, Thomas Jefferson, and other colonial leaders, who met to discuss politics, philosophy, science, and engineering. All of these enterprising men had multiple interests. They believed in the humanist concept of the universal man. Franklin was both a statesman and an inventor. Rush was a doctor and an environmentalist although the term had yet to be coined. He was ostracized for insisting that yellow fever was caused by poor sanitation. Jefferson was trained in philosophy and law, but he was also deeply interested in farming, engineering, and architecture.

In 1770, *The Virginian Gazette* reported, "the house of Thomas Jefferson, Esq . . . was burnt to the ground, together with all of his furniture, books, papers, etc." Jefferson was devastated by the loss of his books and papers, but had no regrets about the destruction of the buildings. He disliked the house he had inherited from his family, and he may have even been relieved, for the fire left him free to create a new structure according to his own design.[11] He began by searching for an architectural style that symbolized American values. It had to express democracy and scientific theory, and it also had to be practical for plantation life. Most importantly, it had to be free of all British concepts, especially references to King George.

The only style that appealed to him was neoclassicism, which he discovered by reading Palladio. For Jefferson, architecture was a philosophical medium. In building a house, he would be establishing a way of life. The house would be real, but it would also be a metaphor for his values—expressing his belief in a civilized world. Part of his interest in Palladio lay in the fact that his work was inspired by humanism and the democratic culture of ancient Greece.

Jefferson called his house Monticello, Italian for "little mountain," as it was built on a hill. The design was based on Renaissance principles of symmetry and axis and French neoclassical concepts, but the house also had an American quality. It was made of red brick, built close to the ground, and had few ornamental details. The plan of the building had a duality that reflected both sides of his intellect. The west side had a formal entrance, appropriate for a statesman; the east side opened to an informal courtyard with service areas for a working plantation.

Throughout Jefferson's life, he and Alexander Hamilton debated concepts of the ideal environment for a democratic culture. Hamilton favored a strong central government with an emphasis on large cities. Jefferson championed the notion of an agrarian society of small towns, controlled more by state and local authorities. The strains of this debate would continue into the twentieth century through the architectural work of Le Corbusier, who preferred cities, and Frank Lloyd Wright, who believed in rural towns.

Thomas Jefferson, Rotunda
of the University of Virginia,
Charlottesville, Virginia.

Jefferson was also committed to the concept of the grid, which he considered a
democratic form. In 1803, as president, he purchased the Louisiana Territory, which
doubled the size of the United States. He acquired over a million square miles of
land from Napoleon at a price of fifteen million dollars. To encourage the partici-
pation of new settlers, the government then created the National Land Ordinance,
a system that divided the land into Jefferson's beloved grid. Each section comprised
640 acres. Then the sections were subdivided into 160-acre farms and sold for two
dollars an acre.

The major problem with this system was that some tracts of land were more valuable
than others. Despite the problems arising from the differences, the grid provided
an efficient way to manage land expansion. Jefferson's national grid also influenced
the planning of many American cities, which were also built on a gridiron pattern.
Historian Frederick Jackson Turner later credited the accessibility of inexpensive
land as a major factor in the growth of the United States. [12]

1.9 The Industrial
     Revolution

*The splendors of this age outshine all other recorded ages. In my lifetime I have seen
wrought five miracles—namely, 1. the Steamboat; 2. the Railroad; 3. the Electric
Telegraph; 4. the application of the spectroscope to Astronomy; 5. the Photograph.*
—Ralph Waldo Emerson [13]

The eighteenth century was not only a period of political revolution; it was also an
era of industrial revolution as the traditions of manual labor were slowly replaced
by new systems of machine production. The Industrial Revolution began in England,
then affected America, and eventually reached continental Europe. Several technologies played a key role in the early stages. In 1709, Abraham Darby, an iron
manufacturer, developed a method for using coal, in the form of coke, for power.

He then applied this system to an iron-smelting process. The increased heat produced by coke created a more durable metal, which would later lead to steel production. Coke also was an inexpensive, reliable source of energy. The system was so successful that other manufacturers soon used coke in their factories. Unfortunately, the burning of coke cast a dark shadow over urban areas. It left a thick layer of dust on the surfaces of homes, schools, and community buildings. The use of coke caused lung problems like asthma, pleurisy, and tuberculosis. It also ruined the lives of the young men who were forced to spend most of their waking hours shoveling coal into furnaces. [14]

A few decades later, machines built by Thomas Savery and Thomas Newcomen led to the first working steam engine. This was improved on by James Watt in 1765, and became a driving force in industrial expansion. Coal-fired steam engines were also noisy, dirty, and inefficient systems, but they soon powered ships, trains, factories, and heating systems.

As each new system was created, the printing press reported it to an enthusiastic public. In 1704, the first technical encyclopedia appeared. It presented more than 8,000 technologies and became a key reference for engineers. The humanist scholars Denis Diderot and Jean d'Alembert later published a more complete encyclopedia, including cultural topics as well as technology and science.

During this era, the British government introduced incentives to encourage mechanization. Parliament established the right to patent an invention for fourteen years, which created a strong profit motive. New financial systems were also developed to make lending and investing more accessible. Spurred on by cultural approval, British entrepreneurs extended trade routes and expanded the boundaries of the Empire. Ambitious traders brought tea from China, spices from India, and raw materials from the American colonies. The British government also created new laws that ensured that the colonies would be both producers of raw materials and consumers of British goods.

In 1776, the same year as the Declaration of Independence, the British economist Adam Smith published *An Inquiry into the Nature and Causes of The Wealth of Nations*. This landmark book defined the concepts of the new capitalist system. It stressed the importance of free trade and pursuit of personal wealth as key aspects of the emerging economy, and it also helped to establish capitalism in England and the acceptance of laissez-faire principles.

The excitement about industry was not universal. The men, women, and children who toiled in the factories must have cursed the legacy of machines. They were often forced to work seven days a week, thirteen hours a day, for a trifling remuneration. A few American writers studied the impact of industry on women and children. A journalist at *Cosmopolitan* claimed the job of sewing in a sweatshop was, "the most grinding oppression that can be practiced on a woman." In *Harper's*, another writer described the effect of "in home" industries on children, who spent their days stripping tobacco leaves. "Their eyes are dead, a stupor overcomes them, their nerves are unsettled and their lungs . . . diseased." [15]

It was no coincidence that movements like socialism, communism, and anarchism emerged in that era, nor was it any surprise that a series of environmental

Spindle boy in Georgia
cotton mill.

movements also formed as an outcry against the perils of machines. The first environmentalists were also social reformers who attacked labor problems, such as the
chemical hazards of manufacturing and the dangerous conditions of factories.
They also addressed urban problems, such as air pollution, water pollution, traffic
congestion, and the deplorable quality of slum housing.

1.10 Robert Owen

Throughout the eighteenth century, outraged workers initiated strikes, riots, and
protests, but in 1799, the British Parliament passed a law making it illegal to challenge
an owner's policies. A worker could be imprisoned if he tried to raise wages, reduce
the length of shifts, or improve conditions in factories. The situation was dismal.
However, in 1800, one employer testified before Parliament on labor reform. Robert
Owen, a successful textile manufacturer, described conditions at a mill. He focused
on the issue of child labor, which was disturbing to British leaders: [16]

> I found that there were 500 children, who had been taken from poor-houses . . .
> generally from the age of five and six, to seven to eight. The hours at that time
> were thirteen. Although these children were well fed their limbs were very
> generally deformed, their growth was stunted, and although one of the best
> schoolmasters was engaged to instruct these children regularly every night, in
> general they made very slow progress. [17]

Owen later bought the mill and moved his company to its location in New Lanark,
Scotland. There, he developed a model town for his workers. He also improved
working conditions at the mill, and naturally his most famous reforms concerned
child labor. He increased the age of employment to ten and reduced the schedule to
ten hours a day. He also provided a basic education for the children. His revisions
were considered generous at the time and were widely publicized.

Although many politicians supported his concepts, other factory owners and political conservatives were opposed to them. One of his greatest critics was the economist Thomas Malthus who claimed that if the poor were given better treatment,

they would have more children and thus increase the problem of overpopulation. Malthus's theory, which was published in 1798, stated that the rate of population growth was increasing as never before and predicted it would soon outdistance the world food supply. Although his theory was popular in London for several years, in 1803, the influential economist was forced to modify his views. Increased application of birth control had reduced the birth rate, and better farming techniques had improved the efficiency of agriculture. Malthusian theories were thus disproved, and Owen's philosophy survived its strongest opposition.

Owen was one of several visionaries who were later called "Socialist Utopians." They supported labor reforms, built alternative communities, and improved working environments for the poor. The model town that Owen created around his factory in New Lanark contained parks, housing, schools, and sanitation systems. By modern standards, it was far from perfect, but it was a great improvement over the dark, decaying slums of most industrial cities.

In 1825, Owen inaugurated another community, this time in the United States. He purchased a large tract of land in Indiana and established the town of New Harmony, which housed 1,200 people. There, he established public schools, a free public library, and the first kindergarten in the country. He also provided adult education and created other amenities for workers. The town plan was based on rational principles. Housing was arranged around a large open square. Collective buildings like the school, common dining room, and children's dormitory were placed in the center. New Harmony offered a good standard of living in a healthy environment, but its inhabitants were subject to strict rules and the community failed after only three years.

1.11 The Socialist Utopians

In 1808, the French philosopher Charles Fourier published a concept of a utopian community. He envisioned a town of 1,600 people, living in a large collective building, or *phalanstery*. The structure would have many wings arranged around courtyards. The plan was based on Versailles, a somewhat ironic choice for a socialist society.

25

In Fourier's conceptual town, the workers are shareholders in the farms and industrial ventures, which gives them an incentive to succeed. They are also free to choose their own occupations and recreational activities. He believed that most utopian ideas had failed because they denied human nature and imposed too many restrictions on the residents. Social harmony could only be achieved if people were allowed to follow their own natural passions. He listed twelve types of passions that should be recognized and included them in the community plan.

Fourier never built a community himself, but others did implement his ideas. Brook Farm, a utilitarian community in Massachusetts established in 1841, was based on his concepts. Its members fostered a rich intellectual dialogue through eminent visitors like Horace Greeley and Ralph Waldo Emerson and published a weekly newspaper on utopian ideas.

Jean Godin, a French manufacturer of stoves and heaters, founded an industrial town based on Fourier's concepts near his factory in Guise in the 1840s. The workers' families were housed in a large communal building with a courtyard in the center

Henri Demare, Cartoon of
Jean-Baptiste André Godin,
originally published in *Les
hommes d'aujourd'hui.*

and were permitted to choose their own jobs and leisure activities, based on
Fourier's theories. When Godin died, he bequeathed his factory to the workers,
who continued the community for many years.

In the nineteenth century, the Socialist Utopians were very influential. In the
United States, they created three Owenite towns, seven Fourier phalanxes, and
other related settlements like the Christian communal town of Oneida. Each community had different rules and served as a cultural experiment or prototype. As a
group, the collective towns offered an inventory of alternative systems.

The experimental communities were both admired for their good intentions
and criticized for the failures of their policies. Marx and Engels were opposed to
such schemes, as they saw no reason to write "cookbooks for the kitchens of the
future." They also believed that the workers' autonomy was repressed by the patriarchal systems of the communities. [18] Novelist Emile Zola also rejected utopian
towns. He felt the freedom of ordinary life was restricted in these rural enclaves of
civilization. In his novel *La Terre*, one of the characters cynically remarks, "The
people are going to be forced to be happy in spite of themselves."

1.12 Company Towns

Although there was much skepticism about the idea of planned communities,
a few entrepreneurs decided to develop company towns for workers. In some cases,
the town emerged from the necessity of providing facilities for enterprises in isolated
locations, such as mining operations. Other company towns were the result of an
employer's desire to improve the life of his workers.

Anonymous, *Port Sunlight,*
Works & Village, 1905.

The most famous corporate town in America was Pullman City, built by George
Pullman in 1864 for his railroad car workers in the Chicago area. The community
had parks, schools, a library, and a theater. There was also a large shopping arcade,
based on the Crystal Palace. The infrastructure of the town was impressive. All of
the houses were equipped with running water and sewage systems. Pullman proudly
publicized the plan by exhibiting models at two world's fairs. Despite the quality
of the facilities, the community failed because of Pullman's authoritarian attitude,
which prevented the employees from having private lives.[19]

In 1879, George Cadbury, an enlightened chocolate manufacturer, built a
community for his workers in England. It was a charming village, based on an
organic plan of curving streets, rustic cottages, and large parks. It also had a swimming pool, a gymnasium, and gardens to encourage healthy activities. Unlike
Pullman, Cadbury invited an equal number of outsiders to live in the town, who
established independent businesses that helped the community to grow in a more
natural fashion.[20]

From the 1870s to 1890s, Alfred Krupp, a manufacturer of steel products, created
several residential communities for his employees in Essen, Germany. These towns
were based on picturesque medieval villages with rich landscapes that appealed to
his workers. Unlike most industrialists of his era, he did not impose an ideological
system on his workers or try to limit their activities.

In 1888, soap manufacturer William Lever established the town of Port Sunlight
for his employees. Lever was a social reformer and took great pride in the design in
which neighborhoods were built around a quadrangle or "central park." The main
streets were lined with fireproof brick buildings and were wide enough for a few
horsedrawn vehicles to pass; pedestrians used quiet treelined paths. King Leopold II

of Belgium was so impressed with Port Sunlight, he built similar towns for his workers in the Congo.[21]

In spite of these successes, the practice of creating company towns was generally abandoned in the late nineteenth century, with the exception of towns related to construction of infrastructure or military projects. Most companies chose to build factories near existing cities and contribute to the local communities, rather than own the whole town. They donated parks, gymnasiums, daycare centers, health clinics, and educational programs, but did not get involved with housing or infrastructure. As private industry withdrew, the challenge of building water, power, and transportation systems fell on local government. Although industries depended on these services and supported them through taxes, they did not have to provide them. Urban authorities also faced the problem of increasing levels of pollution and environmental decay.

1.13 Urban Planning and Infrastructure

The squalor of the industrial city was not exactly a new thing, but the scale and intensity of it was: the roar of furnaces, the clank of machinery, the shrill steam whistles, the speed of locomotives, the coal smoke and the soot that fell like black snow everywhere, the frightening new size of new buildings, and the mushrooming population, which strained the physical boundaries of cities everywhere.
—James Howard Kunstler[22]

In the nineteenth century, most urban areas were plagued by environmental problems. Air pollution was a major issue. Cities had a horrible stench, mixing the smoke of coal-fired factories with the smell of hundreds of thousands of horses, and the toxic fumes of substances like kerosene, sulfur, and ammonia. Water pollution was another issue. In most cities, residential wastes were thrown directly into the streets, which ruined local wells. Rivers and streams were also contaminated with industrial chemicals. As a result of these practices, there were frequent outbreaks of diphtheria, typhoid, and smallpox.

To address these problems, cities invested in water and sanitation systems, built parks, and established zoning laws to separate industrial areas from residential neighborhoods. In London, where industrial development was most intense, public officials made constant improvements in the infrastructure. As early as 1762, the Westminster section of London had systems for street cleaning and trash collection. An underground sewerage system also improved public health. Other neighborhoods followed this lead, but they were unable to address the most difficult problem: the issue of traffic congestion.

As industrial production grew, the number of horses, carriages, and delivery carts also increased. It sometimes took hours to traverse the city. In response, urban authorities created several new systems to relieve traffic congestion. Street numbers were assigned to make deliveries more efficient. Maps were made available to help travelers find their way. Highways reduced the travel time between farms and cities. Canals allowed for the delivery of heavy freight. But the most important innovation of the era would be the railroad.

Drawing of an elevated train
in Franklin Square, 1878.

1.14 The Victorian Engineers

The concept of the railroad emerged in sixteenth-century German operations. Individual cars were filled with heavy materials and moved along iron rails to delivery points. The development of stronger metals, better steam engines, and greater access to coal led to broader applications of the concept. In 1808, railroad cars were transformed into comfortable vehicles for passengers, and a steam engine was installed in the lead car to create a locomotive.

The first experimental passenger train was a small circular track that carried people around the city of London. The concept was soon expanded into a network of lines. Although the early trains were a popular form of travel, they caused severe environmental damage. Large parcels of land were absorbed in the stations and yards, causing holes in the urban fabric. Factories were clustered along railroad lines, causing concentrated pockets of pollution. Neighborhoods were cut in half to make way for the trains, which created poor areas on the "wrong side of the tracks."

But there were myriad advantages. Food could be delivered from the farms to the cities in a matter of days; mail moved more swiftly than ever before; and regional trade suddenly expanded. No other system moved people more quickly, or freight more efficiently, than trains.

Throughout the nineteenth century, engineers looked for ways to improve the relationship of the train to the city. They tried overhead systems, which only exacerbated the problem. They later began creating tunnels, which reduced the impact

29

of the railroad on urban communities by bringing trains into the center without disturbing the streets above and reduced the amount of noise, vibrations, and pollution. The engineers of this era also developed the concept of the train station as a major urban center. These handsome buildings became facilities for buying tickets, finding information, dining, shopping, and preparing for travel and led to a new type of structure made of iron and glass. These lightweight prefabricated structures, which emerged from the market at the Galerie d'Orléans and the greenhouse at Kew Gardens, became train sheds, sheltering passengers boarding or disembarking from trains. These dramatic structures integrated industrial materials with neoclassical forms. The waiting areas of the linear platforms were supported by a continuous line of columns and arches. The roof structure was often a huge arch that integrated skeletal ironwork with glass panels. The large areas of glass provided an abundance of natural light and as well as an indoor/outdoor space that was ideal to its purpose. The iron and glass concept of these structures would later be applied to other types of buildings, such as marketplaces and exhibition halls like the Crystal Palace.

1.15 Baron Georges Haussmann

In the early nineteenth century, Paris was a medieval city suffering from industrial pollution, congested street patterns, and rat-infested slums. The old neighborhoods were overcrowded, and many buildings were in disrepair. The decayed quality of the city led to many protests.

In 1848, Karl Marx and Friedrich Engels published *The Communist Manifesto*, a powerful book outlining a new cultural vision, urging labor to unite, overthrow the bourgeoisie, and build a new society based on communist theories. That same year, a group of workers, including Marx himself, rebelled against the authorities and briefly overran the government of Paris. But the Paris Commune, as it was called, barely had time to establish a new regime. They were defeated a few months later by the army of Napoleon III, who quickly sought to consolidate his authority. His friend Baron Georges Haussmann convinced him that the development of a modern urban plan would provide better control of the population and would also solve some of the environmental problems that afflicted the city.

In 1853, Napoleon III arranged for Baron Haussmann to rebuild large areas of Paris. His master plan was based on a baroque system of wide boulevards with symmetrical lines of axis, enhanced by neoclassical buildings and formal parks. The major avenues would meet in traffic circles, arranged in a radial pattern. Haussmann also built a new water supply and sanitation system. The full implementation of his plan took seventeen years.

Some of his reforms were inspired by the utopian novel *Travels in Icaria*, written by Etienne Cabet. The novel portrays a visionary city that is designed to provide a healthy environment. The streets are washed regularly; the water supply is carefully monitored; and zoning systems are introduced that separate industrial areas from residential streets. [23]

In developing his vision of a modern city, Haussmann also eliminated medieval neighborhoods like Ile de la Cité, where activists met to discuss ideas. Opposition came from urban planners who advocated the preservation of historical communities and picturesque designs, instead of geometrical systems, and accused him of

Aerial view of the Arc de Triomphe, built in 1836, and *rondpoint*, created during Baron Haussmann's rebuilding of Paris, 1853–69.

catering to the emperor. Haussmann ignored the criticism and developed his own concept. His ambitious reconstruction of Paris improved traffic flow, provided clean water and sanitation systems, and established a series of major urban centers, based on a radial street plan. It also created impressive boulevards that appealed to the conservative residents of the city. In the twentieth century, however, when traffic reached unexpected levels, many Parisians regretted his use of a radial plan, instead of a grid.

1.16 Frederick Law Olmsted

In 1850, New York reformers began to lobby for a public park. They convinced politicians that a park would not only serve the poor; it would also increase the real estate values in neighborhoods around the park. This argument appealed to the wealthy landowners in the midtown area, so the park proposal was approved and a site of 840 acres was designated in mid-Manhattan.

Frederick Law Olmsted and Calvert Vaux won the competition for the design of the park with the Greensward Plan, a proposal for a romantic natural landscape inspired by Rousseau, which broke away from the rigid geometry of the New York City grid, and an innovative circulation system that segregated pedestrian, equestrian, and vehicular traffic and suppressed the transverse roads.

The construction of Central Park was extremely difficult, extending over a twenty-year period. The land was filled with shantytowns, swamps, and herds of wild animals; there were also several groups of homeless people. Olmsted and Vaux methodically emptied the site, drained the swamps, and created a handsome, organic plan featuring curving paths, undulating ponds, and clusters of trees that framed picturesque views. This was the first major park ever built in the United States and an important model for the future.

After Central Park was completed, Olmsted designed parks and college campuses throughout the United States. His projects included plans for the World's Columbian Exposition in Chicago and for the Chicago suburb of Riverside, which became a

Aerial view of Central Park,
New York, begun 1857.

model town. In Riverside, he planted thousands of trees along curving residential
streets and lined the railroad tracks with trees to reduce noise and pollution. His
design emphasized nature and relaxation rather than speed and efficiency and provided varied views and picturesque intersections instead of standardized blocks.

1.17 Nineteenth-Century
Trade Expositions

*We are living in a most remarkable period of transition, laboring forcefully toward that
great aim indicated everywhere by history; the union of the human race ... Gentlemen, the
exhibition of 1851 shall give a vivid picture of the stage at which humanity has arrived.*
—Prince Albert[24]

The idea of a trade fair began in the Greek agora and the Roman forum as annual
religious festivals and markets where traveling merchants sold their goods. These
activities were part of the definition of an early city. The fair continued in the
medieval era as an event that provided opportunities to buy special foods,
clothing, and handcrafted products, but in the seventeenth and eighteenth centuries, the popularity of fairs diminished as permanent markets were established
in enclosed buildings.

In the nineteenth century, at the peak of the Industrial Revolution, when innovative
companies needed a system for marketing their products, the notion of the fair
was revived as an international exhibition of products, technical inventions, and
intriguing designs. The trade exposition was also considered a way to improve
political relationships, stimulate global exchange, and support technological development. It became a symbolic ritual that measured the level of scientific progress as
well as the architectural sophistication of an era and provided an opportunity to
showcase the lifestyle of the leading cities that produced the fairs.

1.18 The Crystal Palace

The first world's fair was held in London in 1851, and its success established an ongoing tradition of similar events. The public excitement over the vast range of products later led to the development of department stores and specialized trade shows that focused on products in a given field. The first department store was Bon Marché, which opened in Paris in 1869. It was followed by Wanamaker's and Macy's in the United States and Selfridges in London. [25]

In 1850, England had the largest manufacturing companies in the world. In celebration of their industrial success, British leaders proposed the creation of a world's fair, or an international exposition of new products and designs. The planning committee was led by Prince Albert, the husband of Queen Victoria. Although the proposal appealed to the aristocrats and industrial leaders, there was opposition to the plan of holding the fair in Hyde Park, whose great lawns and ancient trees were an important public amenity in the dark industrial environment of London. The proposal had almost been defeated, when Joseph Paxton, a horticulturalist and greenhouse designer, proposed a huge iron and glass building that could house the exhibits and accommodate the crowds without disturbing the landscape and planting in the park.

Known as the Crystal Palace, the building was eight city blocks long and nine stories high. Many consider it to be the first modern building because it introduced the curtain wall, the flat roof, and standardized prefabricated systems. It also unified the classical formality of the past with the minimal technology of the future.

The Great Exhibition of the Works of Industries of All Nations, as the fair was called, contained more than 14,000 exhibits and introduced both new products like Krupp steel and Otis elevators and the emerging medium of photography. Over six million visitors attended the exposition in Hyde Park, where it remained for five months. The Crystal Palace was then moved to Sydenham Hill, where it remained a popular tourist attraction until it was destroyed by fire in 1936. [26] The design became a model for other exhibits and public events and would inspire twentieth-century buildings based on green design.

33

Joseph Paxton, The Crystal Palace, London, 1851.

Eiffel Tower, built for the
World's Fair of 1900.

1.19 The Eiffel Tower

In 1885, the French government decided to hold a world's fair to mark the centennial
of the Revolution. Gustav Eiffel, a prominent engineer, proposed the construction
of a great tower in Paris. At its completion in 1889, Parisians were caught off guard.
Although the plans had been openly discussed for several years, the finished structure had an even more imposing quality than had been expected. It is twice as high
as the Washington Monument, which had previously been the tallest structure in the
world. It contains more than 12,000 individual wrought iron struts and seven million
rivets, each fabricated to carry a specific load. It is a remarkable feat of engineering,
which was fully evident in the design.

Many Parisians toasted the dramatic structure and proclaimed a new era in archi-
tecture, predicting that buildings would be taller and urban landscapes transformed.
The poet Apollinaire called it the "shepherdess of the clouds" and compared it to
Notre Dame and other great structures.

Others protested the huge iron monster. The novelist Victor Hugo was offended by
the intrusion of a strutting industrial colossus in his elegant city. According to leg-
end, Hugo ate lunch everyday in a café beneath the Eiffel Tower because it was the
only place in Paris he could dine without having to look at the arrogant monolith.
But despite his protests, the public grew fond of the tower and adopted it as a cultural
symbol, and the café received so much publicity that it was renamed Victor Hugo
Café, an ironic gesture that permanently linked his name to the structure.

Hugo was opposed to technology in general. He felt that industrialization produced
inferior products and reduced workers to mere extensions of machines. As he stared
at the impregnable tower, he saw the mystery and poetry of medieval architecture
being replaced by cold industrial forms and elegant European cities being polluted

by the relentless growth of industrial neighborhoods. He saw talented craftsmen forced to close their shops, as mass production rendered them obsolete. He blamed the printing press, which began the Industrial Revolution, for the end of civilization, declaring, "architecture is dead, hopelessly dead, killed by the printed word."[27]

1.20 The World's Columbian Exposition and the City Beautiful Movement

The World's Columbian Exposition, held in Chicago in 1893, celebrated the 400th anniversary of the discovery of America by Christopher Columbus, but it had the larger ambition of surpassing the great expositions held in London and Paris. The Chicago firm of Burnham and Root, led by Daniel H. Burnham and John Wellborn Root, and Frederick Law Olmsted were selected to develop the overall plan, but Burnham quickly enlisted other prominent designers, including Richard Morris Hunt, Charles Follen McKim of McKim, Mead & White, Louis Sullivan, and Augustus Saint-Gaudens to garner national support for the concept. The plan was based on a series of water features with the main exhibition buildings, built with a uniform cornice line and designed in a classical vocabulary, arrayed around the Grand Basin. In the rush to complete the buildings before opening day, all were sprayed white, creating the mirage of the White City on Lake Michigan.

Rivaling the Crystal Palace and the Eiffel Tower for structural innovation was the original Ferris Wheel, designed by William Ferris, an engineer from Pennsylvania. The giant wheel, almost 300 feet in diameter, carried 2,000 passengers, and as it rotated up into the air, it provided incomparable views of the fair.

The Beaux-Arts planning and classical idiom of the World's Columbian Exposition gave rise to a new direction in urban planning known as the City Beautiful Movement. Burnham became the chief proponent, working for the McMillan Commission to restore and expand L'Enfant's plan for Washington, D.C., and developing plans for San Francisco and Chicago. There he unveiled an elaborate vision for rebuilding the city by integrating modern technology with neoclassical structures featuring wide boulevards with baroque skyscrapers and templelike buildings.[28]

35

Overview of the World's Columbian Exhibition, Chicago, 1893.

A significant number of voices dissented from this conservative approach. The loudest protest came from Louis Sullivan who wrote, "The damage wrought by the World's Fair will last for a half century from its date, if not longer. It has penetrated deep into the constitution of the American mind, affecting there lesions significant of dementia."[29]

Perhaps the most surprisingly influential building of the World's Columbian Exposition was the Japanese Pavilion, a small teahouse structure based on traditional woodcraft system that had been the only building on the island in the lake behind the Court of Honor. The craft concept of this traditional teahouse would influence the work of Frank Lloyd Wright, a visitor to the fair, and the Greene brothers who later created the California craftsman style of design.

1.21 Tall Buildings

The invention and perfection of the high-speed elevators make vertical travel, that was once tedious and painful, now easy and comfortable; development of steel manufacture has shown the way to safe, rigid, economical constructions rising to a great height; continued growth of population in great cities, consequent congestion of center and rise in value of ground stimulate an increase in number of stories . . . Thus has come about that form of lofty construction called the "modern office building."
—Louis Sullivan [30]

From the 1850s to the 1870s, architect and theorist Eugène Viollet-le-Duc lectured at the Ecole des Beaux-Arts on the importance of expressing truth in architectural style. Although he believed in the continued use of handcrafted details and historical references, he also urged students to create a new architectural language that reflected the "true function" and "true structure" of a building.

Viollet-le-Duc used technology as a source of inspiration. He particularly favored the flying buttresses of the Gothic period that expressed both the religious function and the structure of medieval cathedrals. He was also impressed with new iron and glass train sheds, and the Crystal Palace, which fused modern function and structure. He insisted that the next generation of architects should develop rational systems that unified these two major issues of design. This philosophy had a particularly strong influence on William Le Baron Jenney and Louis Sullivan, both Chicago architects who were among the first to develop the idea of tall buildings.

Two inventions made possible the rise of tall buildings, which emerged in the next few decades. In 1856, the English inventor Henry Bessemer developed a new process for producing inexpensive steel. This system facilitated the creation of bridges, railroads, and other infrastructure in the late nineteenth century. In 1852, Elisha Graves Otis engineered the first passenger elevator safeguarded by a cable system. He introduced his invention at the New York Crystal Palace exhibit in 1854. The first applications were in New York and Chicago, which were growing at an incredible pace. The multistory building allowed these cities to increase density without expanding beyond their existing urban boundaries.

Dankmar Adler and Louis
Sullivan, Guaranty Building,
Buffalo, New York, 1895.

1.22 Louis Sullivan

In developing his own design theory, Sullivan merged the idea of true function and
true structure with the pragmatism of William James, an American philosopher
who advocated a close relationship between theory and practice. These two sources
led to Sullivan's famous credo, "form should be derived from function."

As Chicago was recovering from the great fire of 1873, new office buildings
were being constructed in its business districts by developers who wanted flexible
space that could be rented to a variety of tenants and tall buildings to maximize
their investments. Sullivan became a leading spokesman for the development of
such office buildings, with his partner, Dankmar Adler, engineering the structural
systems. Grids of steel columns provided open plans that could be partitioned to
suit individual tenants. He also used fireproof steel-cage construction to avoid future
catastrophes and developed floating foundations to compensate for the weak soil
conditions in the Chicago area.

Sullivan realized that logical systems of structure were only the first step in a successful architectural expression. In defining the form of these buildings, he used
neoclassicism as a metaphor. He organized the vertical expression of the structure
into three general areas: the ground, midsection, and skyline, divisions based on the
three sections of a column. One of his most famous buildings, the Guaranty
Building in Buffalo, New York, clearly illustrates this principle.[31]

37

38

He also interpreted the facade of a building as a grid of panels. Some panels held
windows; others contained intricate decorative details based on patterns in nature,
which add a rich element of refinement to his buildings. Sullivan's rational system
influenced many architects, including Frank Lloyd Wright, who worked in his
office for many years.

1.23 Harvey Wiley
       Corbett

Corbett, a New York architect, was another important advocate of skyscrapers. In
partnership with Frank J. Helmle, Corbett designed in a neoclassical style based on
the Beaux-Arts tradition, but he also introduced modern theories in his work. He
believed that the new skyscrapers made cities more efficient by establishing a dense
business district and thus reducing the need for transportation. He knew that most
city workers had to commute to their jobs, but he claimed that once they arrived in
the business district, they would move only within a concentrated area of the city.

He also felt that skyscrapers should have multiple uses including housing, stores,
and recreational facilities. In an article on future cities, he wrote, "When a man left
his office, he could take an elevator home." He added that the upper-story residences would be very desirable, because of their access to light and air, and their
dramatic views. [32]

Corbett also explored the idea of the multilevel street. He felt that pedestrians
should be separated from vehicular traffic, and his drawings included elevated sidewalks as well as bridges that linked towering structures. Although Corbett's real

Future New York, "The City
of Skyscrapers."

Future New York "The City of Skyscrapers," New York.

buildings were designed in a traditional Beaux-Arts style, his interest in neoclas-sicism was not reflected in most of his conceptual drawings. In 1913, *Scientific American* published an elegant drawing by Corbett presenting a section through a tall urban building that contained overhead bridges, multilevel sidewalks, and intriguing skyline designs. It also showed how subways and underground facili-ties could be integrated in vertical structures.

1.24 The Debate on
Skyscrapers

Some urban leaders actively opposed skyscrapers. They felt the towering structures created traffic jams, cast giant shadows on the narrow streets below, and required large amounts of power and water, which placed a burden on public resources. Major Henry Curran, a resident of Chicago, declared, "Is it good sense not to have a dollar for any other city need, to pour it all into more traffic facilities to take care of a coagulated bunch of skyscrapers?" [33]

Other critics had aesthetic objections. Author Henry James disliked the random locations of tall buildings. While riding on a Hudson River steamship, he described Manhattan as a "pin cushion in profile." He was not alone in this view. Chicago urbanist C. M. Robinson also stated that skyscrapers should be located in strategic positions, according to a city plan.

A few publications encouraged dialogue on the subject by presenting visionary concepts of tall buildings. The most famous drawings of this era were presented in a series of books by Moses King, a turn-of-the-century publisher who specialized in urban histories and guidebooks. In 1908, he created *King's Views of New York*, the first of several publications that featured conceptual drawings of the future skyline filled with huge skyscrapers, linked by bridges high above street level. Many of the tall buildings included intriguing roof terraces visited by airships and balloons flying over the city. The dramatic drawings implied that the next era of urban planning would introduce an entirely new concept of the city. These images inspired many architects, including the designers of the visionary film *Metropolis*.

1.25 Turn-of-the-Century
     Urban Visions

Cut down the pleasant trees among the houses, pull down ancient and venerable buildings for the money that a few square yards of London dirt will fetch; blacken rivers, hide the sun and poison the air with smoke and worse . . . that is all that modern commerce, the counting house forgetful of the workshop will do for us.
—William Morris [34]

By the late nineteenth century, most major cities had become endless metropolitan areas of unprecedented scale. The development of tall buildings had increased the density of business districts and generated more stores, restaurants, offices, and housing. The streets were overflowing with carriages, streetcars, and delivery vehicles. The science fiction writer H. G. Wells, who was generally in favor of technological progress, described the streets of Chicago as "simply chaotic-one hoarse cry for discipline." [35]

At the time, American cities were struggling with a massive wave of immigration. From 1870 to 1895, ten million immigrants entered the United States, and this dramatic rise in population placed new burdens on cities. Tenements were overcrowded; schools were overfull; hospitals were insufficient; and there were never

40

Traffic jam at Randolph
and Dearborn streets,
Chicago, 1905.

enough parks. The demand for energy, water, and transportation systems also grew, as well as the requirements for food, clothing, and other products.

The housing in working-class neighborhoods was usually constructed with the cheapest materials and often lacked the basic necessities, such as running water, light, and air. According to journalists of this era, the rooms were infested with rats and roaches; the privies were filthy; and the cellars contained goats and pigs as well as human inhabitants. Ironically, the rents on the tenement flats were sometimes a third more expensive per square foot than the spacious apartments in prosperous uptown neighborhoods. [36]

The literature of this period reflected the struggle of minorities and the working class. In 1888, the three most successful books in America were *Uncle Tom's Cabin*, *Ben-Hur*, and *Looking Backward*, all political novels that appealed to immigrants and working-class intellectuals. The first two address the issues of slavery and religious persecution. The third, Edward Bellamy's *Looking Backward*, presents a utopian vision.

In this compelling novel, a nineteenth-century man is transported to Boston in the year 2000. There, he finds a highly evolved society where individualism is fully expressed. To his surprise, Boston has become a communist city. Like most utopians of the era, Bellamy was a communist. His concept is presented through a Platonic dialogue between the transported Bostonian and a helpful doctor who explains the system. In his ideal society, industries are owned by the community and operated by its citizens. All the residents serve in the industrial workforce until their mid-forties, when they are able to retire on pensions earned in their youth. Men and women receive the same education and hold comparable jobs.

The government is controlled by a few experienced officials, who are past retirement age, but continue to serve like philosopher kings. The political concept was the weakest part of the scheme, for the quality of justice depended on the goodwill of a patriarchal class.

Bellamy's vision of a communist Boston had a distinctly twentieth-century quality that offended some nineteenth-century reformers. Unlike the Socialist Utopians, who believed in small towns, he delighted in the possibility of a large city and describes the environment with enthusiasm: "At my feet lay a great city. Miles of broad streets, shaded by trees and lined with fine buildings . . . not in continuous blocks but set in larger or smaller enclosures, stretched in every direction." [37]

Looking Backward had an impact on American politicians. Bellamy Clubs were formed in towns throughout the United States and helped define the platform of the Populist party. The book was translated into more than twenty languages and inspired intellectuals worldwide. Bellamy would also influence several utopian designers, who emerged in the late nineteenth century.

1.26 Ebenezer Howard

Howard, the son of an English shopkeeper, was among the millions who read Bellamy's book. He was raised on the dark streets of industrial London and had very little formal education, but he understood Bellamy's socialist principles and later applied them to the development of a practical plan for a future city.

Ebenezer Howard, "The Three Magnets," diagram originally published in *To-morrow: a Peaceful Path to Real Reform*, London, 1898.

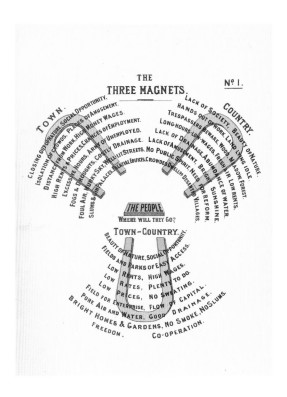

In 1871, Howard emigrated to the United States with two friends. Through a relative, the three found jobs on a Nebraska farm, but within a year, Howard realized that he was not suited to farming. He moved to Chicago and studied shorthand to become a court reporter. Five years later, he returned to London, where he also worked as a court stenographer.

While making a living in the British courts, Howard was exposed to the problems of taxation and land ownership. He also became aware of the dialogue among reformers on urban issues. He spent a decade developing the concept of a garden city, and in 1898, he published the book *To-morrow: A Peaceful Path to Real Reform*. It was reissued a few years later as *Garden Cities of To-morrow*.

The term "garden city" had already been used to describe pastoral communities endowed with rich landscapes, but Howard applied the phrase in a new way. Rather than creating cities with gardens, he created diagrams of a city in a garden, or surrounded by a greenbelt. His brief experience in farming had made him aware of the interdependence of cities and regional agriculture, and in his text, he showed the benefits of a cooperative arrangement.

In his scheme, the greenbelt is as important as the urban center. It is protected from development by zoning regulations. Local greenbelt farms deliver dairy and other foods to the city at an economical price, and the costs of transportation are kept low by the proximity of the farms to the city. Greenbelt areas also offer access to nature, which is essential to the health of urban residents. The city and greenbelt become a unified regional area, called a garden city.

In 1919, the Garden Cities and Town Planning Association collaborated with Howard on a definition of his concept: "A Garden City is a Town designed for healthy living and industry; of a size that makes possible a full measure of social life, but not larger; surrounded by a rural belt; the whole of the land being in public ownership or held in trust for the community." [38]

Like most utopians, Howard was horrified by crowded conditions, so the population of his garden cities would be limited to 32,000 people. If the number of inhabitants grew, rather than expand the boundaries of the city, he proposed that a new city or a satellite town be created, separated by another greenbelt. The communities would be linked by a railroad system to provide easy access between the main city and the satellite towns.

Howard's doctrine also espoused socialist ideas. The community would be a collective culture that owned all of the land and rented individual properties to its citizens; income from the real estate should be used to provide funds for improving the infrastructure and facilities of the city.

Howard's book was very influential. Garden City associations were formed throughout the United States, Europe, and Russia. Two real garden cities were realized with his help, one of them being Letchworth, England, where he lived for many years. Howard's theories came to be associated with Arts and Crafts, as the buildings of Letchworth were designed by Unwin and Parker in a rustic Arts and Crafts style.

1.27 Tony Garnier

At the turn of the century, another utopian labored at the drawing board: French architect Tony Garnier. Unlike Howard, who focused on planning issues, Garnier created an extensive architectural design. Garnier was born in the industrial city of Lyon. He came from a working-class family and supported his education by becoming a draftsman. He studied architecture for several years in Lyon and completed his degree at the Ecole des Beaux-Arts. He was awarded the coveted Prix de Rome scholarship and studied at the Villa Medici from 1900 to 1904. As part of the requirement for the award, he was expected to design a project in the Beaux-Arts style, but instead, Garnier developed his Cité Industrielle, a conceptual city of the future.

Each aspect of the plan showed how architecture could serve a utopian lifestyle. His industrial city is located in a manufacturing community near a river, much like his home city of Lyon. The plan is based on environmental considerations. It is arranged on an east-west axis to give all the buildings a southern exposure. All the rooms have windows for natural light and ventilation. Each building occupies only half of its site with the remaining area landscaped as a garden or a lawn. Most of the streets are lined with trees; some lead to public parks.

Garnier's city is unconventional in many ways. The urban center contains structures that emphasize the activities of the mind, body, and spirit of the workers. Rather than a shopping center, it features a huge outdoor assembly hall, built into a hill, like a Greek theater. There are also a few office buildings and stores, as well as a greenhouse, a library, and a museum.

Garnier was inspired by the work of Rousseau, Fourier, and Zola, who emphasized the importance of nature. The city also has a hydrotherapy center with public baths,

Tony Garnier, Metallurgical factories and blast furnaces, in *Cité Industrielle*, 1901-1917.

44

a pool, a track, and a gymnasium. All of the buildings have modern conveniences like running water, hydroelectricity, and street cleaning systems, based on Haussmann's improvements of Paris.

Some facilities have special sites. The hospital is immersed in "curtains of greenery" and built behind a mountain to shelter it from the wind. The schools are located on landscaped streets. There are primary and secondary schools for students up to the age of twenty. Education was important to Garnier. There were also two professional schools for college-age students, an art school to teach crafts like ceramics and carpentry, and an industrial school to educate students in the manufacturing processes for the local industries of metal and silk. The two types of schools are his attempt to solve the ongoing struggle between industry and handcrafted systems. [39]

His architectural designs introduced a new style that anticipated modernism. The buildings were based on the idea of a "white box in nature," which would later become a popular theme among modernists. Most of the structures were made of reinforced concrete, using standardized modular systems, flat roofs, and minimal details. The planning concepts were also modern. Residential areas were separated from industrial zones, and several different types of housing were provided.

Garnier also developed the philosophical concept of the city. He was a socialist with radical ideas. Cité Industrielle has no police force, no jail, and no court. He based his theories on the work of nineteenth-century socialist-anarchist Peter Kropotkin, who believed that crime was the result of economic deprivation. Garnier's conceptual city has a socialist system in which no one was deprived; therefore, the system eliminated criminal behavior and had no need for punitive measures. Garnier also eliminated religion, emphasizing health, science, and education instead. His project was as much defined by what he left out, as by what he included in the design. His philosophical concept was outlined in a program, which was presented in the prelude to the project.

Tony Garnier, Residential quarter in *Cité Industrielle*, 1901-1917.

Garnier submitted his drawings of the Cité Industrielle to the Prix de Rome committee as his official project, but the project was rejected. He then designed a traditional plan for reconstructing an ancient city in a Beaux-Arts style to satisfy the requirements. In 1904, he returned to France and joined an architectural office. He continued to develop his conceptual city, which was finally completed and published in 1917. Garnier's project would influence many architects and planners, including Le Corbusier, who visited him in Lyon.

1.28 The Reaction Against Industrialization

Men were not intended to work with the accuracy of tools . . . the kind of labor to which they are condemned is verily a degrading one, and makes them less than men.
—John Ruskin [40]

45

Throughout the nineteenth century, reformers wrote fierce essays, assessing the impact of the Industrial Revolution on cultural values and environmental conditions. Art critic John Ruskin was especially critical of the dehumanizing affect of most factory work. He felt the job of cutting a straight line ten hours day reduced a man to a mere "animated tool." It caused the worker's "soul and sight (to) be worn away, and the whole human being (to) be lost." [41]

In contrast, he felt the job of the craftsman, "made a man of him." Although the craft system was undoubtedly less efficient, it allowed workers to think about their task and create some of their own details. Ruskin believed that if the working class were to maintain a creative way of life, the entire culture would benefit. He disapproved of standardized systems that destroyed individual expression and urged an appreciation of the importance of nature in design.

His essays influenced many architects and designers, especially William Morris, a writer and designer who helped establish the British Arts and Crafts movement. His firm, Morris & Co., was an association of artisans who were committed to developing handcrafted products—textiles, furniture, wallpaper, and decorative objects—at a reasonable price.

Morris also established a small independent press that published his essays on a variety of issues from the low quality of mass-produced objects to the lack of art in modern society. He also attacked the immorality of the capitalist system and advocated socialism. He later wrote the utopian novel *News from Nowhere*.[42]

The writing of Ruskin and Morris would influence many designers, especially those that had not yet accepted industrial culture. Even though structures like the Crystal Palace and the Eiffel Tower had an impact, most nineteenth-century designers were not yet ready to move on to an industrial style.

1.29 Art Nouveau

The art nouveau style emerged in nearly every western European country. Leaders of the movement included Henry van de Velde and Victor Horta in Belgium, Josef Hoffmann and Otto Wagner in Austria, Hector Guimard in France, and Antoni Gaudí in Spain. It also included Charles Rennie Mackintosh and his partners Herbert MacNair and Margaret and Frances Macdonald in Scotland. Each of the leading architects in the movement had a unique style based on a cohesive expression of industrial and regional themes.[43]

The art nouveau designers introduced the new concept of combining modern structural systems with handcrafted details and expanded the use of industrial materials like iron and glass through the creation of colorful, romantic details that made reference to nature. Their elegant designs were also inspired by late nineteenth-century artistic developments, especially the work of the postimpressionists. The vivid colors of Van Gogh and Matisse encouraged a break from realism, as well as a more dramatic use of color. The intricate drawings of Aubrey Beardsley demonstrated the power of linework to the movement.

Guimard's entrances to the Paris Metro are a classic example of art nouveau. In this project, Guimard created intriguing organic forms in iron and glass. His designs were developed by combining skeletal iron structures with a delicate interplay of etched glass, framed by enameled steel. They integrate industrial materials with sophisticated expressions of natural forms and elegant craft techniques and present a dramatic new concept in urban decoration that appealed to the public. They became instant icons in Paris.

Mackintosh and his collaborators applied the Japanese notion of combining nature and the grid in elegant designs that were not overly ornate. They also fostered the notion of the total environment, in which a single style is expressed in all aspects of the design and individual elements are subordinated to the general concept.[44]

Belgian architect Victor Horta created several townhouses in the art nouveau style. In these luxurious private residences, he introduced large curving staircases with elaborate iron balustrades that contained rich organic forms. He later designed the Maison du Peuple, a more subdued building that provided a center for the Belgian Socialist party. The design combined local masonry materials with intricate iron details. The main space is a large auditorium, enhanced by elegant iron balconies.

Hector Germain Guimard,
Metro Porte Dauphine, Paris,
1900.

1.30 Antoni Gaudí

One of the most controversial architects of this era was Antoni Gaudí, who was
born in the Catalonia region of Spain. Although his work is associated with art
nouveau, it is so unconventional that he is often regarded as a lone visionary. He
was raised in a small town, and due to ill health, he spent many hours alone, con-
templating nature. He later studied architecture in Barcelona and remained there
after completing his studies.

His work was influenced by the theories of both John Ruskin and Viollet-le-Duc.
He was also inspired by the views of the wealthy industrialist Eusebio Güell, who
became his patron. In 1892, Güell commissioned Gaudí to develop a community
for the workers in his textile factory. Although the community took many years to
build, Gaudí's success in the first stages of the project led to other commissions,
including an elaborate palace for the Güell family.

Eusebio Güell also became interested in the Garden City philosophy and arranged
for Gaudí to create Park Güell, intended to be middle-class housing around a large
public park. Although the housing was never completed, the park was planned in
an organic manner, which combined a rich landscape with artistic elements made
by local craftsmen. Most of the perimeter was defined by an undulating wall inset
with shards of broken pottery. The central area is a covered marketplace, supported by sixty-nine columns of various sculptural shapes. [45]

47

Antonio Gaudí, Church of the
Sagrada Familia, Barcelona,
begun 1882.

Gaudí was dedicated to supporting the regional traditions of Catalonia and the artisans of northern Spain. All of his projects featured the handcrafted ironwork and colorful pottery of local craftsmen. He also emphasized concepts of nature in all of his work. He once said, "the straight line belongs to man, the curved line belongs to God." Gaudí's buildings contain highly plastic forms, such as leaning columns, undulating facades, and an endless variety of sculptural details. His engineering concepts were extremely sophisticated, especially his use of leaning columns and curving walls, which later influenced some of the deconstructivist architects.

Gaudí's most famous design is that of the Church of the Sagrada Familia, where he incorporated principles of Gothic architecture with forms that were entirely his own. After he died in 1926, the people of Barcelona continued working on the church. The project held great importance to the city, as it was not only conceived as a place of worship, but also a school for local children, a facility for religious research, and a training program for local craftsmen. The people of Barcelona hoped to keep the craft tradition alive, and they realized that the design of the church expressed a unique creative vision.

Among architecture critics, Gaudí's work was extremely controversial. Although his projects are associated with the art nouveau movement, his eccentric style differed from the restrained approach of most of the other architects of this era. Some critics disliked the bizarre quality of his designs; others were inspired by the passionate intensity of his vision. [46]

1.31 The Debate on the Machine

The boundless evil caused by shoddy mass-produced goods is like a tidal wave sweeping across the world. We have been cut adrift from the culture of our forefathers and are cast hither and thither by a thousand desires and considerations. The machine has largely replaced the hand and the businessman has supplanted the craftsman. To attempt to stem this torrent would seem like madness . . . Yet for all that we have founded our workshop.
—Josef Hoffmann and Koloman Moser [47]

As the twentieth century began, the dialogue on industrialization became more heated. The designers who favored Arts and Crafts became more vehement in their arguments against mechanization. Several young Viennese designers played an important role in this transitional period. They included the architects Josef Maria Olbrich and Josef Hoffmann and the painters Gustav Klimt and Koloman Moser. This emerging group was inspired by Otto Wagner, who trained both Hoffmann and Olbrich and by Charles Rennie Mackintosh and his associates. Their handsome projects combine a modern sensibility with elegant Arts and Crafts details.

In 1897, Olbrich, Hoffmann, Klimt, Moser, and their associates decided to mount an exhibition of their work, but instead of showing their projects at the traditional Kunstlerhaus, which exhibited established Austrian artists, they developed an alternative venue known as the Secessionhaus. The building, which was designed by Olbrich, expressed the new style.

In 1903, Hoffmann and Moser formed the Wiener Werkstätte, a workshop intended to produce handcrafted furniture, light fixtures, textiles, and decorative objects based on the principles of Ruskin and Morris. These elegant products became fashionable among upper-class consumers, which led to the creation of similar workshops in Dresden, Munich, and other cities.

In 1910, architect Adolf Loos began to denounce the art nouveau style and the principles of the Wiener Werkstätte. He felt their products had become so expensive, they no longer reflected the values of Ruskin and Morris. He published "Ornament and Crime," an article in which he asserted that ornament was appropriate for children and tattooed savages, but had no place in modern society. He also said, "Freedom from ornament is a sign of spiritual strength." [48]

Loos asserted that the use of decorative details increased the price of an object without adding real value to it. He urged, instead, the development of a new design vocabulary based on industrial culture. He felt that the goal of modern designers should be the creation of simple, inexpensive products that could be mass-produced for the working class.

Unlike Hoffmann and Moser, who thought machines were monstrous assemblies that destroyed the lives of the worker, Loos was in favor of technology. He considered mass production to be a way of creating inexpensive products that would

"The Demon which is destroying the People," undated political cartoon.

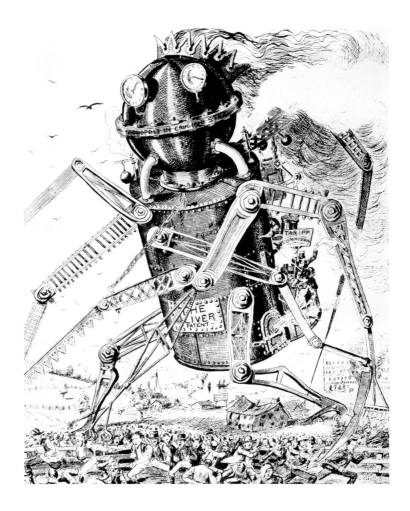

enhance the life of the worker and his family. He also felt that the Arts and Crafts style was no longer appropriate in the twentieth century.

Loos continued his assaults on the Wiener Werkstätte for many years. In a speech in which he denounced their decorative style he declared, "I warn the Austrians against identifying with the Wiener Werkstätte movement . . . The modern spirit is a social spirit, and modern objects exist not just for the benefit of the upper crust, but for everybody."[49]

Loos became known as the "Wrathful Anti-Christ of the Wiener Werkstätte." But he was not alone in his opinion. By the early twentieth century, radical designers throughout Europe and Russia were expressing similar views on industrialization. They were rejecting the fussy style of Arts and Crafts and creating simple objects that could be mass-produced for working-class families. As the concepts of modernism and mechanization became more accepted, the art nouveau designers began to seem decadent and old-fashioned. In the next few decades, their views were cast into obsolescence by the unwavering determination of machine-age designers.

Notes

1. Desiderius Erasmus, *Adagia*, quoted in Fred Shapiro, Joseph Epstein, *The Yale Book of Quotations* (New Haven: Yale University Press, 2006), 247.

2. Serge Bramley, *Leonardo* (New York: Harper Collins Publishers, 1991), 420.

3. Bramley, 100.

4. Sir Thomas More, *Utopia* (Harmondsworth, Middlesex, England: Penguin Books Ltd., 1965), 86.

5. Jean-Jacques Rousseau, quoted in Will and Ariel Durant, *Rousseau and Revolution* (New York: Simon and Schuster, Inc., 1967), 162.

6. Will and Ariel Durant, *The Age of Voltaire* (New York: Simon and Schuster, Inc., 1967), 260.

7. Durant, 252.

8. Christian W. Thomson, *Visionary Architecture* (Munich: Prestel Verlag, 1994), 51-54.

9. Thomson, 56-58.

10. Ruth Eaton, *Ideal Cities* (New York: Thames and Hudson, Inc., 2002), 110-15.

11. William Howard Adams, *Jefferson's Monticello* (New York: Abbeville Press, 1983), 8.

12. Spiro Kostof, *The City Shaped* (New York: Bulfinch Press, 1991), 121.

13. Ralph Waldo Emerson, quoted in Lewis Mumford, *The Myth of the Machine: The Pentagon of Power* (New York: Harcourt Brace Jovanovich, Inc., 1964), 207.

14. Lewis Mumford, *The City in History* (New York: Harcourt, Brace & World, Inc., 1961), 447-48.

15. Otto L. Bettmann, *The Good Old Days—They Were Terrible!* (New York: Random House, Inc., 1974), 73-74.

16. Durant, *Rousseau and Revolution*, 82.

17. Robert Owen, quoted in Document 10, http://www.historyteacher.net/EuroProjects/DBQs2002_ReformMovements.htm

18. Karl Marx, quoted in Eaton, 125.

19. Francoise Choay, *The Modern City: Planning in the 19th Century* (New York: George Braziller, Inc., 1969), 29.

20. Eaton, 131-32.

21. Eaton, 131.

22. James Howard Kunstler, *The Geography of Nowhere* (New York: Simon & Schuster, Inc., 1993), 36-37.

23. Choay, 19.

24. Donald J. Bush, *The Streamlined Decade* (New York: George Braziller, Inc., 1975), 155.

25. David Raizman, *History of Modern Design* (Upper Saddle River, NJ: Prentice Hall Inc., 2004), 52.

26. Freddy Langer, ed., *Icons of Photography: The 19th Century* (Munich: Prestel Verlag, 2002), 32.

27. Choay, 103.

28. Howard Mansfield, *Cosmopolis: Yesterday's Cities of the Future* (New Brunswick, NJ: Center for Urban Policy Research, 1990), 32.

29. Louis Sullivan, "The Autobiography of an Idea," quoted in John Szarkowski, *The Idea of Louis Sullivan* (New York: Bulfinch Press, 2000), 126.

30. Louis Sullivan, "The Tall Office Building Artistically Considered," quoted in Szarkowski, 73.

31. William J. R. Curtis, *Modern Architecture Since 1900* (Englewood Cliffs, NJ: Prentice Hall, Inc., 1987), 42.

32. Mansfield, 5.

33. Mansfield, 3.

34. William Morris, "The Lesser Arts," in *The Industrial Design Reader* edited by Carma Gorman (New York: Allworth Press, 2003), 38.

35. H.G. Wells, quoted in Bettmann, 31.

36. Bettmann, 43.

37. Edward Bellamy, *Looking Backward* (New York: The New American Library, 1960), 43.

38. F. J. Osborn, preface to *Garden Cities of To-Morrow* by Ebenezer Howard (Cambridge, MA: The MIT Press, 1965), 26.

39. Dora Wiebenson, *Tony Garnier: The Cite Industrielle* (New York: George Braziller, Inc., 1969), 111.

40. John Ruskin, "The Stones of Venice," in Gorman, 15.

41. Ruskin, 15.

42. David Raizman, *History of Modern Design* (Upper Saddle River, NJ: Prentice Hall Inc., 2004), 111.

43. Francesca Prina and Elena Demartini, *One Thousand Years of World Architecture* (Milan: Mondadori Electa Spa, 2005), 276.

44. Anthony Jones, *Charles Rennie Mackintosh* (London: Studio Editions, 1990), 70.

45. Kenneth Frampton, *Modern Architecture: A Critical History* (London: Thames and Hudson Ltd., 1985), 66.

46. Prina and Demartini, 290.

47. Josef Hoffmann and Koloman Moser, *The Work Program of the Wiener Werkstatte*, in Gorman, 62.

48. Ulrich Conrads, *Programs and Manifestoes on 20th-Century Architecture* (Cambridge, MA: The MIT Press, 1964), 19-24.

49. Adolf Loos, quoted in Jocelyn de Noblet, *Industrial Design Reflections of a Century* (Paris: Flammarion/ADAGP, 1993), 114.

51

THE MACHINE AGE IN EUROPE

Every innovation, be it in the sciences, culture, the arts or architecture . . . consists on the one hand of building up piece by piece a new image of the world, while on the other hand an old world image is being broken down.
—Theo van Doesburg[1]

In the early twentieth century, dozens of new inventions appeared: the Zeppelin, the first rigid-frame airship, electric-powered bicycles, automobiles, consumer products and appliances like razor blades, light bulbs, dial telephones, refrigerators, and washing machines. Each new product was an engineering challenge. The manufacturers not only developed the concept; they also designed the production, packaging, and distribution systems. Any mistakes in planning or presentation could mean financial failure. Existing factories were inadequate for mass production, and new types of buildings were needed to accommodate the larger systems.

Though many Europeans were skeptical of machines, there was no alternative. As the century began, most continental countries suffered from widespread unemployment, a high birth rate, and a limited educational system. Industry was still dominated by handcrafts and controlled by the medieval guilds. As a result, these countries were unable to compete with British and U.S. manufacturers, and they lacked the infrastructure to modernize their cities.

Russia had even greater problems. Over half its population was descended from serfs, whose living conditions were reportedly the worst in Europe. They had no skills or education and struggled daily with the threat of starvation. In 1881, Count Leo Tolstoy visited the Moscow slums and was so disturbed by the poverty of the serfs that he established 250 kitchens for the poor. He dressed like a peasant, worked in the fields, and renounced his land, income, and title. Prince Peter Kropotkin also rejected the military career and privileges of his title. In the 1890s, he wrote essays on anarchism and socialism, advocating the idea of a brotherhood of worker-artists in modern industries.[2]

The political ideals of this era impacted designers. They were not only challenged by the goal of adapting to machine technology, they were also determined to help the working class by improving factory, housing, and urban environments. Some were dedicated to Marxist values. Others were inspired by the romanticism of Friedrich Nietzsche, who proclaimed that true artists were visionaries who would lead society out of darkness into an enlightened era.

Franz Kruckenberg,
The Railway Zeppelin,
1929–30.

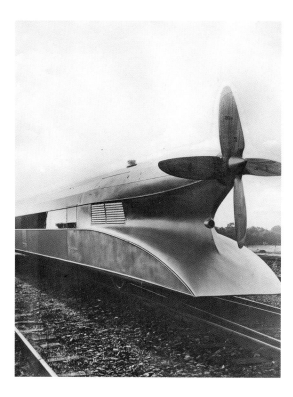

54

In the late nineteenth century, several European designers recognized the need for a new approach to the design process based on mechanical systems. Gottfried Semper, a German architect and political exile, wrote a pamphlet describing his impressions of the 1851 London exhibition in which he concluded that many of the products could have been improved. Semper believed that the traditions of hand-crafted systems should be completely abandoned and that it was necessary for designers to find a new process that would integrate art and industry. The techniques of handcrafted production did not apply to the machine. Mechanization would succeed only if it were accompanied by new materials, new manufacturing systems, and new concepts in design.

These ideas did not have an immediate impact, but within a few decades Semper's writings became seminal works for the German avant-garde. In the early twentieth century, German designers and industrialists formed the Deutscher Werkbund, an organization dedicated to developing a new language in design. The Werkbund publications inspired architects throughout Europe. Within a decade, new design groups emerged across the continent including the Futurists in Italy, the Modernists in Germany, the Constructivists in Russia, and the De Stijl movement in the Netherlands. These inventive designers created housing concepts based on mass production, and new types of household products that were affordable for the working class. They also wrote manifestos that expressed a new cultural vision, and their political commitment added to the integrity of their work. Avant-garde architects felt their true role was greater than the creation of products and structures; their real purpose was to build a new social order based on mechanization. As a result of this belief, they introduced an era of intense visionary movements, characterized by political idealism, artistic innovation, and a tireless commitment to technological progress.

Paul Citroen, *Metropolis*,
photomontage, 1923.

2.1   Italian Futurism

*We declare that the splendor of the world has been enriched by a new beauty . . . the beauty
of speed. A roaring motorcar, which seems to run on machine-gunfire, is more beautiful
than the winged victory of Samothrace.*

—Filippo Tommaso Marinetti[3]

At the turn of the century, the Italian working class suffered from extreme poverty
and unemployment. Industries were not yet utilizing modern technology and were
still controlled by medieval practices. Italian architects were also burdened by the
weight of history. Their work was steeped in Renaissance tradition, and their cities
were encumbered with the remnants of aging infrastructure. Although most educated Italians wanted to modernize their way of life, they needed a new movement
to foster their views. In 1909, Filippo Tommaso Marinetti, a rising young poet,
wrote a Manifesto of Futurism. In a list of eleven powerful statements, he presented a dramatic new concept of Italian society based on images of modern cities,

mechanized industries, and new transportation systems. In this stirring declaration, he announced that the new era would be characterized by energy, speed, and technological vision.

He also demanded that the people of Italy turn away from the traditions of the past and destroy reactionary institutions like museums and libraries, declaring, "We are on the extreme promontory of the centuries! What is the use of looking behind at the moment when we must open the mysterious shutters of the impossible? Time and Space died yesterday . . . "[4]

Marinetti published this document in *La Figaro*, hoping to inspire others to join him. Some were offended by the bombastic character of his statement, but it attracted the attention of many artists and designers. The cubist painter Umberto Boccioni was the first to pledge his allegiance to the new movement. In 1910, Marinetti and Boccioni collaborated on a Futurist Manifesto of Painting. In the next few years, other artists joined the movement, adding, in 1912, a Futurist Manifesto for Sculpture, and in 1916, a Manifesto for Futurist Cinema.

2.2 Antonio Sant'Elia

In 1914, Marinetti collaborated with Antonio Sant'Elia, a dedicated young architect, on the development of the Messaggio, a statement that became the equivalent of a Futurist manifesto of architecture. Sant'Elia was inspired by the heroic designs of American factories and skyscrapers and intrigued with Jules Verne's science fiction novels and Tony Garnier's visionary city. His writing expressed a bold new concept, integrating technology and design:

> The problem of Futurist architecture is not a problem of linear arrangements. It's a question of creating the Futurist house . . . with the aid of every scientific and technical resource . . . establishing new forms, new lines, a new harmony of profiles and volumes . . . This architecture cannot be subject to any law of historical continuity. It must be as new as our frame of mind is new . . . [5]

During that period, Sant'Elia also worked in an architectural office and participated in a group of innovative young architects called Nuove Tendenze with colleagues such as Ugo Nebbia and Mario Chiattone, but after collaborating on the Messaggio, he joined the Futurists. He also created drawings of a visionary city, which he aptly called La Città Nova. The images had a new vitality, unlike the static drawings of the past. The machine aesthetic dominated all of his work whether in drawings of a rough industrial character or sophisticated renderings of modern structures. Made of modern industrial materials, such as steel, concrete, and glass, his designs had a minimal quality, free of unnecessary ornament or detail. His skyscrapers featured sleek towers, curving balconies, and glass elevators, and his train stations had wide expanses of multilevel tracks.

The technological vision of the Futurists inspired not only artists and writers; it also attracted the interest of the rising dictator Benito Mussolini. He appeared in several newspaper articles with Marinetti to promote technological development. At the time, Mussolini was still a Socialist, committed to economic growth and expansion of the working class.

Antonio Sant'Elia, *Power
Station*, 1914.

Mussolini sponsored two exhibitions of Futurist designs. One in Rome included
an urban planning competition in which architects were asked to submit designs that
addressed the housing and traffic problems of modern cities. Sant'Elia developed
a powerful group of drawings for the event. Mario Chiattone also devised some
interesting images. In *Construction for a Modern Metropolis*, Chiattone provided a
surprisingly realistic vision of a modern city.

During these years, automobile manufacturers, such as Fiat, Lamborghini, and
Alfa Romeo, created dramatic modern concepts. In 1913, designer Carlo Castagna
developed the Alfa Romeo 20/30 for Count Mario Ricotti. Its aerodynamic, stylish
form was a testament to the visionary talent of the era and would later inspire the
American streamlined designers.[6]

The Futurist movement was suspended when World War I began. Sant'Elia was
killed at the front, but after the fighting was over, his dramatic drawings were
circulated among European architects, and his concepts became very influential.
He was the first architect to say a house should be "similar to a gigantic machine,"
a statement that may have influenced Le Corbusier.

Carlo Castagna, Alfa Romeo
20/30, created for Count Mario
Ricotti, 1913.

Giuseppe Terragni,
Casa del Fascio, Como, Italy,
1936–39.

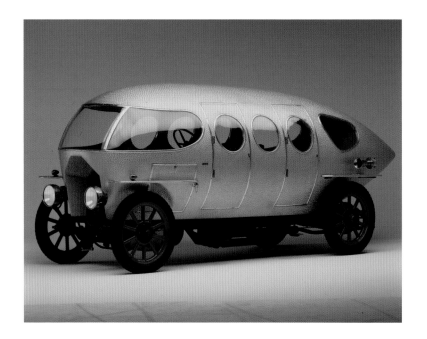

2.3   Italian Rationalism

In the aftermath of war, Italy was torn in half by the struggle between two political parties, the Fascists and the Socialists. The Fascists envisioned a unified Italian culture under a national party. The Socialists wanted to form an international government of workers. The Socialists held power for a few years, but they were unable to stabilize the economy, which allowed the Fascists to seize control.

By 1922, Mussolini had become a Fascist and abandoned his early beliefs. He led a march on Rome with an army of "black shirts" that was such an intimidating front that King Victor Emmanuel III was forced to capitulate. After establishing his government, Mussolini rejected the radical proposals of the Futurists and criticized the movement and censored their work. A defiant Marinetti wrote a book called *Futurism and Fascism*, claiming that Futurism had inspired the Fascist party, but his angry statements failed to rejuvenate Mussolini's interest in the group.

In the mid-1920s, several young architects who wanted to work for Mussolini's party formed a new movement called Italian Rationalism dedicated to the principles of Fascism. Their designs had a modern quality, but were based on the monumental forms of classical Roman buildings. Unlike the Futurists, the Rationalists were not interested in conceptual design; they wanted to build. The Futurists took credit for inspiring their style, a claim refuted by Alberto Sartoris, who stated, "Italian Rationalism is more closely related to . . . cubism, Suprematism, Constructivism, surrealism, and neo-plasticism . . . It would be ridiculous to deny Futurism's share in raising the new architecture to its present form, but its claim to have created the rationalist trend . . . is a blatant untruth."[7]

The Rationalists later broke into several groups, the most prominent of which was Gruppo 7 of Milan, who formalized a Fascist concept in design. Giuseppe Terragni, a leading member, created disciplined structures, defined by strict concepts of geometry and proportion. Terragni built Casa del Fascio (1936–39), a government building that became a centerpiece of the Fascist regime. The design is a courtyard scheme based on the geometry of the square. It has the controlled institutional quality of a well-resolved structure, but none of the passionate energy of Futurism.

| 2.4 | The Russian Avant-Garde | *The social role of architecture is essentially as one of the instruments for the building of socialism by means of the collectivization of life, by means of the rationalization of labor, by means of the utilization of scientific data . . . we believe that what is needed is not the invention of an art . . . but work on the organization of architecture, proceeding from the data of economics, science, and technology. It is to this great work that we call . . . the architects of the Soviet Union.* |

—F. Yalovkin, a member of ASNOVA[8]

On a cold January morning in 1905, Father Gapon, a determined priest, led a group of poor workers and their families to the Winter Palace in St. Petersburg to deliver a petition to the czar. They had been taxed to the breaking point to support a futile war and wanted to beg for decent food and wages. The czar's troops met them on horseback and fired relentlessly into the crowd. The massacre, which was known as "Bloody Sunday," was followed by months of riots, protests, and strikes. This was the beginning of the Russian Revolution, a unified effort of the workers that had been fermenting for years. The fighting continued until 1917, when the workers finally overthrew the czar and executed his family. Vladimir Lenin returned from exile in Western Europe and formed a Bolshevik government. Lenin had to address the shortages of food, housing, and medical services as well as the longer-term issues of building industries and restoring cities. However, the greatest challenge was to define a vision of the new country and create a cultural revolution in the hearts and minds of a predominantly ignorant society. The revolutionary leaders disagreed among themselves on the best direction for the future, and two more years of war followed between the Whites, who rejected communism, and the Reds, who embraced it.

When the fighting ended, Lenin established a program to introduce revolutionary propaganda to the people. He asked artists, designers, and filmmakers to develop projects on communist themes. Many responded to this initiative, but most of their efforts failed because the distance between the intelligentsia and the proletariat was so great that meaningful communication was almost impossible. Several filmmakers

The citizens of Vladivostok gather after the Russian Revolution to support the new Soviet leaders, Lenin and Trotsky, 1922.

tried to communicate through political films. Director Sergei Eisenstein created *The Battleship Potemkin*, a rousing film based on revolutionary themes. It was elegantly composed, using sophisticated cinematic techniques of montage and rhythmic editing, but when Eisenstein showed the film to a general audience, the result was a failure. Many peasants had never seen a film before and thought the characters died when they went off screen.[9]

The only approach that succeeded was graphic design. Since so many Russians were illiterate, dramatic images on posters became a popular form of communication. The posters of the constructivists Vladimir and Georgii Stenberg were striking compositions of modern symbols. In *Symphony of a Big City*, they presented a skyscraper, camera, typewriter, airplane, and clock in a single dynamic composition. Their powerful collages inspired other experiments in graphic arts.

The failure of communication with the peasants led to endless debates on the cultural dilemma. As early as 1906, some artists generated working-class culture through a movement called "Proletcult." Their good intentions led to a revival of crafts, but did not advance the Revolution or the goal of industrial development. A few architects proposed neoclassical buildings that the peasants would understand, but the avant-garde felt that neoclassicism was counterrevolutionary and that ornamental design was dead. Anatoly Lunarcharsky, a leading intellectual, stated the Bolshevik position as "all that is frivolous in decorative art, all that is merchandise for the market, the literary subtleties which have really nothing to say, all that has no other use than to sustain parasites must be annihilated."[10]

2.5   Suprematism

In the early 1920s, there were few funds for real buildings, so architects developed conceptual designs instead. Several stylistic elements characterized this work: many designs were placed on a diagonal to eliminate the concept of symmetry, which was reminiscent of art under the czar. The diagonal also generated more dynamic images, which implied movement into a new era. In addition, most conceptual works included industrial symbols, or a text that stated Russia's intention

Vladimir and Georgii Stenberg,
Symphony of a Big City, 1928,
lithograph.

to modernize. Dutch architect and writer Theo van Doesburg later said of their heroic work, "The Russian national character, founded on the extreme stresses of tragedy and suffering, draws its reserve strength mainly from abstraction, dreams and utopia."[11]

As the Soviet government began to construct buildings, a new set of questions arose. Architects wondered if the new buildings should be based on emerging technological systems or the traditional construction methods the workers understood. They also disagreed on whether the designs should feature individual styles or purely functional ideas. Several different groups of designers formed around these issues.

El Lissitzky, *Lenin's Tribune*, 1920.

El Lissitzky, *Lenin's Tribune*, 1920.

62

One of the first to emerge were the Suprematists. This collective defended the idea of individual artistic visions and never fully accepted the socialist agenda. Many of their projects were abstract in nature. Konstantin Malevich, a founding member, built sculptural models of pure geometrical forms, and his elegant projects inspired other architects to experiment with formal exercises.

El Lissitzky, another Suprematist designer, lived in Europe for several years, serving as an intermediary between European and Russian designers. His own experimental paintings, which he called "Prouns," or "Projects for Affirmation of the New," combined painting and architecture. A few examples of his work were published in the Dutch avant-garde magazine *De Stijl*. He also planned an orator's platform for Lenin featuring a small stage perched on an industrial tower that resembled a crane. The sleek industrial form became an iconic image.

2.6 ASNOVA

The Association of New Architects, or ASNOVA, led by Konstantin Melnikov, took a formal/psychological approach to design. Its members were considered more conservative than the other designers, and their projects explored aesthetic issues and individual visions rather than socialist themes. The bourgeois quality of their work alienated the more radical Bolsheviks, who felt that design should incorporate a political agenda.

Ilia Golosov, Zuev Workers
Club, the clubhouse of streetcar workers, Moscow, 1930s.

Melnikov's design for the Soviet pavilion at the 1925 International Exposition of
Modern Industrial and Decorative Art in Paris was a sophisticated building that
expressed both proletarian and industrial themes. His design for the Rusakov
Workers Club also attracted international attention. The building was a center
for the trolley car workers of Moscow, and the design featured a powerful series
of projecting forms that contained meeting rooms for the group.

The multitalented designer Alexander Rodchenko also participated in the 1925
Paris Exposition. He created an interior design for a Workers Club, which illustrated a new concept for enhancing the life of the collective culture. Since his concept
was more accessible than most of the avant-garde proposals, it became a more
popular exhibit.

Ilia Golosov, an architect who originally worked with Melnikov, designed the Zuev
Workers Club in Moscow, an industrial building with a dramatic facade. The design
expresses the bold geometry of the era in two basic forms, a cylinder and a cubelike
volume that encases it.[12]

2.7   OSA

The Association of Contemporary Architects, or OSA, emerged a few years later.
This group emphasized socialist principles, and the movement it espoused was called
Constructivism because it focused on creating socialist propaganda, collectivist
architecture, and industrial production. This influential group included prominent
artists such as Vladimir Tatlin, gifted architects like Moisei Ginsburg and the Vesnin
brothers, and talented graphic designers like Georgii and Vladimir Stenberg.

63

Vladimir Tatlin, Model of
the Monument to the Third
International, on exhibit in
Moscow, 1920. Tatlin stands
in the foreground, holding
a pipe.

Although the Constructivists claimed their work was not driven by aesthetic considerations, their visual concepts were powerful. In 1919, Tatlin was commissioned
to create a sculpture that would serve as a monument to the Third International, a
major conference on socialism. He designed a huge double helix structure, which
was expressed through a dynamic intersection of two spirals, rotating upward at
a provocative angle. Tatlin intended the tower to be 1,000 feet tall, higher than the
Eiffel Tower, but it was never constructed because the cost would have been prohibi-
tive. Tatlin was later criticized for the impractical, bourgeois nature of his concept.
Van Doesburg wrote in a review that the construction of the tower "would require
more slave labor than was necessary to build Cheops's pyramid." But his model was
exhibited, and, bourgeois or not, it became a symbol of the Revolution.[13]

A few Constructivist urban planners were inspired by the French utopian socialists
Fourier and Garnier. Others admired Ebenezer Howard's concepts. However, they
all felt that Russia needed its own leaders to define a vision for the new collective

community and so studied the socialist/anarchist theories that Peter Kropotkin and Mikhail Bakunin developed in the nineteenth century. Kropotkin's essays were very influential. In *The Conquest of Bread*, 1892, he advocated the abolishment of private property and development of a collectivist culture. In a reinterpretation of Darwinian theory he claimed that culture is not based on survival of the fittest species, but rather on survival of the most social species, such as a flock of birds, a herd of cattle, or a school of fish.[14]

Neither of these philosophers offered a real definition of the new society. Since the concept of the collective culture had not yet been defined, it was difficult to plan communities. As a result, there were controversies among various design groups regarding the best direction for the future and raising fundamental questions about life. Architects debated whether families should live in individual houses or collective dormitories and whether cities should be built around industry, culture, or nature. They discussed how the new society should socialize—whether clubs, sports, or culture should be emphasized. They also argued about aesthetic concepts. Should the new design movements feature artistic ideas or promote purely functional designs?

In 1929, a competition for a Green City of 100,000 people was held based on Ebenezer Howard's concepts. Constructivist architects Ginsburg and Mikhail Barsh collaborated on a linear design of a city arranged along a highway with a series of zones for factories, dormitories, and urban and leisure spaces. However, the plan was awkward, despite its simplicity. The housing consisted of studio apartments raised on columns, and the height of the structures made them difficult to reach.

In 1930, the Vesnin brothers produced several plans for the town of Kuznetsk. Their concept included a text based on socialist utopian theories. One layout, designed for 35,000 people, was similar to Garnier's Cité Industrielle. It called for a linear city, arranged along a main street, lined with rows of facilities, including a factory, a market, schools, and a train station, and emphasized landscape. The Vesnins replaced Garnier's private houses with collective dormitories and introduced communal kitchens and bathrooms.[15]

2.8 Yakov Chernikhov and Ivan Leonidov

Yakov Chernikhov, the most prolific conceptualist of the era, produced more than 17,000 drawings in a unique style that was not easily classified. Some of his images were associated with Futurism and Constructivism, but his architectural fantasies contained exploding abstract forms unlike any prior style. His projects also contained sophisticated urban visions that would later inspire the deconstructivist designers.[16]

Ivan Leonidov created pure architectural forms. In his conceptual design for the Lenin Institute, he proposed two lightweight structures, a transparent skyscraper containing a library and offices and a transparent sphere for a reading room. The two forms are held in tension by wires and express a vision of universal elements that transcended stylistic considerations. This project would become another icon of the era.

65

Yakov Chernikhov,
architectural concept.

Boris Iofan, Palace of the
Soviets, model of winning
design, Moscow, 1931–33.

In the early 1920s, Lenin's artistic policies provided opportunities for avant-garde designers, but at the end of his life, Lenin rejected the visionaries he had earlier promoted. He announced, "I cannot follow the works of the expressionists, Futurists, and cubists, nor all the other 'isms' in which artistic genius awakens. I do not understand anything about it. It leaves me cold." After Lenin's death in 1924 and the installation of his successor Josef Stalin, the creative period in Russia ended, as other Party members were even less tolerant of conceptual explorations.[17]

In 1931, a competition was held for the new Moscow Palace of the Soviets, which attracted proposals from leading modernists, such as Gropius, Auguste and Gustav Perret, Le Corbusier, Ginsburg, and Melnikov, but the winning project by Boris Iofan shocked the avant-garde. It was a tall neoclassical building composed of ascending tiers like a wedding cake crowned by a huge statue of Lenin that embodied an official rejection of the visionary movements. After this competition, most government buildings followed neoclassical concepts, and housing and commercial buildings became mundane functional designs.

From the mid-1930s until the fall of the Soviet Union in the 1980s, the visionary architecture of the 1920s was suppressed and unknown in the West. When the Cold War ended, this innovative work was rediscovered, and the powerful images of the Constructivist architects had an impact on the work of the deconstructivist era. Other Russian projects inspired new directions in graphics, film, and industrial design.

Peter Behrens, AEG Turbine
Factory, Berlin, 1909.

2.9 The Deutsche
     Werkbund

*The fortunate progress of the arts and crafts movement, which has . . . breathed fresh life
into handicrafts and imparted fruitful inspiration to architecture, may be regarded as only
a minor prelude to what must come. For in spite of all we have achieved we are still
wading up to our knees in the brutalization of forms.*
—Hermann Muthesius[18]

At the turn of the century, the German government became interested in supporting industrial research. From 1896 to 1903, architect Hermann Muthesius served as
a cultural attaché to the German embassy in London to report on British art, architecture, and industrial systems. Muthesius admired the British Arts and Crafts
movement, but while living in London, he also began to recognize the possibilities
of machine production. Muthesius returned to Germany with a new concept for
German industry. In 1907, he surprised the members of an Arts and Crafts organization by giving a lecture on mass production in which he asserted that mechanization was essential to the economy and that the quality of machine-made products
could be held to the same standards as handmade goods.

His lecture led to the formation of the Deutsche Werkbund, whose goal was "the
improvement of professional work through the cooperation of art, industry and the
crafts, through education, propaganda, and united attitudes on pertinent questions."[19]
The Werkbund began with twelve representatives from the major craft industries
and prominent designers, such as Josef Hoffmann, Peter Bruckmann, Bruno Paul,
and Joseph Maria Olbrich. Within a year, membership grew to five hundred architects, designers, and manufacturers.

67

Architect Peter Behrens was a founding member. Behrens began as an Arts and Crafts designer, but in 1907, he turned his attention to industrial projects. His first major commission was a turbine factory for the huge electrical conglomerate AEG, where he developed a heroic building, combining lightweight steel systems with classical proportions and sturdy Romanesque forms. Emil Rathenau, the founder of AEG, encouraged the development of new products using electrical power, and he supported innovative design. Between 1908 and 1914, Rathenau commissioned Behrens to build several more factories and hired him as a consultant in the design and marketing of his company's products.

Belgian designer Henry van de Velde became an important member of the Werkbund. He had come to Germany at the request of Grand Duke Alexander to improve the craft industry of Weimar, and through the support of the aristocracy, he had created a successful Weimar Arts and Crafts School, which also gave seminars to local industries.

The diverse membership of the Werkbund led to provocative exhibitions, lectures, and publications on design, and debates on important issues, such as the role of the individual designer in an age of standardization. The majority of the designers, including Van de Velde and Behrens, felt that products should be based on the work of the individual artist or designer, while Muthesius and most of the manufacturers believed in the importance of standardization as a way to establish high-quality designs and efficient production systems.

The Werkbund was an extremely effective organization, despite the differing opinions within the group. Through Muthesius's influence, it later received government funding to develop architectural experiments and constructed a series of avant-garde museums and experimental housing projects. Its building program helped to launch the careers of major architects, including Walter Gropius and Ludwig Mies van der Rohe.

2.10 German Expressionism

The designers of this era were also influenced by the Expressionist movement and the attitudes of German artists, who expressed intense emotions in their work. Architects approached the idea of Expressionism in different ways. Some designs were based on distorted shapes that elicited emotional responses. Others were associated with natural environments, such as mountains, caves, and crystalline forms. A third group of expressionist designs were derived from medieval themes or utopian concepts. In the early twentieth century, several architects built massive industrial structures that had a forbidding quality like medieval fortresses. The Frankfurt gasworks by Behrens and the Luban chemical factory by Hans Poelzig are powerful examples of this haunting style.

The most famous expressionist building is Eric Mendelsohn's Einstein Tower, an observatory near Potsdam. This structure has a strange, biomorphic shape that is difficult to interpret. Some historians believe it was drawn from organic forms found in nature; others claim it was based on Gothic concepts, or the medieval view of science as a mystical activity. Mendelsohn made no public statement on the origin of the design.[20]

Eric Mendelsohn, Einstein
Tower, Potsdam, Germany,
1920–21.

In 1914, Bruno Taut designed a Glass Pavilion for a Werkbund exhibit in Cologne.
His interest in glass was partly inspired by the poet Paul Scheerbart, who believed
that a new kind of architecture should be developed based on the use of glass.
Scheerbart felt that glass would foster a closer relationship with nature and a more
open culture in which nothing was hidden. In 1914, Scheerbart wrote, "Our culture
is in a sense the product of our architecture. If we want our culture to rise to a
higher level, we are forced . . . to transform our architecture. This can only be done
through the introduction of glass architecture that lets the sunlight and the light of
the moon and the stars into our rooms not merely through a few windows, but . . .
through every possible wall."[21]

Taut designed several conceptual glass structures, which he dedicated to Scheerbart.
He later developed the Glass Chain, a correspondence among modern architects
interested in glass that included established designers like Behrens, as well as
emerging architects like Gropius. In the process of assembling this group, Taut also
discovered Mies van der Rohe, a young architect, who was creating glass skyscrapers.

Ludwig Mies van der Rohe,
Glass Skyscraper, project,
Friedrichstrasse Skyscraper
competition, Berlin, 1921–22.

70

2.11 Ludwig Mies
van der Rohe

Ludwig Mies came from a working-class background. He was the son of a stonemason in Aachen, Germany. As a young boy, he earned money working as a runner
on building sites. When he finished elementary school, he went to a trade school to
study construction systems. At fifteen, he left school to work as a draftsman in an
architectural office. When he began working in architecture, he added his mother's
maiden name, van der Rohe, to his own name.

He then moved to Berlin and worked for Bruno Paul, a leading furniture designer
and an important member of the Werkbund. Two years later, he was commissioned
to build a house as a designer/contractor. The project was so successful, he was
offered a job working for Behrens, who, by that time, was the leading modern
architect in Europe.

In the Behrens office, Mies was introduced to the new technologies for industrial
buildings and exposed to the neoclassical planning techniques that Behrens utilized.

He also met two other young architects, Walter Gropius and Charles-Edouard Jeanneret (later Le Corbusier). In 1921, Mies entered the Friedrichstrasse Skyscraper competition with a visionary design that attracted the attention of Taut and other Werkbund members. As a result, he was invited to become involved in the Werkbund, which led to several major commissions that established his career.

In the mid-1920s, Mies was selected by the Werkbund to plan a large housing exhibition called Weissenhof. It was to include thirty-three residential buildings that would demonstrate new housing systems. Mies created the master plan, outlined ground rules for the project, and designed one apartment block himself. He then invited Gropius, Behrens, Le Corbusier, Taut, Oud, Hilberseimer, and other modernists to design the other structures. His management of the project was masterful, and his decision to include other modernists made the project even more important.

In 1928, he designed the German Pavilion at the Barcelona International Exhibition, a sleek glass box with sensitive spatial divisions and rich materials that expressed the essence of his style. Conservative Barcelona officials tried to diminish its importance by placing it on a small site surrounded by a fence and disqualified the building from the architectural competition, claiming it was not architecture. Nevertheless the Barcelona Pavilion achieved international fame as the first glass house ever built, and it became a major landmark in design.[22]

2.12 Walter Gropius

Walter Gropius came from a wealthy Prussian family of architects and military officers. He first studied architecture in Munich at the age of twenty, but he disliked school and stayed only a semester. He then joined the military service but left when he was not promoted. Gropius returned to architecture school, this time in Berlin. Once at school, he faced another problem: he could no longer draw. A psychological impediment caused his hand to become cramped whenever he tried. Determined to become an architect, he hired a draftsman to help him at school. He never finished his degree, but while he was living in Berlin he read Werkbund magazines and became intrigued with the heroic quality of industrial forms and more specifically with the projects of Behrens.[23]

He worked briefly in Behrens's office, where he was exposed to the practical issues of building industrial structures. After leaving Behrens, Gropius wrote articles on modernism that brought him to the attention of the Werkbund. He also opened an office with the architect Adolf Meyer. In the next few years, Gropius and Meyer developed two successful modern buildings: the Fagus shoe factory and the Cologne Werkbund Pavilion.

The design for the Fagus shoe factory was drawn from the industrial concepts of nineteenth-century train sheds. It utilized neoclassical planning principles, but featured industrial details and glass walls. The Werkbund Pavilion in Cologne, commissioned by Hermann Muthesius, had a dynamic, machinelike quality. Both projects were well received, but the promising partnership was interrupted when World War I began. During the war, Gropius thought about teaching. He knew that Henry van der Velde had been forced to leave the Weimar Arts and Crafts School, because Germany was at war with Belgium, and he applied for the position as director of the school. Nothing was decided for several years, but toward the end of the war, he received the appointment.[24]

73

Walter Gropius, Monument for the March Dead, Weimar historic cemetery, erected in 1922.

In the early 1920s, Gropius and Meyer entered the competition for the Chicago Tribune Tower with a modern glass skyscraper somewhat reminiscent of Louis Sullivan's work but without ornament. Instead, it was a sleek cubist structure with balconies, expressed in shifting planes that served as a basis for much of his later work.

During the same years, Gropius developed an abstract sculpture for a memorial to the nine workers who were killed in the Kapp Putsch. His dramatic design had an expressionist quality different from his other projects. The memorial was erected in 1922, destroyed by the Nazis in 1933, and rebuilt in 1945.

72   2.13   The Weimar Culture

Walk through our streets and cities and do not howl with shame at such deserts of ugliness . . . All our works are nothing but splinters . . . created by practical requirements . . . (they) do not satisfy the longing for a world of beauty . . . But there is one consolation for us: the idea, the building of an ardent, bold forward-looking architectural idea to be fulfilled by a happier age that must come.
—Walter Gropius[25]

In 1919, Walter Gropius, Bruno Taut, and cultural critic Adolf Behne curated an exhibition on "unknown architects." They also wrote essays distributed at the event that eloquently expressed the strange mixture of hope and frustration that characterized German artists and architects immediately following World War I. They were critical of the world around them but still hopeful for the future.

The war had a devastating effect on German culture. The Treaty of Versailles required Germany to pay war reparations, despite the fact that the economy was depleted. Paul von Hindenburg, who had dominated the government for many years, stepped aside. A national assembly convened in the city of Weimar, and a new constitution was drafted. The leaders of the Weimar government were Socialists, who improved conditions for the working class by accepting trade unions and creating an eight-hour workday and encouraging artistic expression, intellectual activity, and industrial growth.

Walter Gropius, Bauhaus,
Dessau, 1925.

During the Weimar era (1918–33), Germany had a liberal atmosphere. Controversial subjects were openly discussed. There were exhibitions of expressionist art. But the art of the 1920s was different than the art created before the war. Art critic G. F. Hartlaub referred to this era as "die Neue Sachlichkeit," or the New Objectivity, characterized by a cynical attitude among artists and a sense of realism among architects and designers.

The Bauhaus, arguably the most important design school in the twentieth century, operated from 1919 to 1933, coinciding almost exactly with the Weimar Republic. It passed through several different stages, beginning in the heated era of German Expressionism and ending in the more sober period of Neue Sachlichkeit.

2.14 The First
Bauhaus Era

In 1919, Gropius assumed the leadership of the Weimar Arts and Crafts School. The position gave him some freedom to introduce new ideas, but his policies were subject to the approval of the local government, which supported the institution. He renamed the program "Bauhaus," a word that referred to medieval building and implied that it would remain a traditional crafts school, even though the curriculum would focus on modern design.

Gropius announced that the school would create industrial prototypes to help restore the German economy and would develop ideas for the "building of the future." In 1919, he issued the Programme of the Staatliches Bauhaus in Weimar, which included an idealistic statement of principles, and wrote an enthusiastic Bauhaus manifesto, outlining his goals:

> Architects, sculptors, painters, we all must return to the crafts . . . There is no essential difference between the artist and the craftsman . . . Together let us desire, conceive, and create the new structure of the future, which will embrace architecture and sculpture and painting in one unity and which will one day rise toward heaven from the hands of a million workers like the crystal symbol of a new faith.[26]

73

Oscar Schlemmer, costumes
for the Triadic Ballet, photograph originally published in
the *Wieder Metropol*, 1926.

Woman seated in a chair,
designed by Marcel Breuer.
She wears a mask, created
by Oskar Schlemmer.

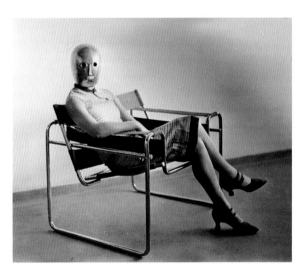

Gropius also promised to eliminate the traditional university rules that hampered
creativity. Some members of the crafts school faculty stayed on, but new teachers
were recruited including Paul Klee, Oskar Schlemmer, Johannes Itten, Lyonel
Feininger, Georg Muche, Josef Albers, László Moholy-Nagy, and Wassily
Kandinsky; Theo van Doesburg became a lecturer in 1921. All were distinguished
artists with different views that frequently conflicted with those of the original faculty. The two groups debated whether the Bauhaus should create art or commercial
products and discussed the role of mechanization in design. The local politicians
who supervised Bauhaus funding also participated in these discussions and pres-
sured Gropius to provide a practical, rather than an artistic, education.

Although Weimar was a cultural center, its residents were conservative. The parties,
the playful antics of the students, and the political rallies at the school offended the
middle-class community. The socialist views of the faculty also caused objections.
Gropius had powerful friends in government, but he was constantly working on
public relations and fighting for financial support.[27]

In 1923, Gropius arranged for the school to host a major exhibition on art and design, which he hoped would improve their image. He introduced the slogan, "Art and Technology, the New Unity," as the exhibition's theme. Although only a few projects reflected that theme, the exhibit was extremely successful, attracting prominent members of the European art world and getting glowing reviews. The most popular event was a performance of Schlemmer's Triadic Ballet based on his theory of "dance Constructivism." [28]

After years of financial struggle and ideological debate, the government announced in 1925 that the school would close. In an unexpected turn of events, Fritz Hesse, the mayor of Dessau, convinced his government that the Bauhaus would bring artistic prestige to their quiet city. He invited the school to move to Dessau and courted the faculty with offers of artistic commissions. Gropius, who wanted to build an architectural practice, was given the chance to create housing and university buildings. Other faculty members were commissioned to develop paintings, furnishings, and interior designs.

The Bauhaus closed its workshops in Weimar and reopened shortly thereafter in Dessau. Gropius designed a dramatic industrial building for the school in a reinforced concrete structure with a three-story wall of glass with the atmosphere of a creative factory. All of the Bauhaus workshops contributed to the design. The lighting and industrial details were made by the metal workshop. The glass workshop, run by Albers, developed several design details. The print workshop provided the signs and the brochures. The joinery shop, supervised by Marcel Breuer, produced the furniture, and his tubular steel chairs were quite popular. Schlemmer's theater group performed at the grand opening of the school. Critics praised the building, as well as the houses for the Bauhaus masters, also designed by Gropius.

At this point Gropius added the study of prefabricated housing to the Bauhaus curriculum, hoping it would lead to real projects. A short time later, he received a contract to build low-income houses on the nearby Torten estates, but the commission led to more problems. The contractors claimed the project should have been awarded to local architects, and labor leaders objected because the prefabricated designs reduced the number of jobs. They tried to defeat Gropius by slowing down the construction process, which raised costs. Eventually, Gropius exceeded his budget, which caused so much protest from the community that he was forced to resign. [29]

75

2.15 The Second Bauhaus Era

Mayor Hesse reluctantly chose the Swiss architect Hannes Meyer to replace Gropius. Meyer was part of a Swiss avant-garde group that published the journal *ABC*. He believed in function over form and pragmatism over aesthetics; he was also a communist who felt practical issues were more important than individual art. To make the curriculum conform to his views, Meyer eliminated the painting workshop, reassigned art classes to smaller workshops within commercial design, and focused the curriculum on practical production. Several faculty members resigned abruptly. Moholy-Nagy left, and Meyer replaced him with Marianne Brandt, a gifted lighting and product designer, who also understood mass production. [30]

Herbert Bayer was asked to develop an advertising workshop. Bayer had done interesting experiments on the relationship between signs and buildings and was

Herbert Bayer, *Newspaper Kiosk*, project depicting the relationship between architecture and advertising, 1924.

76

also interested in "Lichtarchitektur," light architecture, an intriguing new trend in urban design. In the postwar period the government installed electric lights on city streets throughout Germany, and light became a creative medium and established a new type of advertising. It not only promoted industrial products; it made the cities safer at night and created a more positive mood.[31]

Meyer felt the Bauhaus should participate in this effort and saw no conflict between art and advertising. He also moved disciplines like printing, photography, and exhibit design to the advertising faculty. Under Meyer, the Bauhaus seemed to have a more

The Young Theatre at the
Bauhaus, performing in the
"Bauhaus Review," 1929.

orderly system, but the commercial orientation did not inspire the rich creativity
of the previous era. The outward order also hid another issue at the school: as a
dedicated Marxist, Meyer encouraged communism among the students despite the
fact that the local government specifically prohibited political activism at universities. By 1930, the Bauhaus was seen as a Marxist institution. The community
of Dessau was so incensed that Mayor Hesse was forced to dismiss Meyer.

2.16 The Third
Bauhaus Era

Throughout this time, Gropius had worked quietly in the background. When Meyer
left, he arranged for Mies van der Rohe to take charge of the Bauhaus. By this time,
Mies was a respected member of the avant-garde and an important figure in the
Werkbund. Unlike Meyer, Mies had little interest in social causes; his whole life was
dedicated to architecture.

His first challenge was to transform the Marxist image of the school. He and Mayor
Hesse closed the Bauhaus and reopened a few weeks later with a new program.
That year, an economic panic had affected the whole country. The value of the
mark had fallen dramatically, unemployment had soared, and the German economy
was thrown into chaos. The workers staged many protests over the loss of jobs,
which enabled the Fascist party to defeat the Socialist regime. In 1932, the Nazis
swept the local elections. A short time later, they closed the Dessau Bauhaus.

Mies was invited to move the school to Leipzig or Magdeburg, but he chose to
reopen in Berlin, using his own funds. The final version of the Bauhaus was a small
private school in a factory building. In this era, architecture became the major
focus. Other workshops were marginalized. Mies invited urban planner Ludwig
Hilberseimer to teach in the department. Hilberseimer presented a systematized
style of planning and design, but he also included parks, south-facing terraces, and
vegetable gardens in the projects. The Berlin Bauhaus lasted only nine months
before the Nazis closed its doors.

Ludwig Karl Hilberseimer, Highrise City, project, perspective view of North-South street, 1924.

Ludwig Mies van der Rohe with Philip Johnson, Seagram Building, New York, 1954–58.

2.17 The Bauhaus Faculty
in America

When the Nazis closed the final German Bauhaus in 1933, most of the remaining faculty emigrated to the United States, where they were greeted with generous support. The Museum of Modern Art was their strongest ally. Philip Johnson, the curator of architecture and design, and Alfred H. Barr Jr., the director, actively supported their work. Johnson had visited Germany and was familiar with their history.

He had also been the co-curator with Henry-Russell Hitchcock of "Modern Architecture—International Exhibition," a major show at MoMA in 1932, which included work by Gropius, Mies, and Le Corbusier. Johnson had also collaborated with Hitchcock on *The International Style*, a book that introduced a heroic vision of European modernism.

With Johnson's help, American universities opened up positions for leading members of the Bauhaus faculty. Gropius became the dean at the Harvard Graduate School of Design; he also established a successful architectural office known as The Architects Collaborative. Mies became the dean of the architecture school at the Illinois Institute of Technology and developed a successful architectural practice in Chicago. Albers went to Black Mountain College and taught color theory. Moholy-Nagy tried to start a New Bauhaus in Chicago, but ultimately founded a more American-style school called the Institute of Design in New York. Breuer practiced in New York, and Bayer became design director at the J. Walter Thompson advertising agency.

In 1938, Gropius arranged another exhibition at MoMA. This time, chairs by Gerrit Rietveld, Breuer, Mies, and Le Corbusier were prominently displayed, and Bauhaus designs for products, such as lamps, flatware, pottery, and textiles, were also exhibited. Posters from the printing workshop were also shown. In the United States, the Bauhaus faculty realized many of their ambitions and became what they had always hoped to become in Europe: a major influence on the future.

2.18 Expressionist
Cinema

In the 1920s, German Expressionism also engendered a rich era in cabaret, theater, and cinema exploring a variety of themes. Some films portrayed the corrupt environments of European cities in the era between the wars. Other films, like *Metropolis*, presented issues of mechanization and class struggle. A third group of films explored the political conditions of that complex period through haunting medieval environments.

The Cabinet of Dr. Caligari, produced in 1920, depicts the brutal acts of a mad killer in sets containing strange painted images on paperlike walls of a distorted city. Russian director Sergei Eisenstein described the film as a "dismal fantasy . . . showing us a future as an unrelieved night crowded with sinister shadows and crimes." Cultural critic Siegfried Kracauer wrote about the implications of the designs, claiming the flimsy sets were a comment on the vulnerability of 1920s culture and anticipated the rise of Nazism. Kurt Tucholsky had another view; he felt the sets were a revealing probe into the experience of dreams.[32]

Der Golem, designed by the architect Hans Poelzig with Marlene Moeschke and Kurt Richter, portrayed the story of a mythical figure that protected the Jews in a sixteenth-century ghetto. The designers built a medieval village with narrow streets and handcrafted cottages, the interior spaces of which resembled caves.

Production still from the film
Woman in the Moon, 1929.
Director: Fritz Lang.

Another group of filmmakers introduced Weimar street films, which portray cities as dark, shadowy environments, where innocent men become victims of circumstances. The sets were based on real buildings, but they were reconstructed in studios to exaggerate their shabby, depressed quality. The Weimar street films also used dramatic lighting techniques to express danger in a style later utilized by film noir.

The urban environment was a major issue in the films of the 1920s. In turn, the film industry had an impact on urban design. European theater districts featured huge posters and electric signs based on the New York models of Broadway and Times Square. Dramatic billboards adorned with actors and movie scenes brought flamboyant glamour to the streets. In observing an enormous poster of Greta Garbo, journalist/designer Adolf Behne wrote, "Not since antiquity have there been such images of gods and goddesses."[33] As promotional tools for film, billboard designs were often rich and complex using photomontage to portray not only the performers, but also the cinematic themes and environments. The design journal *Deutsche Bauzeitung* called the lure of the posters "Blickfangwerbung," the ability to capture the gaze and imagination of the crowd.[34]

2.19 De Stijl Movement

The artists of today, all over the world, impelled by one and the same consciousness, have taken part on the spiritual plane in the world war against the domination of individualism, of arbitrariness. They therefore sympathize with all who are fighting spiritually or materially for the formation of an international unity in life, art, and culture.
—Theo van Doesburg[35]

In 1917, a small group of Dutch artists, furniture designers, and architects formed a new movement, which they called De Stijl, or "the style." They felt the overwhelming destruction caused by World War I had shifted the priorities of art from subjects exploring individual ideas to the search for universal expressions. In 1918, Theo van Doesburg and other members of the group developed the first of several manifestos in which they declared their political position.

Gerrit Rietveld, Red and
Blue Chair, 1918.

Gerrit Rietveld, Rietveld-
Schroder House, 50, Prins
Hendriklaan, Utrecht, 1924.

This group rejected German Expressionism and its highly emotional imagery. They
felt expressionism had a medieval quality and a relationship to Arts and Crafts.
Instead, they advocated a new type of universal art, removed from the reality of
natural forms, which they described as an abstract style of pure art, or neo-plasticism.

81

Piet Mondrian created revolutionary works that explored grid compositions in primary colors without any literary or cultural references. His work was influenced by
the ideas of the mathematician M.J.H. Schoenmackers, who tried to define the world
in purely mathematical terms. Mondrian was also dedicated to an idea of truth as a
purely objective concept. The Belgian painter George Vantongerloo and the Dutch
painter Bart van der Leck experimented with nonrepresentational art. Their projects emphasized ideas of harmony using minimal compositions of geometrical
forms. They limited their colors to a vocabulary of primary hues—red, yellow, and
blue, as well as white, gray, and black. Architects and furniture designers, including Gerrit Rietveld, Jan Wils, Cornelis van Eesteren, Robert van't Hoff, Theo
van Doesburg, and J.J.P. Oud, applied these principles in three-dimensional forms.

2.20 Gerrit Rietveld

In 1917-18, Rietveld designed the famous "manifesto chair," a three-dimensional
expression of a chair structure. Each plane is placed at a dramatic angle, and each
joint is clearly articulated through color and construction. He later explored
similar themes in light fixtures and other pieces of furniture developed in the same
aesthetic language.

Cornelis van Eesteren and
Theo van Doesburg, shopping
arcade with a cafe, and apartments on upper floors.
Competition project for a site
in The Hague, 1924.

In 1924, Rietveld met Truus Schröder-Schräder, who commissioned him to build a
house based on the idea of the manifesto chair. The Rietveld-Schröder House, a
striking cubist composition, is a rich geometrical exercise in the design and assembly system of a white box. Three-dimensional shifting of planes is emphasized by
simple industrial rails; accent lines in primary colors articulate various elements in
the design. The interior explores other machine age concepts, such as the use of
flexible walls and prefabricated elements. The floor and walls are painted gray,
black, and primary colors to emphasize the geometrical layout of the design. The
furniture is based on similar principles. Many of the shelves and seating areas were
built into the walls, maintaining a minimal aesthetic.

2.21   Theo van Doesburg
        and Cornelis van
        Eesteren

In 1918, van Doesburg established *De Stijl*, a journal that published articles on the
new movement, as well as projects by artists, architects, and furniture designers. As
its editor, he became the leading spokesman of the group. He also created paintings
and architectural projects, including the dramatic design of the Café Aubette, which
he developed in collaboration with Jean Arp and Sophie Taeuber-Arp.

Van Doesburg wrote numerous articles on design and planning. He also traveled
through Europe campaigning actively on behalf of modern architecture and spent
several years in Weimar, lecturing at the Bauhaus. Van Doesburg later collaborated
with Cornelis van Eesteren, a talented architect and urban planner. Together, they
created drawings and models of architectural compositions. None of the designs
were ever built, but they served as striking illustrations of De Stijl principles.[36]

Alvar Aalto, Finnish Pavilion
at the New York World's
Fair, 1939–40.

2.22 Alvar Aalto

*The most difficult problems do not occur in the search for form, but rather in the attempt
to create forms that are based on real human values.*
—Alvar Aalto[37]

Finnish architect Alvar Aalto integrated the functional planning approach of
European modernism with the themes of nature and traditional Finnish woodcraft
systems. Trained both as an architect and a furniture designer, Aalto formed
a design company called Artek with his wife, Aino Marsio, and Harry and Marie
Gullischen. Aalto created a variety of products for Artek, including bentwood
furniture and glassware that inspired Charles and Ray Eames, Eero Saarinen, and
other mid-century modernists. His elegant curving forms were distinctly modern
but also included organic elements.

Aalto's first major building was a sanatorium in Paimio, Finland, built in the late
1920s. Although the form was based on the white box, the interior featured intriguing wood details. The terraces contained planted areas and views near the site. A
sauna and greenhouse were also constructed on the grounds.

Aalto won a competition to design the Finnish Pavilion at the 1939–40 World's Fair
in New York. The main feature of the exhibition space was a masterful curving
wall, which leaned at a striking angle. This dramatic undulating wall was composed
of wooden slats that provided a textured background for the display of Finnish
craft products. In the same period, Aalto also designed the Villa Mairea for the
Gullichsens. This handsome house combined the cubist white box with the use of
local materials, such as wood and stone. It featured a grass-covered roof, then an
indigenous concept in Finland and today an important element of green architecture.

83

Alvar Aalto, Villa Mairea,
Noormarkku, Finland,
1938–39.

In 1939, Aalto addressed the Nordic Architectural Conference giving his views
about nature: "I have said before that nature herself is the best standardization committee in the world, but in nature, standardization is almost exclusively applied to
the smallest possible unit, the cell. This results in millions of flexible combinations
that never become schematic. It also results in unlimited riches and perpetual varia-
tion in organically growing forms."[38]

Aalto was sometimes described as a humanist, and sometimes as a rationalist. His
work represented a different approach to modernism, but was fully accepted by the
leading modernists.

84

2.23 Le Corbusier

*The use of technical analysis and architectural synthesis enabled me to draw up my
scheme for a contemporary city of three million inhabitants. The result of my work was
shown in November 1922 at the Salon d'Automne in Paris. It was greeted with a sort of
stupor; the shock of surprise caused rage in some quarters and enthusiasm in others.*
—Le Corbusier[39]

Le Corbusier (born Charles-Edouard Jeanneret) began as a student at a Swiss art
school, preparing for a career as an engraver in the clock industry, but after taking
art classes with an innovative professor, he decided to become an architect. Professor
L'Eplattinier introduced him to the work of avant-garde designers and engineers,
and he also arranged for Jeanneret to design a villa to earn money to travel and
study architecture.

The fees supported a remarkable series of apprenticeships. In 1907, he went to
Vienna to visit Josef Hoffmann. After touring the city, he realized that he disliked
the fussy details of the art nouveau style. He was offered a job in Hoffmann's office,
but he decided not to stay. He then traveled to Lyon to meet Tony Garnier. He was
intrigued with the white concrete buildings in Cité Industrielle and with Garnier's
use of conceptual design to present a rational approach to urban planning. That

Auguste and Gustave Perret, drawing, Paris, 1922.

Le Corbusier, *Contemporary City for Three Million Inhabitants*, Paris, 1922.

year, he also visited the Charterhouse of Ema and was impressed with the logical systems of the collective community.

In 1908, he moved to Paris and met Auguste and Gustave Perret, who had just completed the Rue Franklin apartment house and moved their office to the ground floor. He worked as a draftsman in their office for almost two years. There, he learned about the modern concepts of open plans, steel structures, and reinforced concrete systems. In 1910, he moved to Berlin, where he discovered the Deutsche Werkbund publications and the industrial language of bridges, factories, and grain silos. He also worked briefly as a draftsman in Peter Behrens's office, where he met Walter Gropius and Ludwig Mies van der Rohe, who were also in the midst of their apprenticeships. He then went to Italy and Greece to visit ancient buildings and found himself moved by their formal clarity and elegant proportional systems. He developed dozens of drawings of classical structures and then returned home to work on his own ideas in painting and design.[40]

All of these experiences affected his approach to design. In 1917, he returned to Paris and visited Auguste Perret, who introduced him to the cubist painters Amédée Ozenfant and Fernand Léger. Together, they created *L'Esprit Nouveau*, a journal that promoted modern art and design. They also formed a new movement, which they called Purism. It was based on cubism, but focused on geometrical compositions.

Through the process of writing articles for *L'Esprit Nouveau*, Jeanneret developed several new concepts. Paris, like most European cities in the 1920s, had a severe housing shortage. It also suffered from traffic jams, especially in the tourist season, when five million visitors descended on the city. In 1921, he wrote an article called, "Building by Mass Production," in which he described a house as a "machine for living in." He also asserted that houses could be mass-produced, which would help to solve the problem of the housing shortage.[41]

In 1922, he was asked to develop an exhibition on town planning at the Salon d'Automne. Organizers expected him to show a few details like traffic signs or public art. Instead, he created a conceptual city for three million inhabitants called Ville Contemporaine, featuring a grid of white skyscrapers surrounded by parks and highways, and wrote a manifesto describing his design as a "vertical garden city."

85

Le Corbusier, Villa Savoye,
Poissy, France, 1928–30.

By 1923, his direction was clearly defined. He changed his name to "Le Corbusier," which meant the "crowlike one." He also published *Towards a New Architecture*, a book that restated his belief that buildings were "machines for living in." He also wrote a set of principles, which he called the "Five Points of a New Architecture," in which he outlined his priorities in design. He claimed that buildings should be based on the following concepts:

1. Pilotis: Structures should be lifted off the ground on columns

2. Roof garden: Roof areas should be developed as terraces for recreation and planting

3. Free plan: Structures should be supported by columns so the walls can take any shape and be located anywhere in the plan

4. Ribbon window: Facades should have a continuous line of windows to increase natural light

5. Free facade: Structures should be supported by columns, so exterior walls can take any shape

In 1928-30, he designed the Villa Savoye, a weekend house that would become one of the best examples of the application of these points. Built on a hill above the town of Poissy, about fifty miles from Paris, the reinforced concrete structure is a pristine white box, which originally stood alone on an open field. It was raised on pilotis, supported by steel columns and adorned with a roof terrace. The building integrated machine-age concepts with sculptural elements. The lower level was curved to accommodate the arrival of an automobile. Inside the building, there was a central ramp, which added a diagonal form to the design. The plan was based on a grid that resembled a Mondrian painting. It featured a large open salon, which combines the dining and living areas. Many of the furnishings were built-in, which reinforced the minimal concept. Although Villa Savoye filled all the functional requirements of the client, it was also a complex exercise in three-dimensional design.

Le Corbusier, Chapel Notre-
Dame-du-Haut, Ronchamp,
France, 1955.

Throughout his career, Le Corbusier adhered to the five points in most of his projects, but in the 1950s, he designed an organic form for a church at Ronchamp. This haunting structure embodies none of the five points. Its walls are both curving and inclined at unusual angles. Its floor slopes downward, following the terrain of the site, and its roof has an organic shape. The windows of the building are also unusual. They are small punched openings, arranged in an abstract manner. Some contain stained glass panels.

When questioned about the origin of the design, he said the form of the roof was inspired by Père Ubu, the absurdist character developed by playwright Alfred Jarry. The curves were supposed to be related to the character's ears. He also claimed that the roof had acoustical properties, but this explanation was never fully accepted. Some critics attributed the expressionistic shape of the roof as a reference to nature, perhaps to the grass roofs of his childhood in the Swiss Alps.

The unusual form was very controversial. Many architects were disturbed by the fact that he had briefly abandoned his Cartesian roots and created an irregular form. But the public didn't mind. The Chapel Notre-Dame-du-Haut became one of his most popular buildings. It also became a cultural icon that appeared on French stamps and tourist brochures. It symbolized a modern concept of a spiritual structure and a softening of the cubist form.[42]

2.24 The Reaction
against Modernism
and the Creation
of CIAM

The undersigned architects . . . have joined together with the intention of seeking to harmonize the elements that confront them in the modern world and of setting architecture back on its true program, which is of an economic and sociological order, dedicated solely to the service of the human being . . . in this way that architecture will escape the sterilizing hold of the Academies.
—First Congress, "The Declaration of La Sarraz," 1928[43]

Though modernism ultimately dominated twentieth-century design, most machine-age architects had to struggle for success. Their concepts initially met with resistance because they were so different from the design traditions that were firmly established in Europe. They also made enemies in the Arts and Crafts community. Adolf Loos alienated many prominent Arts and Crafts designers through his famous article, "Ornament and Crime." In it, he alleged that decorative designs were "a waste of human labor, money, and material . . . Freedom from ornament is a sign of spiritual strength."[44]

Le Corbusier also offended several Arts and Crafts designers, especially Frank Lloyd Wright. In a lecture at the Chicago Art Institute, called "Young Architecture," Wright declared, "Oh yes, young man; consider well that a house is a machine in which to live, but by the same token a heart is a suction pump . . . architecture begins where that concept of the house ends."[45]

As a result of the hostility and the widespread resistance to their work, the machine-age architects had a difficult time attracting clients. Though their projects frequently appeared in exhibitions and magazines, they had very few real commissions. They were also unable to succeed in design competitions, though they often submitted proposals. In 1928, there was a major competition for a new Palace of Nations in Geneva. Many modern architects submitted proposals, including Le Corbusier, whose project attracted a great deal of attention. But the jury, which included art nouveau designers like Josef Hoffmann, rejected all the modern proposals. Instead, they awarded the commission to a team of neoclassical architects, whose design was considered mediocre.

Le Corbusier was infuriated by the choice. He tried to sue the League of Nations, but was unable to proceed because no court in the world would address his complaints. He later commented, "The importance of the competition was felt by many, since 377 schemes arrived in Geneva, which, set out side by side, would have extended for more than six miles."[46]

As a result of this event and other similar rejections, Le Corbusier and other modernists created the organization CIAM, the International Congress of Modern Architecture, which included designers from twenty-three nations who were determined to promote the new style. CIAM became an influential organization that sponsored conferences, exhibitions, publications, and research. In the 1930s, they produced The Athens Charter, a comprehensive proposal on planning, infrastructure, and environmental issues. Its concepts were widely applied.

CIAM was an active organization for about thirty years. Its conferences were attended by many leading modern architects, and its research projects were widely read. Throughout that time, Le Corbusier and the other modernists began to penetrate the design establishment. After World War II, modernism became an established style in Europe, the United States, India, Brazil, Japan, and parts of Africa. By 1959, most members felt the organization had achieved its goals, and CIAM was officially disbanded.

Notes

1. Theo van Doesburg, "Architecture and Revolution—Revolutionary Architecture?" in *Het Bouwbedrijf*, vol. 5, no. 20 (September 1928): 395.

2. P. A. Kropotkin, "The State: Its Historic Role," in *Selected Writings on Anarchism and Revolution*, ed. Martin A. Miller (Cambridge, MA: The MIT Press, 1970), 220-31.

3. Filippo Tommaso Marinetti, *The Futurist Manifesto*, in Gorman, 72.

4. Marinetti, in Gorman, 73.

5. Antonio Sant'Elia and Filippo Tommaso Marinetti, "The Futurist Manifesto," in *Programs and Manifestos on 20th-Century Architecture*, edited by Ulrich Conrads (Cambridge, MA: MIT Press, 1995), 35.

6. Donald J. Bush, *The Streamlined Decade* (New York: George Braziller, Inc., 1975), 99.

7. Alberto Sartoris, quoted in Theo van Doesburg, "Origins of Italian Rationalism," in *Het Bouwbedrijf*, vol. 6, no. 10 (May 1929): 201-3.

8. F. Yalovkin, quoted in William J. R. Curtis, *Modern Architecture Since 1900* (Englewood Cliffs, NJ: Prentice Hall, Inc., 1987), 138.

9. Stefan Sharfin in conversation with the author.

10. Lunacharsky, quoted in Theo van Doesburg, "Architecture and Revolution—Revolutionary Architecture?" 398.

11. Van Doesburg, 438.

12. Francesca Prina and Elena Demartini, *One Thousand Years of World Architecture* (Milan: Mondadori Electa Spa, 2005), 327.

13. Van Doesburg, 400.

14. Marshall S. Shatz, ed., *The Essential Works of Anarchism* (New York: Bantam Books, 1971), 184-85.

15. Ruth Eaton, *Ideal Cities* (New York: Thames and Hudson Inc., 2002), 195-96.

16. Eaton, 193.

17. Van Doesburg, 395.

18. Hermann Muthesius, "Aims of the Werkbund," in Conrads, 26.

19. John Heskett, *Industrial Design* (New York: Oxford University Press, 1980), 88.

20. William J. R. Curtis, *Modern Architecture Since 1900* (Englewood Cliffs, NJ: Prentice Hall, Inc., 1987), 122.

21. Paul Scheerbart "Glass Architecture," in Conrads, 32.

22. Peter Blake, *The Master Builders* (New York: Alfred A. Knopf, 1961), 185-87, 198-200.

23. Elaine S. Hochman, *Bauhaus: Crucible of Modernism* (New York: Fromm International, 1997), 5-8.

24. Penny Sparke, *A Century of Design* (Hauppauge, NY: Barron's Educational Series, Inc., 1998), 88-89.

25. Walter Gropius, "New Ideas in Architecture," in Conrads, 46.

26. Walter Gropius, "Programme of the Staatliches Bauhaus in Weimar," in Conrads, 49.

27. Hochman, 150-51.

28. Magdalena Droste, *Bauhaus* (Koln: Taschen GmbH in association with Bauhaus-Archiv Museum fur Gestaltung und Benedikt, Berlin, 1993), 122-26.

29. Hochman, 209-15.

30. Droste, 166-72.

31. Janet Ward, *Weimar Surfaces* (Berkeley, CA: University of California Press, 2001), 101.

32. Dietrich Neumann, editor, *Film Architecture: Set Designs from Metropolis to Blade Runner* (Munich/New York: Prestel Verlag, 1999), 52.

33. Neumann, 37.

34. Ward, 166.

35. Theo van Doesberg, "'De Stijl' Manifesto I," in Conrads, 39.

36. Carsten-Peter Warncke, *De Stijl 1917–1931* (Koln: Benedikt Taschen Verlag, 1991), 149-52, 208.

37. Alvar Aalto, interview by Philip Herrera, "The Maestro's Late Works," *Time* magazine, Aug. 25, 1975.

38. Alvar Aalto, quoted in Louna Lahti, *Alvar Aalto 1898–1976* (Koln: Taschen GmbH, 2004), 11.

39. Le Corbusier, *The City of To-morrow and its Planning* (New York: Dover Publications, Inc., 1987), 163.

40. Blake, 18-19.

41. Le Corbusier, *The Modular* (Cambridge, MA: MIT Press, 1954), 28-29.

42. Charles Jencks, *The Iconic Building* (New York: Rizzoli, 2005), 56-57.

43. First Congress, "The Declaration of La Sarraz," quoted in Le Corbusier, *The Athens Charter* (New York: Grossman Publishers, 1973), 6.

44. Adolf Loos, "Ornament and Crime," in Conrads, 21-24.

45. Frank Lloyd Wright, "Young Architecture," in Conrads, 124.

46. Le Corbusier, *The Athens Charter* (New York: Grossman Publishers, 1973), 3-4.

THE MACHINE AGE IN AMERICA

*I was amazed at the chasm between the excellent quality of much American production
and its gross appearance, clumsiness, bulk, and noise . . . I could not imagine how such
brilliant manufacturers . . . could put up with it for so long . . . I imagined that a time
would come when I could combine an aesthetic sensibility with my professional background in engineering.*
—Raymond Loewy[1]

In the 1920s, American manufacturers introduced a new technological era that
promised to provide more comfort and convenience than any other age in history.
They invented remarkable new products that offered greater access to information,
faster transportation, and easier household maintenance.

Two inventions laid the groundwork for this dramatic era. The first was a practical
system of electricity, created by Thomas Edison. The development of electricity
required not only the design of the lightbulb, but also a stable supply of power, a
network of circuitry, and linkage systems, such as sockets, switches, wires, and
fuses. Edison completed the entire system in 1879 and illuminated one square mile
of New York City with electric streetlights.

The system was extremely successful—and it made the city safer at night. Edison
also demonstrated that electricity could provide power for the new subways and
skyscrapers that were just being planned. Investors like J.P. Morgan saw the potential and established the Edison General Electric Co., which soon supplied energy to
cities across the United States. Edison's system of direct current eventually would
be replaced with Nikola Tesla's system of alternating current, which was less costly.

The full implications of electrical power were not understood until the twentieth
century, when the U.S. government brought power to the homes of average consumers, first in urban areas and later rural communities. In 1910, only 24 percent of
American homes had electricity. By 1940, it was available in 90 percent of the
nation's households.[2]

Electrification led to many new products, such as refrigerators, washing machines,
tractors, and manufacturing systems, with each new product having an impact on
modern life. Between 1912 and 1929, the work hours of average Americans were
reduced from seventy to forty-eight per week, and as work became more efficient,
ordinary Americans had more free time to explore personal interests.[3]

Hugh Ferriss in his studio, completing the painting *A Street Vista of the Future*, from the series Vision of the Titan City, 1975.

The new leisure time brought a sense of prosperity to average families. They could afford to own radios, cameras, and clocks; even cars were within their reach. They also had time to see films, which portrayed a glamorous new image of American culture. The 1920s was the beginning of the age of mass production, mass advertising, and mass communications. It was also the beginning of the consumer society, which soon defined the American way of life.

Each invention had to be designed, manufactured, and marketed, which led to the new profession of industrial design. These designers had a broader role in product development than nineteenth-century craftsmen: they clarified the idea of the product, decided on its form and color, and refined its functional systems. They also chose the materials and assembly processes. In 1932, Norman Bel Geddes described the job of an industrial designer in his book *Horizons*:

1. Determine the specific design objectives: the intended function of a product, the way it is made, sold and serviced.

2. Visit the client's factory and determine the capacity and limitations of the machines and the workers. Perform a cost analysis of the manufacturing, distribution and promotion of the product.

3. Research the competition, surveying the consumers' attitudes, and test the competitive product to determine its good and bad points.

4. Consider the opinions of salesmen, engineers, advertisers, and other specialists.[4]

This period also witnessed the emergence of the automobile. Henry Ford imagined a society in which anyone could own a car and travel across the country on open roads. In 1913, Ford observed the new assembly line system of processing in a meat-packing factory and applied the same concept to automobiles in his factory. The assembly line reduced the time it took to put a car together from 12.5 to 1.5 hours, which significantly lowered the price of the vehicle.[5]

In 1914, Ford raised the wages of his workers from $2.34 to $5 per day. The higher wages meant workers were able to buy cars, which stimulated the economy. From 1912 to 1920, Ford's production levels rose from 78,000 to over one million cars annually.[6] During these years, Ford manufactured only one design, the Model T, a reliable black car. His efficient manufacturing system depended on a standardized design. In the 1920s, Ford's approach was challenged by General Motors. Their industrial designer, Harley Earl, developed several different styles of automobiles for various types of consumers. He also came up with a production system that allowed GM to manufacture the different styles using the same parts, which maintained lower prices. He even arranged to make cars in a variety of colors.[7]

As a result, manufacturers were forced to diversify their lines and generate products for various consumer groups, working with industrial designers to develop the style and marketing of their new concepts. These designers brought energy and creativity to the marketplace, introducing many innovations, including the sleek look of the streamlined era. Within a decade, business statistics indicated that design played a major role in the success of a product.

| 3.1 | The Streamlined Designers |

Originally, the word streamlining was a term of hydrodynamics. About the year 1909, the science of aerodynamics borrowed it to describe the smooth flow of air as well as the form of a body which would move through air with a minimum of resistance.
— Norman Bel Geddes[8]

In the 1920s, the most dramatic innovation of the new industrial designers was the development of streamlined forms, or the use of curves derived from the shape of birds and fish, which were ideal forms for moving through air or water. The concept had been studied by nineteenth-century engineers, such as Ludwig Mach, who observed the path of cigarette smoke in a wind tunnel and discovered that the smoke naturally formed a cylindrical shape when moving at maximum speed. In 1852, the American sculptor Horatio Greenough wrote about streamlining:

"If we compare the form of a newly invented machine with the perfected type of the same instrument, we observe . . . how weight is shaken off where strength is less needed, how functions are made to approach without impeding each other, how straight becomes curved . . . till the straggling and cumbersome machine becomes the compact, effective, and beautiful engine."[9]

William Van Alen, Chrysler
Building, New York,
1928–30.

In the 1920s and 1930s, American industrial designers transformed the boxy silhou-
ettes of early vehicles into sleek curvaceous forms. The concept was then applied
to trains, ships, and airplanes. This style also appealed to manufacturers, who
developed streamlined clocks, radios, and other consumer products, even though
the shape had no bearing on their performance. Streamlined design brought new
sophistication to American products and expressed the national obsession with
speed and efficiency. The shapely vehicles also fostered the art deco style, which
introduced curving forms into the designs of buildings, furniture, and interior environments. The era produced a glamorous new image of American culture, defined
by fast cars, modern buildings, and fashionable interiors. Streamlined forms also
seemed to match the seductive sounds of jazz. Throughout this period, Broadway
shows and Hollywood films presented musical performances staged in elegant
vehicles and art deco sets.

Norman Bel Geddes,
The Streamlined Ocean Liner,
model, 1932.

3.2   Norman Bel Geddes

Bel Geddes was the first major industrial designer to establish an independent office in New York. He not only developed a successful practice as a consultant to business clients, he also created a variety of conceptual projects and wrote articles promoting streamlined design. At the time, there were many opportunities for young designers. Every department store needed a window dresser. Every public event required poster designs. There were also theatrical projects. The New York theater community put on as many as 300 plays at one time. In 1923, Bel Geddes was was hired to create the set for *The Miracle*. The story takes place in a church, so he turned the entire theater into a cathedral, even replacing the theater seats with church pews.

In 1927, he opened an industrial design office. His first projects included radios for Philco and RCA, automobile prototypes for the Graham Paige Co., as well as kitchen appliances and ship interiors. Throughout his career, Bel Geddes created conceptual proposals including designs for vehicles, buildings, and eventually, a city of the future. Most of his projects were based on streamlined concepts. His 1932 design of a conceptual ocean liner is an extraordinary compact, biomorphic vision of a mechanical great whale, which could move through the ocean at unprecedented speeds. The exterior of the ship is seamless, but sections of the shell could be opened to release streamlined pods containing lifeboats and seaplanes. This conceptual ship would weigh about the same as the *Queen Mary*, but it would be 80 percent longer, 30 percent slimmer, and travel about 25 percent faster than that famous ship.[10]

That year, he also created an aerial restaurant, which was exhibited at the Century of Progress Exposition in Chicago in 1933. The restaurant perches nearly 300 feet above the ground on a structural column, which houses an elevator leading directly to the dramatic circular space. It would have three floors of seating, accommodating about 1,200 people and rotate slowly to offer incomparable views of the surrounding area.[11]

95

Norman Bel Geddes,
Aerial Restaurant, model,
1932.

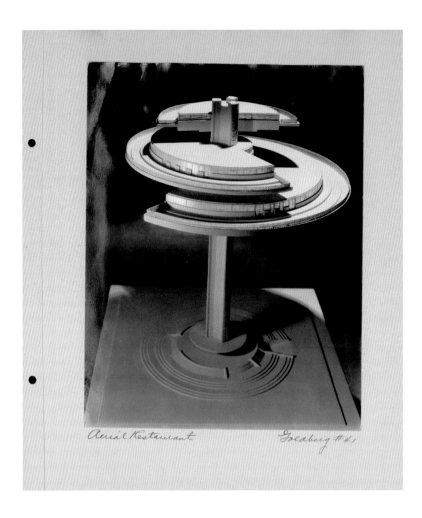

96

In 1934, an article in *Fortune* magazine entitled "Both Fish and Fowl," attacked streamlined design, stating, "advanced designs would cost American industry a billion dollars in retooling." The article was unsigned, but many believed the writer to have been George Nelson, a designer who preferred Bauhaus concepts. Several designers responded by explaining how aerodynamic forms reduced the cost of fuel in vehicles and allowed them to travel faster. The article also provoked some public debate but it failed to dampen the enthusiasm for streamlined concepts. The sleek curving forms continued to capture public interest as the symbol of an era of progress.

3.3   Raymond Loewy

In the late 1920s, French designer Raymond Loewy began approaching businessmen with a card that read: "Between two products equal in price, function, and quality, the better looking will outsell the other." He had to convince potential clients that design added value to a product. His first client was a manufacturer of mimeograph machines who made an awkward piece of equipment. Loewy simplified the function of the machine and built a clay model of an alternative form. His design was so successful that the company produced it for more than forty years.

Loewy's career began in 1908, when he won a model airplane design contest sponsored by J.G. Bennett, a wealthy American flying enthusiast. Using his prize

Raymond Loewy,
Locomotive S1 of the
Pennsylvania Railroad
Company, 1938.

money, fifteen-year-old Loewy redesigned and patented the winning concept, and began manufacturing toy airplanes.[12]

At the age of sixteen, he sold his profitable toy company and used the funds to go to engineering school, but he never completed a degree. After serving in World War I, he moved to New York. Loewy's industrial design practice was extremely success-ful because he not only designed products, he also generated publicity for his clients. His design for the Pennsylvania Railroad was faster and more fuel efficient than most trains, and the interior provided improvements in the comfort of passenger seating and service systems. He later applied similar principles in creating sumptu-ous interiors for luxurious airplanes, such as the *Concorde* and *Air Force One*.

Loewy had a distinct visual style, but he never defined a strict philosophy. He created logos for Exxon and Lucky Strike, cans and graphics for Coca-Cola, and packaging for Nabisco. After completing a study for the U.S. Department of Transportation, he expanded the use of safety features in automobiles and improved sight lines and interior details.

In the 1970s, after conducting exhaustive studies on motion, materials, and propor-tions, he developed improvements in the comfort and functions of the astronauts' cabins on NASA spacecraft. By then, he was over eighty years old, but he was unable to resist the challenge of creating a zero-gravity environment.[13]

97

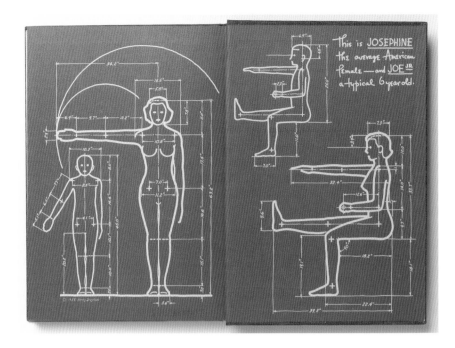

Henry Dreyfuss, human measurements and motion studies, drawing originally published in *Designing for People*, 1955.

3.4   Henry Dreyfuss

Dreyfuss was the first major designer to develop the concept of ergonomics and human scale in design. Coming from a family of costume designers, he was well aware of the importance of individual measurements, and he later applied this knowledge to improve the quality and functionality of products and environments.

Dreyfuss began his career building stage sets, but in 1929, he won a design competition, sponsored by Bell Labs, for a telephone of the future.[14] The competition began a long association with AT&T that enabled him to open his own office. His first telephone was a black plastic model that combined a receiver and a transmitter in a single handset. This classic American telephone was designed to fit neatly between the head and shoulder of the user. It also took advantage of the new science of plastics, which provided a lightweight, durable material that was inexpensive to produce.

Products for other manufacturers included a refrigerator for General Electric, a vacuum cleaner for Hoover, the Polaroid Land Camera, and the famous train, the *Twentieth Century Limited*. Like the other leading designers, Dreyfuss believed in the principles of streamlined forms, which he utilized in many of his designs, but his most innovative work was in ergonomics. In 1955, he published *Designing for People*, outlining the principles of ergonomics as well as the story of his life:

> We bear in mind that the object worked on is going to be ridden in, sat upon, looked at, talked into, activated, operated, or in some other way used by people individually or *en masse*. When the point of contact . . . becomes a point of friction, the industrial designer has failed. On the other hand, if people are made safer, more comfortable, more eager to purchase, more efficient—or just plain happier—by contact with the product, then the designer has succeeded.[15]

His seminal research on proportions brought a more humane approach to industrial design and provided scientific underpinnings for design decisions. In 1969, he published a second book, *The Measure of Man*, which includes more technical charts of proportions and movement studies. Ergonomic theory would become very important in the late twentieth century, when designers began to address health-related problems in design.

Ergonomic systems improved the safety and comfort of cars, furniture, kitchens, computers, and other engineered environments; specialists found they could improve the health of workers by adjusting the height or angle of machines and workstations and providing products that would allow the disabled to participate in the workplace.

3.5	Moral Engineering

The nature of 1920s prosperity; the reason why it ended; the cause of the Great Crash and the Great Depression which followed; and the . . . means whereby the industrial societies emerged from it—all these are still matters of intense argument. The conventional account is largely moralistic: hubris *followed by* nemesis, *wicked greed by salutary retribution.*
—Paul Johnson[16]

The sudden surge of inventions introduced a new vision of the future, a world of speed and efficiency, supported by electrical products. National income rose from $59.4 billion to $87.2 billion in eight years, and per capita income grew from $522 to $716. F. Scott Fitzgerald blithely declared, "America was going on the greatest, gaudiest spree in history."

The industrial expansion also led to new banking practices that provided easy financing and credit systems. Manufacturers approached financial institutions to raise funds for new products, which caused the stock market to rise. Families invested in homes, cars, and large appliances, which led to new credit systems. The advertising industry also grew. Americans were redefined as "consumers" and assaulted with brochures and product information.[17]

99

This growth was concentrated in a specific segment of the population, which eventually led to an imbalance in the economy. Corporate employees flourished, but the farmers, laborers, and civil workers barely remained solvent. As purchasing power diminished, companies were forced to lower prices and lay off part of their labor force. Some companies extended credit, but that just gave the illusion of stability, while the value of the dollar began to fall. Speculation on the stock market increased dramatically. In 1927, over 568 million shares changed hands. By 1929, the turnover had soared to over 920 million shares. Stocks that had sold at ten times earnings rose to a price of fifty times earnings. The stock market bubbled and crashed in 1929, which officially launched the Great Depression.

The federal government tried to bail out some of the banks, farms, and industries that had failed. President Herbert Hoover sponsored bills intended to stimulate the struggling economy and introduced infrastructure projects to provide jobs and improve public works. Most of his programs initially failed. From 1929 to 1934, the unemployment rate rose from 3.2 percent to 26.7 percent. By the mid-1930s, 75 percent of the American companies that had manufactured durable goods were forced to close their doors.[18]

Hoover Dam, dedicated
in 1935.

In 1936, Franklin Delano Roosevelt was elected president after a highly controversial campaign in which he was accused of every kind of perversion. Novelist Thomas Wolfe later described the political process in a satirical commentary, claiming, "I was told that if I voted for this Vile Communist, this sinister fascist, this scheming and contriving socialist and his gang of conspirators, I had no longer any right to consider myself an American."[19] Despite the many insults, Roosevelt prevailed. With his well-tuned political instincts, he used the song, "Happy Days Are Here Again," borrowed from an MGM film, to express his determination to end the Great Depression. 1936 was the lowest point in a desolate period. More than 5,000 banks failed, hundreds of colleges closed, and millions of children were turned away from public schools due to a lack of funds.[20]

Roosevelt succeeded in reviving the economy through a series of aggressive policies. He applied the theories of economist John Maynard Keynes on a deficit spending program and a managed currency plan organized through the Federal Reserve Bank and launched the New Deal, a program designed to stimulate the economy through public works.

The New Deal was developed through the Works Projects Administration (WPA), a government department that organized funding for art, architecture, and numerous other fields. In a five-year period, the WPA built "122,000 public buildings, 77,000 new bridges, 285 airports, 24,000 miles of storm and water-sewers, plus parks, playgrounds, highways, and reservoirs." Projects included landmark structures like the Golden Gate Bridge in San Francisco and the George Washington Bridge in New

Hoover Dam powerhouse,
Nevada wing.

York. The WPA also finished most of the infrastructure projects begun by President
Hoover, such as the Tennessee Valley Authority, a well-engineered system to control
floods, provide power, and bring irrigation to a struggling area.[21]

101

3.6   Hoover Dam

One of Hoover's most important infrastructure projects was the Hoover Dam,
a huge facility on the Colorado River about thirty miles from Las Vegas. The dam
was a $49 million facility, designed to supply water and power to surrounding
areas and prevent flooding in the region. A new town named Boulder City constructed for the workers offered a decent quality of life based on traditional
planning concepts.[22]

The completed dam was not only a major engineering feat; it was beautifully
designed and integrated in the environment. The four intake towers featured art
deco details, and the powerhouse was based on streamlined design. The dam
contained an unprecedented amount of concrete, enough to lay a highway from
Miami to Seattle.

Many conservative Americans considered these government-funded projects
"creeping socialism." Indeed, the infrastructure projects were often accompanied by
other efforts at social engineering, but the WPA projects brought new economic
activity to Depression-era communities and improved the American quality of life.
The dams, powerhouses, and bridges constructed also provided valuable systems
and facilities for the future.[23]

Margaret Bourke-White,
Fort Peck Dam, *Montana*,
1936.

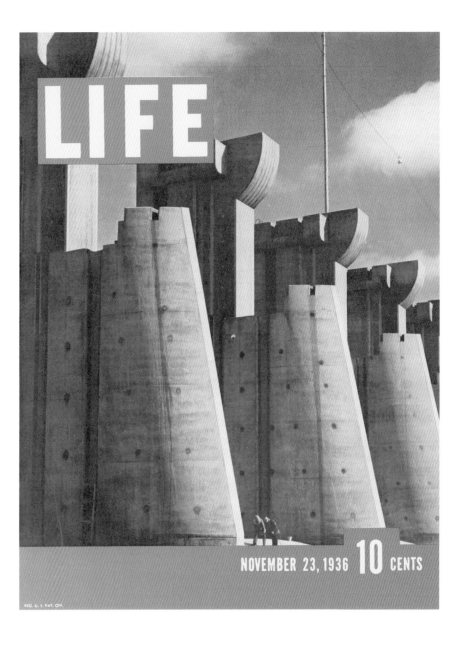

3.7 Industrial
Photographers

Photographers were instrumental in documenting the growth of industry and infrastructure. Their images recorded the handsome designs, technical achievements, and heroic efforts of the workers and provided positive propaganda that helped restore the American spirit. The leading photographers of this era included Andreas Feininger, Arthur Rothstein, Lewis Hines, and Margaret Bourke-White, who captured the drama of industrial forms and structures.

Bourke-White's images are especially poignant. In her varied career, she photographed everything from elegant houses to hog farms, dams, factories, and steel mills. As a staff photographer for *Time*, *Fortune*, and *Life*, she covered many WPA projects. She not only photographed the engineering accomplishments, she also recorded the human issues related to the work. She later went abroad to photograph the rise of communism in Russia, World War II, and the refugee camps in the postwar era.

Construction on a scaffolding, near the top of the 70-story RCA building in Rockefeller Center, New York, 1934.

3.8 Machine Age
      Architecture

It must be realized that at the moment we are only on the threshold of what in a few years will undoubtedly be the universal architecture.
—Norman Bel Geddes[24]

American architects were intrigued with the sleek forms of the streamlined era. At an American Institute of Architects convention in 1930, a heated argument developed between the modernists who supported machine-age designs and the Beaux-Arts designers. The modernists not only advocated streamlined forms, they also supported other machine-age concepts, such as the concrete block buildings of Frank Lloyd Wright and the art deco designs of Robert Mallet-Stevens. They were also interested in the French concept of Style Moderne.[25]

The debate failed to achieve consensus, but it did expand interest in machine-age concepts, especially art deco. This influential style took its name from the 1925 Paris Exhibition of Decorative Arts and was expressed not only in architecture, but also in furniture, textiles, and decorative objects that featured rich materials, intricate geometrical patterns, and exotic details.

American art deco differed from the European concept. In the United States, the style symbolized the new technological era. The greatest concentration of art deco buildings was in major cities like Miami, New York, and Los Angeles, where the style appeared in sophisticated hotels, department stores, and skyscrapers. There were also more modest art deco buildings, such as movie theaters, gas stations, and apartment houses, scattered across the country. The most dramatic structures were the skyscrapers, which became prominent symbols of corporate power. The streamlined details of the facades—curving walls, strip windows, and vertical lines—emphasized their height. Corporate logos in the art deco typography became lively signs and bright canopies that brought advertising to the streets.

Photographs of skyscrapers became promotional images, introducing a new role of architecture as a marketing tool. During construction, workers were photographed

103

Madelon Vriesendorp,
Apres l'amour, 1974.

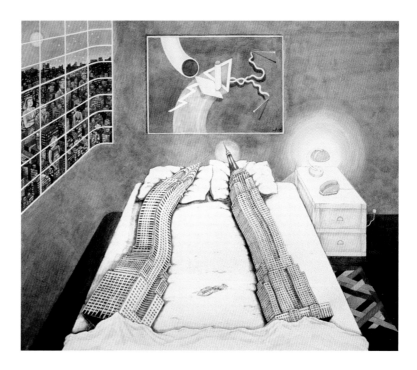

casually eating lunch while sitting on a narrow beam, 800 feet in the air, or catching rivets while precariously perched on a narrow ledge. These acrobatic feats created a heroic association in the public mind between the workers and their corporate employers. The skyscrapers dominated the urban skyline, bringing prestige to the corporations they housed.

Some buildings incorporated exotic architectural details based on corporate products. The Chrysler Building, designed by William Van Alen in 1928-30, is a sleek vertical metaphor of an automobile. The hubcaps, eagle radiator ornaments, and stainless steel skin of the building are all direct references to automobile detailing, and the overall curved shape of the structure expresses the streamlined form of modern cars.[26]

The Chrysler Building was the tallest structure in New York until the Empire State Building surpassed it. Designed by William Lamb in 1931 for the Empire State Bank, the structure contains no explicit references to banking, but its height was a towering expression of capitalist ambition. As the tallest building in the world, it had great symbolic importance, highlighted by the multicolored lights that illuminated its upper stories and the art deco details at street level. This eminent skyscraper was constructed in less than a year, a record time for such an undertaking. The construction system was so efficient, the steel beams often arrived from the mill still warm from the fabrication process. Unfortunately, it was completed in the midst of the Depression, so a large number of its floors remained vacant for many years.

3.9 "Culture of Congestion"

In his book *Delirious New York*, published in 1978, Rem Koolhaas traced the development of Manhattan as a "Culture of Congestion." In describing the creation of the Empire State Building, he noted that the elegant Waldorf Hotel was torn down to clear the site for the new skyscraper, calling the demolition "a form of architectural cannibalism," in which a building was conceived by "swallowing its predecessors." He asserted that in any other culture the destruction of the old Waldorf Hotel would be a "philistine act of destruction," but in Manhattan, "the site is freed to meet with its evolutionary destiny."[27]

The Manhattan design community became committed to historic preservation in the 1970s, but in the 1930s, there was no such feeling. Public sentiment was focused on the future. The romance of the streamlined era was expressed in these enormous structures that represented the pride of inventing something new, the goal of surpassing all other buildings in the world, and the vision of a city of skyscrapers as an environment of the future.

A painting by the Dutch artist Madelon Vriesendorp, reproduced in *Delirious New York*, depicts a whimsical relationship between the Chrysler Building and the Empire State Building, presumably considering them to be male and female versions of the same concept. The painting also expresses the idea of the "Culture of Congestion," in the numerous eyes that peer through a window to observe them.

3.10 Rockefeller Center

Although the public was enthralled with the new heights of skyscrapers, some planners were critical of their impact on urban centers. The towering structures caused traffic jams, reduced the amount of light and air in the city, and offered few amenities at street level. In response, the Rockefeller family, owners of Standard Oil, invested in the development of an alternative approach. Instead of a single skyscraper, they built Rockefeller Center, which was a comprehensive master plan for a community of office buildings.

The new urban concept was constructed through a painstaking series of proposals, designed by a collaborating team of about ten New York architects and developers. The final scheme was a complex of nine buildings with varied heights and setbacks, distributed on a large urban site. At each stage of the project, the design committee debated competing architectural theories from Europe and America. The final

105

Aerial view of Rockefeller Center, overlooking rooftop gardens, New York.

Raymond Hood, Manhattan
1950, model of concept for
expanding New York City
with a ring of apartment
bridges, 1929.

master plan of Rockefeller Center integrated the architecture of American sky-scrapers adorned with art deco details and roof gardens, fountains, and public squares derived from European planning concepts.

Raymond Hood was the principal designer in the group. Before he became involved with the planning, the design was composed of repetitive slab structures. Hood advocated a more diverse arrangement of tall slim buildings, with varying heights and setbacks, creating a more dynamic quality and providing more light and air at street level.

Hood proposed integrating many facilities in a single structure, seeing no reason why a gym, a restaurant, or even housing, could not be located in an office building. He introduced retail space in the large underground tunnels beneath the building for the convenience of tenants, generating additional income for the project. His innovative plan even included activities for evenings and weekends, which would keep the neighborhood busy and safe.

3.11 Manhattan, 1950

One of Raymond Hood's most memorable proposals was Manhattan, 1950, a concept for expanding New York across the water through a ring of "apartment bridges" around the city. Each bridge structure contains housing towers, fifty or sixty stories high, built along a wide street. The bridge housing benefits from clean air, dramatic views, and easy access to the urban center and offers an interesting alternative to the suburbs.

Hugh Ferriss, *Verticals on Wide Avenues*, a drawing commissioned to illustrate "New York's Skyline Will Climb Much Higher," an article by Raymond Hood, originally published in the magazine *Liberty*, April 10, 1926.

107

The idea of bridge structures could be traced back to the shops on the Ponte Vecchio in Florence, but Hood's proposal brought new scale to the concept. His powerful forms establish a new kind of urban landscape, linking the city to surrounding rivers. It would also help to reduce traffic congestion. At the base of each bridge, Hood envisioned facilities for hydroplanes and water transportation that would distribute traffic around the perimeter of the city. If the project had included subways that fed directly into the city, the concept would have been extremely modern.

3.12 *The Metropolis of Tomorrow*

Architectural delineator Hugh Ferriss drafted the renderings of Hood's Manhattan, 1950 and those of many other buildings of the era. His drawings present a unique expression of light and shadow that create moody, haunting images of structures and convey the mystery of a monumental city at night.

In 1916, New York City passed a zoning law that defined the allowable mass of a new building. Ferriss was commissioned by Harvey Wiley Corbett to create a set of drawings to illustrate various massing configurations that conformed to the new regulations. After drafting the possibilities, Ferriss added a text that described the setbacks and forms that adhered to the law so architects could envision a variety of solutions.[28]

In the 1920s, Ferriss developed drawings of a conceptual future city, which were published in *The Metropolis of Tomorrow*. The urban plan is divided into three zones, an Art Zone, a Science Zone, and a Business Zone. Each area contains tall stream-lined buildings, arranged along highways. The project does not provide a new urban theory, but it offers a rich visual experience that has had an effect on several generations of artists, architects, and film designers.

3.13 Frank Lloyd Wright

In 1930, in a lecture on design integrity, Frank Lloyd Wright stated, "We see an airplane, clean and lightwinged—the lines expressing power and purpose; we see the ocean liner, streamlined, clean and swift—expressing power and purpose. Why are not buildings, too, indicative of their special purpose . . ."[29]

Deeply committed to authenticity in architecture, Wright denounced the AIA approval of classical details on modern buildings and criticized the International Style, for he felt the design of a building should be related to its region and culture. For Wright, integrity meant a relationship to nature, a connection to the site, and an understanding of the cultural context in which a building was created.

At each stage of his career, Wright experimented with new design languages. His Prairie houses introduced complex roof systems with deep overhangs. His design for the Oak Park Unity Temple featured pure concrete forms with minimal ornament, which expressed the sculptural quality of concrete. He later created four elegant houses in California using concrete blocks. These handsome structures may have been inspired by the Froebel blocks of his childhood. All of his buildings were based on modern structural grids and organic concepts, but they also incorporated handcrafted details.

Some of the European modernists admired his experiments. His early concrete projects inspired Auguste Perret. His wood details influenced the De Stijl movement. However, minimalists like Loos and Le Corbusier considered him old-fashioned, because of his use of ornamental details.

In 1937, at the age of sixty, Wright designed a building so new that it completely altered their opinion. Fallingwater, commissioned by the Edgar Kaufmann family, is a building that expresses the essence of his organic philosophy. The design unifies the house with nature through a dramatic composition of abstract forms. Wright placed the house on the waterfall and created deep cantilevered terraces, expressing the idea of a ledge over the water. The cantilevers are so deep that a few engineers felt the structure might be unsafe, but the engineering behind the construction was sound, integrating nature with machine-age concepts. The strong horizontal lines of the terraces have a modern, machinelike quality. The use of local materials such as wood and stone link the building to its site. The colors express an autumn palette. The design even appealed to those European minimalists who had previously rejected his ideas. It demonstrated to them how a modern building could relate closely to site and environment and showed that an organic concept could be as modern and machinelike as the white box.

The Johnson Wax Administration Building, which Wright also began in 1937, was based on a sophisticated composition of streamlined forms. The exterior structure is composed of interwoven ribbonlike curves. The main workroom is a vast open

Frank Lloyd Wright,
Fallingwater, Mill Run,
Pennsylvania, 1937.

Frank Lloyd Wright, The
Solomon R. Guggenheim
Museum, New York,
1946–56.

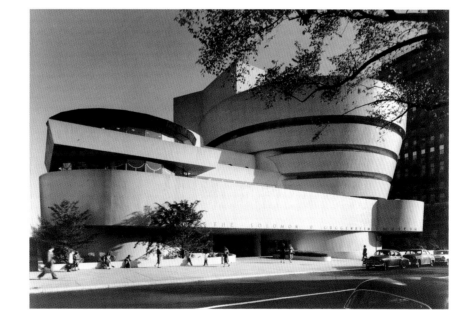

109

space, dominated by white tapered columns that rise up to an enormous skylight
and culminate in circular concrete forms.

The dramatic spiral form of the Solomon R. Guggenheim Museum, completed
in 1956, was based on an earlier conceptual design for the Automobile Objective
Planetarium. That proposal featured a large exterior ramp to bring cars into a
museum complex, but in the Guggenheim design, the ramp is expressed in both
the inside and outside of the building in a powerful streamlined form.[30]

William Van Alen, designer of
the Chrysler Building, and his
wife at the Beaux-Arts Ball,
New York, 1931.

3.14 "Fête Moderne—
A Fantasie in
Flame and Silver"

Around the turn of the century, a group of architects who had studied at Ecole des
Beaux-Arts in Paris formed the Society of Beaux-Arts Architects, a group that later
expanded to include other members of the New York architectural community.
Traditionally, the Society of Beaux-Arts Architects held an annual costume ball
based on a historical theme, but in 1931, the organizing committee decided to
introduce a modern theme. The event was advertised in the *New York Times* as a
"modernistic, futuristic, cubistic, altruistic, mystic, architistic and feministic" event.
A ticket cost fifteen dollars, a hefty amount at the time.

Most of the drinks were in metallic colors, and one hors d'oeuvre, a toasted marsh-
mallow, was designed to look like a flaming meteorite. In addition to the music and
dancing, the ball also included a satirical abstract art exhibit and a mechanical band
with steam pipes and pneumatic riveting machines. The evening culminated with a
living tableau of the New York skyline performed by over twenty architects dressed
in costumes to represent the buildings they had designed. The participants included
Harvey Wiley Corbett, who was dressed as the Bush Terminal, and Raymond Hood,
who appeared as the *Daily News* Building. Arthur Arwine, a heating contractor,
wore a costume, designed to replicate a "low-pressure heating boiler."

At the height of the evening, the group gathered to perform "The Skyline of New York." Most of them wore similar skyscraper costumes, but were distinguished by their individual headpieces. William Van Alen was an exception to the rule. He wore not only a fantastic headpiece, but also an entire costume representing his design of the Chrysler Building. His remarkable costume was made of black patent leather, teak veneer, silver metal cloth, and flame-colored silk. The next day, it was featured in newspaper articles providing amusing photographs of the group.[31]

3.15 Streamlined Films

More than any other visual medium, film, by virtue of the size of its audience and its growing influence over culture as a whole, helped shape popular perceptions of architectural modernism.
—Donald Albrecht[32]

In the 1920s, many Americans had a weekly ritual of going to the movies. The medium of film was so popular that attendance surpassed those at concerts, museums, and most sports events. Movie audiences continued to grow even in the 1930s, when money was scarce. By 1939, America had 17,000 movie theaters, boasting a weekly attendance of 85 million viewers.[33]

Throughout these years, most Hollywood film studios were committed to modern design. Film executives were well aware of the popularity of streamlined forms in cars, trains, and consumer products, and they were also conscious of the public interest in skyscrapers and luxury environments. Since these structures were inaccessible to most Americans, part of the allure of the movies was the experience of entering extraordinary spaces.

The films of the 1930s portrayed extravagant hotels, nightclubs, steamships, and executive suites, which added an element of fantasy to the stories. They also depicted the new trends in fashion and furniture design and provided a glimpse of the lifestyles of successful people.

The preference for streamlined forms even affected the figures of the actors and actresses. In 1931, *Silver Screen* magazine featured an article that proclaimed, "This is the speed age. Motion picture stars, like motor boats, aeroplanes and racing cars are built on greyhound lines . . . A few years ago screen beauties were more generous in build than today. Now diet, exercise and masseurs play important parts in the demand for faster figures."[34]

In the 1930s, struggling Americans enjoyed watching slim stars in fashionable settings. The fanciful stories, centered on the antics of unconventional millionaires who fell in love with their secretaries or actresses who became stars overnight, offered hope for the future and a few hours of relief from the troubled economy.

Another popular theme was the American work ethic. The film based on Sinclair Lewis's novel *Dodsworth* was an incisive satire comparing American and European values. The story portrays the life of an American manufacturer, who sells his company so he can retire and travel abroad. His social-climbing wife is intrigued with European society, but the hardworking Dodsworth prefers American values. At the end of the story, he decides to come out of retirement to start a new company.

Utopian concepts like *Lost Horizons* were also a popular antidote to the Depression. The art deco design developed in the film brings a timeless quality to the visual enactment of the story. Science fiction films like *Things to Come* and *Just Imagine* also created idealistic images of the future enhanced by elegant designs.

The 1930s were an era of lavish musicals staged in fantasy environments. An entire genre was developed in the elegant setting of New York nightclubs and hotels that provided perfect environments for light comedies, witty dialogue, and romantic plots. These dreamlike spaces were also extraordinary settings for dance and musical performances. The sophisticated art deco designs included moving walls, curving staircases, and multilevel spaces, enhanced by graceful performers in elegant costumes.

3.16 *Swing Time*

One of the most intriguing art deco sets was the Silver Sandal Club created by Van Nest Polglase and Carroll Clark for the 1936 film *Swing Time*, starring Fred Astaire and Ginger Rogers. Several rows of nightclub visitors are seated at tables on a restaurant floor that descends like a cascade of stairs. The men wear dark dinner jackets, but the women's gowns are all white to accentuate the design. The concept is strengthened by black walls with tiny white lights that resembled the night sky. The design focuses on a pair of black curving stairs, which gives the room a striking geometrical quality. The stairs lead to two cantilevered stages on separate levels. One stage holds the musicians; the other presents the performers. The floor is covered in Bakelite to add a glossy quality to the set, and the flowing quality of the space is enhanced by special effects. A special dolly was created to keep apace with the fluid dancing of Astaire and Rogers.

3.17 *42nd Street*

The gifted director Busby Berkeley created memorable musicals in the 1930s. His films had a distinctive choreography that produced exciting geometrical patterns, which were photographed from dramatic angles. Berkeley had been a drill sergeant during World War I and was fascinated with formations of soldiers marching. He had also worked on Broadway with chorus lines similar to the Rockettes.

In Hollywood, he shot complex patterns of dancers from a variety of angles, and his films contained rich kaleidoscopic forms with a mechanized quality. Some of his images express antifeminist concepts, as the women become machinelike objects, posed in awkward positions.

Berkeley was fascinated with the formal properties of objects. He created interesting patterns of various types of products, such as one film containing images of an endless line of pianos, forming a geometrical pattern of repeated curves. Another film utilizes violins in a similar sequence. The scenes were shot from numerous angles to provide an exciting visual experience.

In 1933, he created a dramatic concept for the filming of the musical numbers in *42nd Street*. Several dozen dancers stand on a staircase, holding posters of skyscrapers. As the music accelerates, they move the posters back and forth, giving the illusion of a city in motion. At the climax, the floor below the dancers becomes one huge skyscraper, shot from above by the ubiquitous Berkeley. The story contains a magical message of hope, driven forward by the American love of technology.

The Silver Sandal Club in the film *Swing Time*, 1936. Director: George Stevens.

Scene from the film *42nd Street*, 1933. Director: Lloyd Bacon.

113

3.18 *Just Imagine*

Just Imagine (1930) is a science fiction musical, a mixture of two genres that are rarely combined. Production designer Stephen Goosson built a huge model of a future city in an airplane hangar, where much of the film was shot. The main set was a futuristic vision of a city that integrated ideas of real buildings with conceptual images by modern architects. Some buildings are arranged along highways that run directly through the urban center, as in Le Corbusier's Radiant City. A few structures resemble Hugh Ferriss's drawings in *The Metropolis of Tomorrow*. Others were

Cityscape in the film *Just Imagine*, 1930. Director: David Butler.

based on real New York skyscrapers. There are even a few overhead bridges, inspired by *King's Views of New York*.

The plot centers on a love story, which depends on the success of a trip to Mars. Since part of the story occurs on Mars, the concepts of the Martian throne room and the scientific laboratory offered opportunities for exotic design. Goosson based the Martian scenes on Russian constructivism.

The influence of American industrial designers is also evident. Several interior spaces are based on streamlined concepts, and an elegant modern airplane serves as a pivotal element in the plot. Though the mixture of styles was based on unrelated ideas, the final design was gracefully integrated. Goosson won an Academy Award for his luminous concept.[35]

3.19 *Things to Come*

In response to the dystopian vision presented in the German film *Metropolis*, Hollywood created films to present positive images of the future. In *Things to Come*, science and technology are portrayed as humanizing influences. Veteran science-fiction writer H.G. Wells wrote the screenplay, and in a 1936 interview with the *New York Times*, he declared, "you may take it that whatever Lang did in *Metropolis* is the exact opposite of what we want done here."[36]

Things to Come traces the history of a British "Everytown" through a series of calamitous events that eventually lead to a utopian society. The story begins on a rainy night in Everytown, when the city is attacked and forced into a disastrous war. When the fighting subsides, all that remains is a primitive cluster of urban ruins. For a while, the devastated city is ruled by roaming warlords, but eventually, engineers emerge from hiding and rebuild Everytown as a sophisticated modern city. They form a utopian society, based on rational principles.

The world of tomorrow in the film *Things to Come*, 1936. Director: William Cameron Menzies.

Director William Cameron Menzies asked Le Corbusier to design the sets, but he declined. Instead, the designs were created through a collaboration of set designer Vincent Korda, painter Fernand Léger, and Bauhaus photographer/designer László Moholy-Nagy.

115

The film presents an evolution through a century of time. The original art deco city is damaged during the war and remains in ruins until the final scenes of the film, when Everytown reemerges as a fascinating streamlined city, built underground. Wells placed the city underground to introduce another important idea: in the story, the natural landscape of the earth is destroyed during the war, and the new society revitalizes the environment to provide clean air, water, and food for the community. The final scenes of the visionary city are luminous. Unlike the sets in *Metropolis*, they portray a calm environment based on Italian futurism and American streamlined design, and free of traffic and pollution.

Everytown is a handsome city, with elegant curving balconies, transparent elevators, and sleek bridges. Light filters down from a huge atrium above. Rich animated footage shows automated construction systems erecting prefabricated buildings. Innovative product concepts are also presented, such as lightweight furniture, curvaceous cars, and educational television.

The plot of *Things to Come* endorses science, technology, and industrialization. It reflects Wells's belief in a rational society of equals as an ultimate goal of scientific progress. The film also expresses American optimism and the belief that technology would ultimately improve their lives.

Joseph Binder, poster
promoting the New York
World's Fair, 1939.

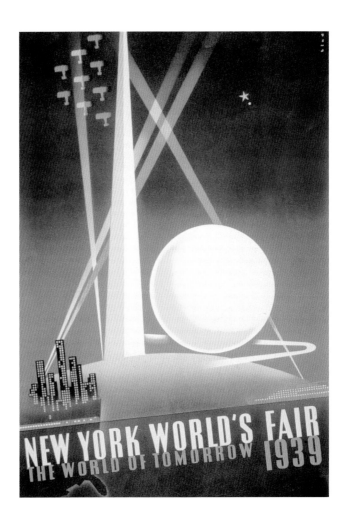

116   3.20 The 1939–40 New
            York World's Fair

*I think there are moments where you can see the world turning from what it is into what
it will be. For me, the New York World's Fair is such a moment. It is a compass rose point-
ing in all directions . . . a world of tomorrow contained in the lost American yesterday.*
—John Crowley [37]

In 1936, New York City officials decided to stage a World's Fair in an effort to lift
the spirits of struggling Americans and improve the troubled economy of the city.
The theme "Building the World of Tomorrow" was intended to give a positive
view of the future based on the concept of technological innovation. Grover
Whalen, president of the New York World's Fair Corporation, declared that the
fair would offer the common man, "a glimpse of the community of the future—
a future conditioned by science."

The committee chose as the location a marshland in Flushing, Queens, that was
being used as a garbage dump, and therefore required several major improvements.
Before the construction could begin, the site had to be cleared and developed. New
water and power lines were needed, as well as parking lots, roads, and a subway
system. Building the basic infrastructure and one permanent structure cost $26.7
million. [38]

While the basic systems were being installed, plans for the construction of the buildings were developed. The fair would be truly international, with exhibits from sixty nations, thirty-three states, and numerous corporations. Germany was absent because the war in Europe had already begun. At the inauguration, Albert Einstein, the honorary chairman, turned on the electric lights. President Roosevelt gave a speech, announcing the fair was officially open. His speech was probably the first public television broadcast in history. An official declared the fair was not "a vague dream of a life that might be lived in the far future, but one that could be lived tomorrow if we willed it so."

Many artists and architects were involved in the exhibitions, but American industrial designers dominated the experience. Walter Dorwin Teague, first president of the American Society of Industrial Designers and reputedly more of a businessman than the other designers, was chairman of the board of design and planned the entire site. In that role, Teague worked with many of the major corporations sponsoring exhibits. He helped define several of the exhibition concepts himself and made certain that other leading industrial designers participated in the project.

The layout of the fair was planned like a small town. Two buildings stood prominently in the center, a 700-foot-high Trylon (or triangular pylon) and a 200-foot-wide Perisphere. The major streets fanned out from the central space in radial lines, leading to seven zones of exhibition—transportation, production and distribution, communications and business systems, food, medicine and public health, science and education, and community interests. Most of the streets were given patriotic names, such as Lincoln Square and Jefferson Place.

The Trylon and Perisphere were used as symbols of the fair in the posters commemorating the event. One of the most popular posters was developed by graphic designer Joseph Binder, who used a streamlined concept in the design. The

Norman Bel Geddes, model of the Metropolis of Tomorrow in the *Futurama* exhibit at the New York World's Fair, 1939.

William Dorwin Teague,
National Cash Register
Building, New York World's
Fair, 1939.

Henry Dreyfuss, Democracity,
drawing of exhibition at
the New York World's
Fair, 1939.

background of the poster is red, white, and blue, in reference to the American flag.
In the foreground are yellow renderings of the Trylon and Perisphere, which provide a striking image of the theme.

Austrian designer Josef Urban developed the color concept in which the colors were
light near the center of the site and became stronger as visitors proceeded down the
main avenues. Each zone was assigned a different color. Constitution Mall began
in rose-colored hues that changed to deeper shades of burgundy. The Avenue of the
Patriots began in soft yellow tones, which darkened to heavy shades of gold. The
lighting was also carefully arranged to enhance each area of the site.[39]

One of the most popular exhibitions was *Futurama*, designed by Norman Bel Geddes
and sponsored by General Motors. It featured an enormous model of a future
community—"the world of 1960"—with experimental farms tucked among
mountains and lakes and a handsome city that dominated the design. Tall streamlined buildings rose in key areas of the plan; busy highways were filled with GM
model cars. Visitors were seated in pairs on a rotating balcony above the enormous
model so that the view was as if they were riding in "a low-flying aircraft." Each
pair of seats had speakers that explained the design below.[40]

Raymond Loewy created an exhibition of streamlined trains for the Pennsylvania
Railroad Company. Several famous locomotives were brought to the site, including
one of his own design, and activities celebrated train technology. In one theater,
there was a dramatic reenactment of the meeting of the railroad tracks of the cross-country line. Kurt Weill composed a musical score for the performance. In another

auditorium, a huge regional model demonstrated 500 types of equipment used by trains. Loewy also created a Rocketport of the Future, which shot a rocket into the air at a climactic moment in a transportation sequence.

Henry Dreyfuss designed an ideal city for AT&T, called Democracity, in the Perisphere. Inside the great sphere, visitors stood on two levels of circular balconies, suspended over a model of a future city. The balconies rotated as music, lights, and a rousing address expressed themes of international brotherhood and industrial progress. He also constructed the Demonstration Call Room, where visitors could make calls to any town in the country. As each call occurred, the destination was illuminated on a large map of the United States.

Teague designed several exhibitions, most notably the Ford Exposition, which included a Road of Tomorrow, on which visitors could test new Ford cars. He also built a huge model of New York City for Con Edison. This dramatic exhibit featured moving subways and active factories in a twelve-minute reenactment of "a day of light" in the city. But his most famous design was the National Cash Register Building, which expressed the capitalist themes of the fair. Its gleaming shape provided a whimsical symbol of the popular exhibition.

The fair promoted the idea of scientific planning and mechanization and advanced the theme of a cooperative relationship between government and industry. Though some critics disapproved of the commercial quality of the event, most visitors were enchanted with the imaginative exhibitions. It was generally considered both a popular and critical success.

The fair logged a record attendance of 45 million people, but after Hitler invaded Poland in September 1939, the awareness of an impending war caused attendance to drop in the second year and the fair was forced to close in October 1940. Over 19 million dollars were lost due to the early termination. The closing of this remarkable event also signaled the end of the great era of avant-garde design and the beginning of World War II.

3.21 The End of the Era

Dr. New Deal is off the case . . . Now it's Dr. Win-the-War.
—President Franklin D. Roosevelt[41]

On December 7, 1941, the Japanese bombed Pearl Harbor. More than 2,500 people were killed in the assault and 1,000 more were wounded. Nineteen naval vessels were destroyed. The next day, the United States declared war on Japan. In turn, Hitler, as an ally of Japan, declared war on the United States. By the end of the week, the United States had committed to the European conflict.

The sudden onslaught of war led to a huge demand for machinery, uniforms, weapons, supplies, and vehicles. American industry became the main source of production not only for its own military effort, but for the European Allied forces as well. Thousands of factories throughout the United States were retooled to manufacture military products. Shipyards stopped making yachts and cruise ships and began building battleships and aircraft carriers. Clothing companies turned away from fashion and produced uniforms instead. Automobile plants were converted into facilities for making tanks, trucks, and aircraft.

Jean Carlu, *Give 'em Both Barrels*, 1941. Poster in support of the war effort.

The funding for military production came from the public coffers. From 1940 to 1945, federal spending in the United States increased from $9 billion to $98.4 billion per year. President Roosevelt's social programs were immediately reduced or eliminated to funnel funds to the war effort. The Great Depression, which had haunted American workers for over a decade, ended abruptly.

When the war started in 1940, approximately 8 million Americans were unemployed. By 1942, there was virtually no unemployment. The number of teenage workers rose from 1 million to 3 million. Women provided an additional 2 million workers. Norman Rockwell's image of "Rosie the Riveter" appeared in magazines as part of a promotional package encouraging women to join the assembly lines.[42]

Graphic designers played a major role in promoting the war effort, creating recruiting posters, magazine covers, and billboards with visual symbols of the patriotic goals. Jean Carlu, a European designer who had emigrated to the United States, created powerful posters using the graphic principles of the Bauhaus and the Russian constructivists. American designer Will Burtin simplified the graphics in a gunners' training manual and refined the illustrations. His visual improvements reportedly cut training times in half.[43]

The industrial designers also played an important role in the war effort. Dreyfuss designed uniforms and equipment for the armed forces. Bel Geddes developed systems for testing military strategy. Loewy improved the design of naval vehicles and other products. Teague planned offices for Allied intercommand headquarters and served as a consultant to several war industries. Many of the innovations they had introduced in previous decades were implemented in the design of vehicles, weapons, and products that helped to win the war.

Notes

1. Raymond Loewy, *Industrial Design* (Woodstock, NY: The Overlook Press, 1979), 10.

2. Richard Guy Wilson, Dianne H. Pilgrim, and Dickran Tashjian, *The Machine Age in America: 1918–1941* (New York: Harry N. Abrams, Inc., in association with The Brooklyn Museum, New York, 1986), 25.

3. Robert A. Caro, *The Power Broker* (New York: Random House, Inc., 1975), 143.

4. Norman Bel Geddes, *Horizons* (New York: Random House, Inc., 1932), 227.

5. Alexander Hellemans and Bryan Bunch, *The Timetables of Science* (New York: Simon & Schuster, Inc., 1998), 913.

6. Charles E. Sorenson, *My Forty Years with Ford* (New York: Collier Books, 1956), 133-34.

7. Donald J. Bush, *The Streamlined Decade* (New York: George Braziller, Inc., 1975), 117.

8. Norman Bel Geddes, "Streamlining," in *Atlantic Monthly* (November 1934), in *The Industrial Design Reader*, edited by Carma Gorman (New York: Allworth Press, 2003), 135.

9. Horatio Greenough, "The Law of Adaptation," in *The Travels, Observations, and Experience of a Yankee Stonecutter* (New York: G.P. Putman, 1852), in Gorman, 12.

10. Bush, 47.

11. Bush, 23.

12. Loewy, 11.

13. Loewy, 205.

14. Bush, 19.

15. Henry Dreyfuss, "Joe and Josephine," *Designing for People* (New York: Simon & Schuster, 1955), in Gorman, 163.

16. Paul Johnson, *Modern Times* (New York: Harper & Row, Publishers, Inc., 1983), 231-32.

17. Johnson, 222.

18. Johnson, 239-46.

19. Johnson, 259.

20. Johnson, 254.

21. Johnson, 256.

22. *The Story of Hoover Dam* (Las Vegas: Nevada Publications, 1931), 25.

23. Wilson, 113-17.

24. Norman Bel Geddes, "The House of Tomorrow," *Ladies Home Journal*, vol. 48, no. 4, (April 1931), quoted in Bush, 134.

25. Wilson, 149.

26. Wilson, 163-65.

27. Rem Koolhaas, *Delirious New York* (New York: Oxford University Press, 1978), 114.

28. Hugh Ferriss, *The Metropolis of Tomorrow* (Princeton, NJ: Princeton Architectural Press, 1986), 152.

29. Frank Lloyd Wright, *The Future of Architecture*, (New York: New American Library, 1953), 141.

30. Robert McCarter, *Frank Lloyd Wright* (London: Phaidon Press Limited, 1997), 306.

31. Christopher Gray, "A New Age of Architecture Ushered in Financial Gloom," *New York Times*, January 1, 2006, http://travel.nytimes.com/2006/01/01/realestate/01scap.html.

32. Donald Albrecht, *Designing Dreams* (New York: Harper Collins Publishers in association with The Museum of Modern Art, New York, 1986), xiii.

33. Albrecht, xii.

34. Albrecht, 86.

35. Dietrich Neumann, *Film Architecture: Set Designs from Metropolis to Blade Runner* (Munich/New York: Prestel Verlag, 1999), 112.

36. Neumann, 118.

37. John Crowley, commentary in *The World of Tomorrow*, documentary film on the 1939 New York World's Fair, produced in 1984.

38. Stanley Appelbaum, *The New York World's Fair 1939/1940* (Mineola, NY: Dover Publications, Inc., New York, 1977), ix.

39. Applebaum, xiii.

40. Bush, 116.

41. Godfrey Hodgson, *People's Century* (New York: Times Books, Random House, Inc., 1998), 168.

42. World War II: The Home Front, Board of Regents of the University of Wisconsin, 1999, http://us.history.wisc.edu/hist102/lectures/lecture21.html.

43. David Raizman, *History of Modern Design* (Upper Saddle River, NJ: Prentice Hall Inc., 2004), 235-36.

THE AUTOMOBILE AGE

"The case of Little Reuben occurred only twenty-three years after Our Ford's first T-Model was put on the market." (Here the Director made a sign of the T on his stomach and all the students reverently followed suit.)
—Aldous Huxley, *Brave New World*[1]

At the turn of the twentieth century, there were fewer than 14,000 cars in the United States. Automobiles were considered extravagant toys for wealthy enthusiasts. But in 1913, Henry Ford introduced the assembly line, which soon made cars accessible to working-class Americans. By 1930, over 26 million vehicles were registered in the United States—1 in every 5.5 Americans had a car.[2]

It was the beginning of the American obsession with the automobile. The popularity of cars soon led to the creation of other types of vehicles. In 1905, the first double-decked buses appeared in cities. Taximeter cabs started plying their trade in 1907. Trucks emerged in 1910. The use of tractors in farming communities also increased. Access to these new vehicles improved the efficiency of agriculture and reduced the sense of isolation felt by many farmers.

Increased traffic also led to new types of infrastructure. Electric traffic signals were introduced in 1914, and highway systems were expanded in cities across the United States. By the 1920s, Henry Ford's vision of a world dependent on automobiles was becoming a reality. His company was producing a million cars a year and shipping to over thirty nations. Ford had factories in Canada, Europe, Asia, South Africa, Australia, South America, and Russia.[3] The utilization of automobiles grew even during the Depression. In the 1930s, the WPA built 664,000 miles of roads throughout the United States, signifying government support of private cars.

Such popularity also led to traffic problems, however, even at Ford Motors itself. The huge Ford factory at River Rouge in Dearborn, Michigan, employed 80,000 people. Most workers commuted in private cars, which caused increased traffic at rush hour. In response, Ford started providing company buses. The factory also faced traffic delays in the delivery of cars across the country. So Ford bought a train to solve the "freight shipment bottleneck." The irony of Ford Motors using public transportation was buried in the annals of automobile history. It did nothing to dampen enthusiasm for cars.[4]

The greatest traffic problems were in urban areas, such as Los Angeles. Its residents wanted both the glamour of a big city and the convenience of a small town, so in the early twentieth century, the city constructed over 900 miles of roads. Some

123

Albert Kahn Associates,
GM Model Production Line.
Developed for the General
Motors Exhibition at the
"Century of Progress"
Exposition, 1933–34.

historians feel Los Angeles was also affected by the ruthless strategy of a few corporations. In 1922, General Motors, Standard Oil, and Firestone Tire and Rubber
Co. established a subsidiary company called National City Lines. It was founded
for the sole purpose of closing streetcar systems in urban areas and promoting the
use of buses and automobiles instead.

In the next few decades, National City Lines bought over "100 electric surface-
traction systems in 45 cities."[5] Then they dismantled the streetcar systems and introduced GM buses along the same routes. These actions eventually led to a lawsuit,
and in 1949, National City Lines was convicted of conspiracy.

By the late 1930s, cars had become a necessity in the United States. The widespread
use of automobiles broke the boundaries of public transportation, which made some
neighborhoods accessible and others difficult to reach. It also brought speed, flexibility, and independence to modern life.

This advancement did require sacrifices. Americans gave up millions of miles of
public land to build parking lots, highways, and gas stations. They raised taxes to
support road repairs, traffic lights, and highway patrols. They also spent thousands
of hours each year commuting to work in private cars. They even learned to live
with traffic jams, accidents, noise, and pollution.

The second phase of the automobile age came with the war era. During World
War II, almost no private cars were manufactured. Automobile plants were retooled
to build jeeps, tanks, trucks, and airplanes, and the demands of war led to the development of more efficient production systems, more durable materials, and more
practical designs. When the war ended, the infatuation with vehicles accelerated
due to the millions of soldiers returning home, eager to purchase cars.

The third phase in the automobile age was the postwar expansion era, when many
new communities were built for returning servicemen and their families. Most new

housing developments were constructed near highways on the outskirts of cities. There was very little public transportation, so the residents needed cars to travel to their jobs, schools, and activities.

By the 1950s, the automobile was not just a vehicle, it was a way of life. It forced people to learn how to read maps and understand the basic layout of cities. It generated new types of buildings, such as shopping malls, gas stations, and parking structures, as well as drive-in movies, drive-in restaurants, and drive-up banks. The drive-in facilities along highways were so convenient and popular that the downtown business districts of many cities deteriorated. The car also encouraged the development of mass-produced homes. Prefabricated housing was cheap and easy to construct, but produced repetitive communities, based on the same unit, which also engendered a culture of conformity.

As the use of automobiles increased, major environmental damage began to occur. Car manufacturing consumed an enormous amount of materials and left a legacy of garbage dumps and toxic waste. Extensive use of cars affected the quality of air, water, soil, and public health. It also caused cultural compromises, especially in cities, where highways were built instead of subways and commuter traffic patterns became firmly established. By the 1960s, some commuters spent four hours a day in their cars, more waking hours than they spent with their families.

The automobile age lasted over forty years. Finally, in the 1960s, protests by urbanists such as Lewis Mumford and Jane Jacobs altered the attitude toward cars. As a result of their critiques, planners and architects began to understand the impact of automobiles. They also undertook the difficult process of revitalizing downtown areas of cities and developing public transportation. But as the American obsession with automobiles subsided, the demand for vehicles grew stronger in emerging countries, repeating the process abroad.

4.1   The First Era of the Automobile

What has New York done about street congestion? Bless your little journalistic hearts—a hell of a lot . . . We have built and are building wide parkways and expressways, bridges and tunnels, without crossings and lights, with service roads for local use and parking, belt and crosstown systems which take through traffic off ordinary streets and enormously cut down congestion.

—Robert Moses, *Herald Tribune*, August 1945[6]

One of the most influential planners of the early twentieth century was the masterful politician Robert Moses, who developed New York City into a sprawling urban region of highways and suburbs. During his forty years in public office, he built 627 miles of highway. In the process of creating these highways, he destroyed several vibrant areas of the city, and even attempted to run a highway through Soho and Greenwich Village, but the project was defeated by community protests.

Despite his extensive highway program, New York's traffic grew more congested during his years in office. According to Robert Caro, author of the definitive biography on Moses, traffic planners studying the problem recognized an ongoing trend in the system—as soon as new highways were built, an enormous number of cars "would pour onto them and congest them and thus force the building of more highways." The Triborough Bridge, for example, which opened in 1936, was built by

Highway Interchange, Los Angeles, California.

Moses to provide infrastructure for about 8 million cars annually. By 1941, it carried 11 million cars per year. By 1949, it carried 23 million cars annually. In 1960, over 46 million cars crossed the bridge. Similar growth was occurring on other road systems throughout the United States.[7]

Instead of questioning the use of cars, most cities kept expanding their highway systems. In 1950, Moses even proposed the idea of building an elevated highway along a major avenue, which would carry traffic right through buildings. Fortunately, this idea was rejected.

Most visionary concepts in this era supported the automobile. They focused on the issues of parking, traffic, and highway access. Some projects featured linear cities; others were based on traffic circles or grids. Leading architects and planners were so convinced of the necessity of automobiles that even the most monotonous designs were considered successful if they improved the flow of cars. The housing concepts developed in these years were also standardized, contributing a repetitious quality to the designs.

4.2   Plan Voisin

In 1935, Le Corbusier visited New York for the first time. A reporter from the *New York Herald Tribune* asked him what he thought of America's largest city, and he replied that the streets weren't wide enough and the buildings weren't tall enough. When asked what he thought of skyscrapers, he called them "acrobatic feats," rather than serious solutions to urban planning, summarizing his view with the words, "New York is a catastrophe . . . a beautiful catastrophe."

Le Corbusier, Plan Voisin, model showing concept for rebuilding Paris, 1922.

Le Corbusier was also amazed by the number of cars. At the time, New York boasted more cars than all the cities of Europe combined. As he toured the United States, he criticized commuter culture and the amount of traffic caused by the American lifestyle. It seems surprising that the most outspoken advocate of the machine was so critical of America's quantity of vehicles. He was also disturbed by a lack of urban planning, specifically the sprawling expansion of modern cities.

In the 1920s and 1930s, many European cities also suffered from traffic. Each day, thousands of cars made their way through the narrow, winding streets of what were essentially medieval cities. Le Corbusier considered these issues to be scientific problems requiring rational solutions. His first urban project, Ville Contemporaine, created in 1922, proposed a grid of highways, housing towers, and parks. In 1925, he presented Plan Voisin, a proposal to demolish the Marais district in Paris and replace it with a new urban concept. His plans reconfigure the streets of the Marais into a grid, then place a housing tower, surrounded by a park, in each section of the grid. The towers are arranged in the shape of a cross to provide maximum light for individual housing units.

Although he described his concept as a "vertical garden city," it lacks the continuous urban fabric of a real city. Highway traffic cuts through the district and destroys the sense of community. Also, there is no continuous facade of stores along the streets, which characterize a traditional city. Fortunately, the Plan Voisin was never implemented, and sixty years later, the Marais district was restored and became a vibrant neighborhood once again.

Nevertheless, the Plan Voisin influenced the design of housing projects in both Europe and the United States. Some applications of similar concepts worked in middle-class suburbs but failed in most urban areas. Le Corbusier later experimented with conceptual projects for linear cities near Algiers and Rio de Janeiro, but the communities were split in half by highway traffic and similarly flawed.

In 1929, Le Corbusier published *The City of To-morrow and Its Planning*. He begins by explaining the importance of the grid and the use of logical planning theory. He notes, "The Romans built WHOLES . . . lucid, strong, simple, and geometrical. They created cities that worked like machines: machines of which the product was action." He goes on to list principles required for sound urban planning:

1. We must de-congest the centres of our cities.
2. We must augment their density.
3. We must increase the means for getting about.
4. We must increase parks and open spaces.[8]

Le Corbusier's insistence on the grid would prove valuable, but his concept of highways and towers caused problems, especially in urban areas. In the 1960s, Jane Jacobs's book *The Death and Life of Great American Cities* discredited many of his urban concepts.

4.3 Rush City Reformed

In 1923 Austrian architect Richard Neutra came to America. Like Le Corbusier, Neutra was struck by the amount of automobile traffic. He traveled across the country, visiting architects whom he admired and compiling information for a book called *How America Builds* or *Wie Baut Amerika*. In it he presented modern concrete buildings by Frank Lloyd Wright and Rudolf Schindler, as well as a few of his own projects, including Rush City Reformed.

The name Rush City Reformed expresses the concept of Neutra's design. He approached the issue of urban planning as if it were a mathematical formula. His conceptual city is designed for speed, but it also contains a few "reforms." It is comprised of endless lines of housing slabs, developed along highways. The repetitive structures have a machinelike regularity, reminiscent of the work of Bauhaus planner Ludwig Hilberseimer. The design also has a fascistic quality, and contains none of the sensitivity of Neutra's architectural work.

There were, however, a few environmental concepts covered in Rush City Reformed. The housing structures face south to provide maximum exposure to the sun. Streets are wider than the height of the buildings, so none of the facades are draped in shadow. Parking is underground to avoid turning large areas of the community into a wasteland of parking lots.

Neutra also establishes sidewalks above street level to separate pedestrians from automobile traffic. He even converts a few major streets into pedestrian malls. But his environmental gestures did not ameliorate the overwhelming theme of machinelike replication that characterized the design. Fortunately, Rush City Reformed failed to attract any supporters.

4.4 Broadacre City

In 1935 Frank Lloyd Wright was asked by the Museum of Modern Art to develop a concept of a future city based on American values. Unlike most architects of this era, he chose to create a decentralized suburban concept, rather than a proposal for

Richard Neutra, Rush City
Reformed, drawing of conceptual city, 1923.

Frank Lloyd Wright, plan of
Broadacre City, 1934.

129

a city, since he himself disliked and rejected urban environments. In the essay
When Democracy Builds, he wrote, "To look at the plan of a great city is to look at
something like the cross section of a fibrous tumor."[9]

He called his project Broadacre City. This rural community is composed of individual houses, built on one-acre lots along tree-lined streets. The community
also has farms, roadside markets, small factories, a university, a skyscraper, and
a church. But in keeping with Wright's anti-urban view, there is no main street or
town center. In his book *The Future of Architecture* he later stated, "Even the small
town is too large."

Wright not only disliked the physical form of the city, he also disapproved of its quality of life. He declared that cities were, "infested with the worst elements of society as a wharf is infested with rats." He also rejected the modern approach to low-income housing. In an essay called "The Passing of the Cornice," he insists "Human houses should not be like boxes . . ."[10]

Wright did approve of the automobile, however. Broadacre City is a decentralized community of private houses with commercial structures spread throughout the town, so its inhabitants would need cars for transportation. He even designed high-tech automobiles for the project. He felt the car was a truly American vehicle, as it offered limitless freedom.

Wright's preference for private houses with yards was based on Thomas Jefferson's agrarian philosophy and Ralph Waldo Emerson's belief in the value of nature, and expresses Depression-era values as well. In discussing his views, Wright declared, "When every man, woman, and child may be born to put his feet on his own acres, then democracy will have been realized."[11] Some of his concepts appealed to developers and were later implemented, but the low-density planning concept led increasingly to urban sprawl and a reinforced dependence on cars.

4.5   The War Years

Production . . . must be raised far above present levels, even though it will mean the dislocation of the lives and occupations of millions of our own peoples. Let no man say it cannot be done. It must be done and we have undertaken to do it.
—Franklin D. Roosevelt[12]

In 1941, America entered World War II. The interests of capitalism were put on hold as thousands of factories were retooled to support the needs of the war. Since most factories were located in cities, over fifteen million Americans moved from farms to cities to work for the war effort. The sudden shift in population caused housing shortages in urban areas, but there was no time to address the issue. The new urban dwellers rented rooms in houses or shared apartment space.

In the first year of the war, automobile plants were reconfigured to produce military vehicles and assembly processes were restructured to generate more efficient systems. The results were remarkable. In 1941, the construction of a B-17 aircraft required 55,000 work hours. By 1944, only 19,000 hours were needed for the same task. Some factories operated twenty-four hours a day, seven days a week, to meet the needs of the war. Airplane production rose more than any other industry. In the 1930s, the United States built fewer than 6,000 planes a year. During the war, over 9,000 planes were produced each month.

Some of the technologies invented in the 1930s became critical instruments of war. The jet engine was among them, followed by the lightweight, maneuverable helicopter. British experiments in wireless technology produced radar, a valuable navigation tool for both airplanes and ships. The first digital computers also emerged in these years, and were used to break codes inscribed in enemy messages.

New materials were also developed based on synthetic compounds that were easy to manufacture and required few natural resources. Plastics, lighter and more durable than glass, were used in dashboards and helicopter hoods. Synthetic rubber was

Woman factory workers
install lights in airplane
nose cones.

utilized in war products ranging from tires to canteens. Nylon stockings replaced
silk stockings, so silk could be reserved for parachutes. Cardboard, instead of
metal, became the preferred packaging material to conserve metal for more important purposes.

Valuable materials like metal, paper, and rubber were recycled to provide resources
for the war effort. For the first time in history, the United States faced economic
scarcity and government control of goods and services. New medicines, such as
penicillin, were developed to fight infection, and the armed services cooperated
with the Red Cross, which carried food and medicine to both sides of the conflict
under a neutral banner.

Agricultural production increased overall, but rationing cards were introduced
for basic foods like eggs, coffee, and meat. Preservatives were developed to sustain
canned goods for longer periods of time. Popular foods like Hershey bars were
also improved so they wouldn't melt at the front. Artificial foods, such as Spam,
debuted as an alternative to fresh meat.

The war even had an influence on fashion. Both men and women took pride in the
idea of wearing uniforms, rather than expressing individuality through clothes.
Women's clothes were trimmed to more efficient designs that required less material.
Skirts were made shorter and narrower in a trend retailers at Neiman Marcus
described as "patriotic chic."

4.6 Photography, Media,   Throughout the war years, the role of mass media grew. Radio became an impor-
      and Communications   tant means of providing public information and improving morale. Leaders like
                                 Roosevelt and Churchill gave frequent broadcasts to garner public support.

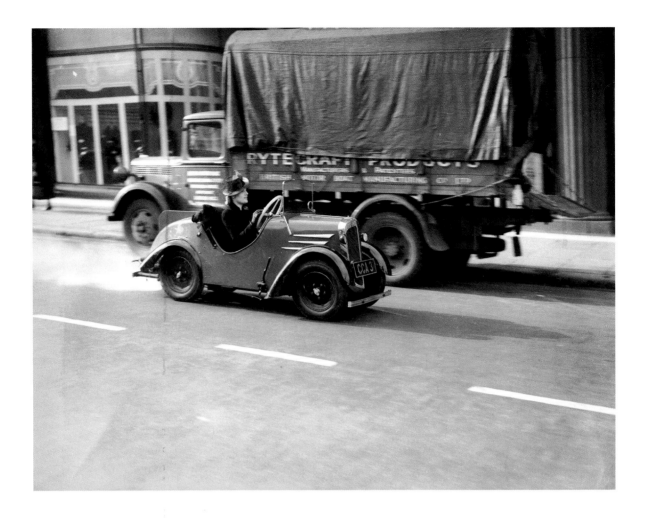

132   A woman driving a small 'Scootacar' during the war era. This vehicle was reputedly capable of traveling a distance of 80 miles on a single gallon of gasoline.

Patriotic songs were played between news reports and political speeches, which added vitality to the war effort. Overseas programs like Radio Free Europe brought hope to millions of Europeans living in the shadow of conflict.

Films were also popular, but the playful love stories of the previous era were replaced with dramas. Fanciful evening gowns and art deco stage sets were put aside while filmmakers created patriotic scenes of battlefields and moving stories of civilian life. Both the Allies and the Nazis used film as propaganda.

Photographers of this era made detailed records of the conflict and war effort. Their images expanded public knowledge of the inhumane activities of war, as well as the environmental damage that occurred. Factory production was also covered, with powerful portraits of assembly lines illustrating the new relationship between people and machines. These images also informed the public of the innovative work being done by manufacturers, the importance of new technology, and the huge industrial production level needed to support supply lines.

4.7 Lightweight Vehicles

During the war era, there was a limited quantity of gasoline available on the home front, and many ordinary citizens faced the problem of finding inexpensive transportation to their jobs. Several manufacturers developed small economy vehicles

Charles Eames, Eames storage unit and desk with fiberglass reinforced plastic chair. Manufactured by the Herman Miller Company, beginning in the late 1940s.

designed to address the issue of gas rationing. These lightweight vehicles were not just smaller copies of traditional cars, many also featured innovative designs that required fewer materials and less maintenance.

Designers found ways to build cars requiring less steel, rubber, glass, and other materials needed in the war effort. Some introduced three-wheeled vehicles or placed the engine in the back of the car. Others utilized alternative materials, such as aluminum alloys and Plexiglas, instead of the steel and glass bodies used in conventional cars. Several of these cars could travel as far as eighty miles on a single gallon of gasoline.

This trend continued after the war, when many returning veterans could not afford large cars. European companies, such as Fiat, Volkswagen, Citroën, Renault, and Saab were among the leading manufacturers of small vehicles. Datsun was one of the first Japanese brands of economy cars. American firms, such as Ford and GM, also created several inexpensive cars, although heavier cars were more popular in the United States.

4.8 New Materials and Manufacturing Techniques

In 1940, the Museum of Modern Art held a competition called "Organic Design in Home Furnishings," organized to encourage the development of new materials and manufacturing systems. The jury included well-known modern architects such as Alvar Aalto, Marcel Breuer, and Edward Durell Stone. Two first prizes were awarded to the team of Eero Saarinen and Charles Eames, who were members of the faculty at Cranbrook Academy.

Their furniture demonstrated how molded plywood, composed of seven to four-teen sheets of veneer connected by layers of glue, could be used to create curved

133

wood forms. The composite material was assembled, placed on a mold, and heated in an oven. It could be shaped to almost any curve or angle and was much cheaper to manufacture than solid wood furniture, providing an excellent substitute for many wood products. They also introduced "cycle-welding," a new process that made it possible to connect wood to other materials like rubber, glass, and metal.

During the war, Eames and Saarinen were commissioned by the U. S. Navy to expand the use of molded plywood for war-related purposes. They created curved wooden forms that were utilized in airplane propellers, crutches, and furniture. One of their most significant designs was a flexible, lightweight leg splint for wounded soldiers.

When their project for the Navy was terminated, Saarinen joined the Office of Strategic Services, and Eames worked on furniture for the Herman Miller company. Saarinen would later create furniture concepts for Knoll and establish an important architectural practice.

4.9   Protective Shelters

Throughout the war era, most European countries built protective structures and emergency products. They manufactured bomb shelters, gas masks, portable bathrooms, folding cots, canned foods, water containers, fire equipment, and medical supplies. The British were especially diligent, as their cities were under constant attack. Throughout Britain, basements in schools, factories, stores, and hospitals were converted into shelters for use during bombing raids. The most popular sanctuaries were the Underground tunnels and stations throughout London. Some were even equipped with beds, food, and medical services.

Manufacturers also created special protective structures for VIPs. The Churchill Egg, for example, was designed by the airplane manufacturer Avro to permit an important passenger to ride in a plane without wearing a gas mask and provided

The Churchill Egg, a pressurized cabin designed to protect the prime minister while he flew at high altitudes during World War II.

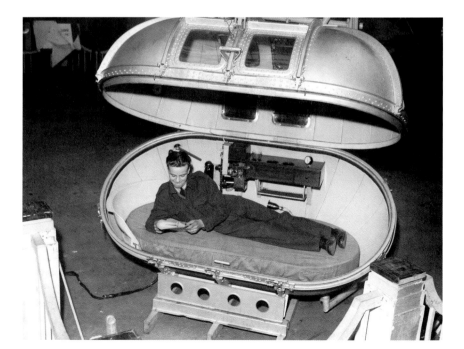

extra insulation against an attack. An extraordinary structure, it was made of aluminum alloy and had eight windows to prevent claustrophobia. It also contained a telephone, drinking facilities, books, and newspapers. It even provided room for its inhabitant to smoke cigars, although it is doubtful that anyone would have survived the experience of smoking in such a small space.[13] After the prototype had been successfully tested, plans were made to install the Egg on a Douglas C-54B aircraft, but the concept was eventually dropped as impractical and politically incorrect. Most British politicians preferred to use the same protective structures as the general public, and Churchill had a particular disdain for special privileges.

4.10 The Housing Shortage in the Postwar Era

East and West have met. This is the news for which the whole Allied world has been waiting. The forces of liberation have joined hands.
—News commentator, April 25, 1945[14]

World War II lasted more than six years. When it ended, the Allies established an uneasy peace. Servicemen from many countries returned to their homes and began the difficult process of rebuilding their lives. They hoped the future would be an era of security and prosperity, but their enthusiasm was somewhat subdued by the fear of another conflict.

They were also horrified by the vast amount of destruction that had been done. World War II left a legacy of overwhelming problems. Hundreds of cities had been destroyed, millions of buildings had been demolished, and tens of millions of people had been displaced.

One of the greatest challenges was housing. The British had lost over 500,000 housing units. France had lost 1.5 million. The Nazi invasion of Russia was even more devastating. German soldiers had bombed an estimated 32,000 factories, 100,000 collective farms, and 5 million housing units. Over 12 million Russians had been evacuated from cities and were homeless refugees. They were living in abandoned trucks, railroad cars, even oil tanks, until new houses could be built. Millions of apartments were also destroyed in Denmark, Belgium, Norway, and Greece.

The Germans suffered from a housing deficiency as well. They had lost over 2.5 million units, 25 percent of their housing inventory. Cities like Dresden and Berlin, which had been heavily bombed, had lost more than 40 percent of their residential buildings. There were similar tolls in Japanese cities.

Although plans for rebuilding were quickly developed, most countries were deeply in debt and could not afford to begin construction immediately. Over $2 trillion had been spent on the war, more than any other conflict in history. Damaged infrastructure and shortages in materials and labor were further concerns.[15] In most cases, the challenges went deeper than men, money, and materials. Prewar design and planning systems were no longer valid. New concepts were needed for cultures emerging in an era of limited resources. Each country took a different approach to reconstruction.

British citizens selected books, which were still intact after the bombing of the Holland House library in London.

4.11 Postwar Housing in
       Europe and Russia

British leaders had a resilient attitude. Lord Balfour declared, "We have . . . thanks to German bombers, a much greater opportunity for physical reconstruction."[16] Throughout the war, British architects and planners visited bombed neighborhoods with sketchbooks and cameras to record the conditions of demolished sites, and in their spare time, also created plans for postwar redevelopment, which they hoped to implement when hostilities had come to an end.

The British government took over the building industry. They established a socialist policy that forbade the development of private buildings for several decades. A New Towns Act was also introduced to create new suburban towns, called development corporations, near cities. The hardworking planners of these agencies produced many grandiose schemes, but only a few new towns were built, due to shortages in materials and funds.

France also faced shortages in money and materials, but their first concern after ridding themselves of the Vichy government was to reestablish governmental authority—all private projects had to be approved by the State. Aesthetics were a low priority. Losses during Occupation had been so severe that the goal was to quickly provide the bare necessities for as many people as possible. As a result, most French projects of this era were repetitive concrete structures that had a prisonlike quality.

Both Britain and France received aid from the United States, but they were still unable to develop a significant amount of housing. Russia, despite refusing aid from the United States, produced far more housing than its European neighbors. In its first five-year plan, which commenced in 1946, the communists built 4 million dwelling units. It was an impressive accomplishment, considering the amount of destruction they had endured.[17]

Soviet prefabricated housing, built in a later phase of recovery at Tushino, USSR, 1967.

The dreary, institutional Russian housing of this era served an immediate purpose, but established lifeless communities that lowered the overall standards of Soviet architecture. The massive blocks of repetitive units cast a grim mood across the Russian provinces and stamped out any vestige of cultural character or artistic expression. The pallor of the postwar years also contributed to the environmental decay of communist countries. It was not until the 1980s, when the Iron Curtain was lifted, that these depressing structures began to be replaced.

137

4.12 Unité d'Habitation

Throughout this era, European modernists proposed many new housing concepts, but avant-garde designs were not generally successful in the postwar years. Most Europeans chose to live in traditional cottagelike homes. Their preference for old world structures stemmed from the years of war and economic turmoil, which caused a return to conservative values. Despite the reactionary atmosphere, a few experimental concepts were realized.

The city of Marseilles suffered severe damage during the war. Besides destroying housing stock, the Germans demolished the Vieux Port, leaving many citizens unemployed. In 1946, an innovative minister of reconstruction chose a twelve-acre site on the edge of the city and asked Le Corbusier to develop a prototype housing project. Le Corbusier was almost sixty when he began. His design for the Unité d'Habitation was the culmination of over thirty years of architectural analysis and was his first opportunity to implement his ideas on a large scale. The building was made of reinforced concrete, utilizing the techniques he had learned from the Perrets. The design was based on the five points of architecture he had defined in the 1920s.

Le Corbusier, Unité
d'Habitation, Marseilles,
1947–53.

138

The building is lifted off the ground on huge pilotis, or pillars. The structure is supported by columns, which provide a free plan and a free facade. The building also contains a roof terrace with recreational areas. This dramatic structure would not only provide housing, it would also introduce a new way of living. The Marseilles block, as it was called, could house a community of over 1,600 people in a single seventeen-floor structure of 337 units, which are more like maisonettes than apartments. The seventh and eighth floors contain public facilities, such as a laundry room, small stores, a restaurant, and a hotel. The roof terrace featured a day care center, swimming pool, gymnasium, running track, and solarium. The ground level opened to a large park with tennis courts and playing fields, as well as a garage. The mechanical systems were located on an enclosed service floor just above the pilotis.

Each unit was constructed individually, then inserted into the master grid. There were twenty-three variations in the apartment plans, which made them appropriate for a wide variety of occupants. There were also other amenities in the design. Each unit had a high ceiling in the living room area; the children's spaces were separated from the adult areas by a central lobby; and the kitchens and closets had built-in cabinets and storage units, so the rooms were kept as open as possible.

A few critics claimed the monolithic structure had an impersonal quality. It certainly contradicted the nineteenth-century cottage concept. However, the project won praise from most modern architects for introducing several new concepts for the future, the most important being the idea that a building could house an entire community.

Unité also held a symbolic place in the difficult era of reconstruction. While most projects were being developed as cheaply as possible, at the lowest level of design, it offered a sophisticated approach. While many buildings were designed for homeless refugees, it introduced a middle-class alternative that could be applied in future developments. It also provided a model for the International Style, a concept that grew increasingly important in the postwar era. The Marseilles block served as a prototype for many "apartment blocks" built in later years.

4.13 Redevelopment of the European Automobile Industry

In addition to housing, there was also a need to redevelop the European economy. The postwar generation not only needed housing, they also needed food, water, jobs, energy, and transportation systems. In 1945, a few British officers decided to resurrect a German automobile factory. There was a need for inexpensive vehicles, as well as new industries that would stimulate growth, so they found a factory that was still intact and capable of producing cars.

They decided to manufacture an economical vehicle that had been developed before the war. In the 1930s, Hitler had asked Ferdinand Porsche to design an inexpensive car that could carry five people and travel comfortably at a speed of about sixty miles per hour. Although Porsche did not agree with the politics of the Third Reich, he was interested in the idea of creating a small, efficient vehicle.

Several European companies were already manufacturing small electric cars, but this car would have a combustion engine. It was called the Volkswagen, or the "people's car." Built according to Porsche's design, it was only produced in small quantities in the 1930s, because it was too expensive for average German workers. It was not manufactured at all during the war. However, in the postwar era, the Volkswagen concept realized its potential.

The factory was reconfigured as an assembly line for maximum efficiency, and produced 10,000 vehicles in its first year, an impressive start. The following year, the British military ordered 20,000 vehicles, which led to expansion of the facilities. Within a few years, Volkswagens were being exported to most European countries. The new models were small, fuel-efficient cars that were affordable for most middle-class consumers. Although other companies in Japan and Europe were producing similar cars, the Volkswagen was the most popular. In the 1950s, the company introduced new lines, such as Volkswagen vans, buses, convertibles, and station wagons, as well as the basic Beetle. This lightweight, efficient car would become even more important several decades later, when oil prices rose to exorbitant heights.

139

Lines of Volkswagen cars and vans, waiting to be shipped abroad on the *Fidelio* at Bremen Harbor, Germany.

Fritz Fend, the Messerschmitt KR200 bubble car, 1956.

The production of Volkswagens stimulated other segments of the German economy. It led to the demand for component parts and required flexible manufacturing systems that could be adapted to build various models of the basic car, an important refinement of the assembly line system.

In the 1950s, other German factories were also retooled to manufacture civilian products. The Messerschmitt facility, which had built fighter planes during the war, was reopened under a different name. Instead of aircraft, it manufactured sewing machines, prefabricated houses, and a few experimental cars, including the Messerschmitt KR 200, designed by Fritz Fend. This three-wheeled vehicle followed in the tradition of the "bubble car." It was produced for about twelve years, until the company turned to other projects.

4.14 Prefabricated Housing In America

Just beg, borrow or steal the money and then build and build.
—William Levitt[18]

When the war ended, the United States faced a severe housing shortage. Over eight million men and women were released from the armed services and returned to their communities, eager to restart their lives. Unfortunately, there were no preparations for their arrival.

In 1946, Congress passed the Veterans' Emergency Housing Act and a few military installations were converted into civilian housing, but these did not offer nearly enough units to meet demand. The government also created several mortgage programs to stimulate new construction. One of the most important was the FHA Mortgage Guarantee, which insured loans for inexpensive housing. It guaranteed up to 90 percent of the cost of an inexpensive house, at 5 percent interest, which provided millions of Americans with the means to invest in a modest home.

Even though funding was available, American builders could not begin new construction immediately because the United States, like other nations, lacked materials and skilled labor. Orders for staples such as steel were sometimes delayed for several years. In response to these issues, a few manufacturers developed a new type of housing utilizing recycled materials. They collected war vehicles, disassembled them, and then reworked the materials into prefabricated housing components.

The prefabricated housing systems of this era spawned an important new direction in housing. Most of the units were built on assembly lines. They were inexpensive and easy to construct. Many were purchased by individual owners, but some were mass-produced for developers, who created whole residential communities based on military housing systems by acquiring land and arranging for schools, shopping areas, and parks to be built nearby. Developers also constructed the water, power, and road systems for the project. The result was the creation of mass-produced neighborhoods that provided all the basic needs of working-class families.

4.15 Levittown

Real estate developer William Levitt was among the most innovative builders of this era. His main contribution was the creation of a standardized construction system to produce good-quality housing at a reasonable price. His approach was based on the assembly line system and provided decent, affordable housing for thousands of American families.

Levitt was raised on Long Island, New York. His father was a developer who built mid-priced houses in the 1930s. During World War II, he served in the navy. After the war, he and his brother, Alfred, joined forces to expand the family company, Levitt & Sons.

Their first project, built in 1941, was a government contract to create 2,350 homes for factory workers in Virginia. They set to work with union labor and traditional construction systems, but within a short time, they fell behind schedule and exceeded the budget. Under pressure to succeed in their first major job, Levitt and his team decided to initiate a new system.

They analyzed the construction process and made a list of twenty-seven steps needed to build a house. Levitt then hired twenty-seven teams of workers, who were each trained to complete one stage of the job at maximum speed. Since the product was housing, they could not build a moving system like the assembly lines used in automobile factories. Instead, they created a construction system in which the workers moved from house to house.

They fully utilized this system for the first time in the development of Levittown, New York. The project began with the acquisition of a large tract of land and the construction of basic infrastructure. The habitable areas of the site were divided into equal lots sixty feet apart. Construction materials were purchased in large quantities to keep costs as low as possible.

When teams of workers were brought to the site, one laid the foundations, another built the lower structure, a third did the framing, and so on. Each team moved from lot to lot, completing a specific task on a row of houses. The most efficient teams received higher salaries, providing an incentive for the workers to maintain a rapid pace.

Although designs were standardized, several different models with prices ranging from $8,000 to $12,000 were available. Levitt also offered financing packages that made it possible for a family to own a house for as little as $60 per month. He later built other successful projects in Pennsylvania, New Jersey, Maryland, Virginia, Florida, and Puerto Rico.

A few of his communities still exist. Levittown, Pennsylvania, a suburb of Philadelphia, is thriving. It originally contained about 17,000 housing units and a population of about 55,000 people. The houses were built along curving roads and divided into forty-one neighborhoods. Although there were six different housing models in the project, the styles were extremely similar, establishing a repetitive pattern.

Some architects wondered if Levitt could have accomplished the same task with more variations, but he was the first to apply an assembly line system to housing,

Aerial photograph of
Levittown, New York.

143

and to utilize a simple design to maximize efficiency. He was responding to the emergency demands of the postwar era, which left little time for aesthetic considerations.

Levitt was criticized for his standardized approach, but his methods were widely publicized and copied by other builders. The repetitive housing, which he and others created, helped to establish the culture of conformity that emerged in the 1950s. Although they cannot be held solely responsible for the conservatism of that era, their projects were a contributing factor. They are sometimes cited as examples of the impact of assembly lines on the American way of life.

4.16 Case Study House
      Program

During this era, many architects and industrial designers studied the issue of mass housing. They not only examined design and construction issues, they also tried to create more efficient systems of manufacturing and transporting new homes. Some companies arranged for wartime helicopters to carry the houses to their intended locations. The heavy-duty Sikorsky Skycrane was capable of hoisting a 4,000-square-foot house to its site.

One California design magazine also played an important role in developing new concepts. In 1943, John Entenza, the editor of *Arts & Architecture* magazine, dedicated several issues to the study of prefabricated housing. He worked with Herbert Matter, R. Buckminster Fuller, and Charles and Ray Eames on a comprehensive

The heavy-duty Sikorsky S-64 Skycrane carries a prefabricated house from the factory to its destination as part of a program that provided instant housing in America, 1970.

examination of mass production systems that could be used in the postwar era. The July 1944 issue included a description of the necessary qualities of the designer: "The architect . . . of the prefabricated house . . . must be the student of human behavior, the scientist, the economist and the industrial engineer."

Entenza and his consultants planned another issue on the Quonset hut as a realistic alternative to conventional homes. Quonset huts were simple timber or metal structures used in military installations, usually having four rooms: a kitchen, bathroom, bedroom, and living room. They also had heating, plumbing, and electrical systems, were 500 to 1,000 square feet, and sold for $2,500 to $6,500 per unit.[19]

In 1945, Entenza initiated an even more important project, a Case Study House Program to support housing experiments. The magazine acted as client for the construction of twenty-five case study homes designed by innovative architects. The projects utilized new materials and construction techniques and gave designers an opportunity to build prototypes of new concepts.

4.17 Case Study House #8 or Eames House

Eames and Saarinen were among the participants in Entenza's experiment, creating Case Study House #8 and Case Study House #9, respectively. They had already collaborated on the design of a prefabricated house based on inexpensive off-the-shelf parts ordered from catalogs, but the steel was delayed for three years due to a shortage of available materials. In 1948, when the steel finally arrived, Charles and Ray Eames were in the process of creating a new prefabricated design, which became Case Study House #8.

Their goal was to enclose a large volume of space using inexpensive materials found in catalogs and to preserve the meadow on which the structure was built. The house contained 1,500 square feet of usable space and was made of a steel frame

Charles and Ray Eames, Case Study House #8, Pacific Palisades, California, built 1945–49.

construction system of slim columns and lightweight trusses that was easy to assemble. The design was based on materials used in industrial buildings, such as factories and airplane hangars. The main frame of the structure was erected in a day and a half. Exterior walls were composed of steel panels, arranged in a geometric pattern reminiscent of the panels in Japanese houses. Some panels were painted with primary colors, which were a direct reference to modernism, specifically to the patterns of Piet Mondrian paintings.

145

The interior space took a few months to construct. It was seventeen feet high, and public areas—the living and dining room spaces—maintained this double height. The kitchen and storage areas were built under a mezzanine composed of a bedroom, bathroom, and dressing area. A prefabricated spiral staircase, found in a naval catalog, connected the floors.

Although the house was based on minimal concepts, the interior was furnished with warm wood finishes to appeal to consumers. It provided an inexpensive system that was easy to build, but did not succeed commercially, so Charles and Ray Eames decided to live in the prototype themselves. They later added a second building to serve as a studio. Their home became a classic example of a creative postwar solution.

4.18 Wichita House

Throughout these years, one inventor/environmentalist contemplated the broader issues of industry and environment. Richard Buckminster Fuller was struck by the amount of wasted materials used in traditional construction. He also disapproved of the inefficient systems that dominated most industries and the vast quantities of resources wasted in poorly designed energy and water systems. He believed that if the world's resources were used properly, it would be possible to provide a decent standard of living for the entire population of the globe.

R. Buckminster Fuller, The Wichita House, under construction. A crane lifts the aluminum top of the ventilator onto the roof of the prefabricated circular structure.

R. Buckminster Fuller was raised on an island off the coast of Maine that contained one farm. As a boy, he learned about boatbuilding, fishing, farming, and conservation. He went to school at Milton Academy, then went to Harvard to study mathematics, but he was sent down from college after two years for what he called "general irresponsibility."

After leaving school, he worked in Canada as an apprentice machinist, then in New York for a meatpacking company involved in importing and exporting. During World War I, he joined the navy and studied navigation, radio transmission, port systems, and aircraft.

Through these seemingly unrelated experiences, he developed a new philosophy of design. He considered aesthetic issues to be old-fashioned, and felt the Bauhaus architects were just replacing one set of aesthetics with another. He also rejected technologies like the wasteful combustion engines built by Ford.

In 1927, he designed the Dymaxion House, an innovative concept home that conserved materials and labor. Its sophisticated, hexagonal tensile structure utilizes a high-strength metal alloy in combination with plastic elements, and is suspended from a central core. The core contains a prefabricated kitchen and bathroom, as well as heating, air-conditioning, and plumbing systems. The outer wall has a ribbon window to provide light. It could have sold for $3,000, but it was never mass-produced.

In the 1930s, he addressed the issue of the automobile. He invented a series of Dymaxion cars, which were more efficient than ordinary automobiles. They required 30 to 50 percent less fuel than regular cars. The design was streamlined and slightly triangular, forming an aerodynamic "teardrop" shape.

Dymaxion cars were exhibited at Chicago's "A Century of Progress International Exposition." A British company planned to manufacture the design, but one of the prototypes was involved in a serious accident. The press exaggerated the incident, destroying the reputation of the car, and the concept was unfortunately abandoned.

In the late 1930s, Fuller worked with the Butler Manufacturing Company on the creation of a new circular housing system based on the Dymaxion House. They reduced the materials needed to a bare minimum and planned to manufacture the unit at a cost of only $1,200 per house. It was approved by the government in 1941, and several factories were designated to build 1,000 units per day. But again the design was never mass-produced. No definite reasons were given. It may have been because steel was unavailable or because the system was so advanced that they felt the public would be uncomfortable with the design.

In 1946, Fuller designed the Wichita House, which was also based on the Dymaxion concept. The weight of the hemispherical structure was only 6,000 pounds, which made it light enough to be airlifted or moved by trailer. He also made certain that none of the parts weighed more than ten pounds to simplify the construction process. He received orders for 3,700 units at a price of $6,500 each, but for some reason, the plans to make the Wichita House were also cancelled.[20]

Despite these setbacks, Fuller created many other inventions and designs. He also wrote several books attacking capitalists for making products without concern for their effect on the environment. It was not until the late 1970s that plastics were commonly seen as a danger to the environment because of the chemicals used in manufacturing the material and the problems associated with its disposal. He gave many legendary lectures on the topic of resource planning and left a legacy of important environmental ideas.

4.19 New Products and Industrial Designs

As millions of new households were established, a new generation of furnishings was also created. Every family needed a refrigerator, washing machine, stove, and telephone. Consumers were eager to exercise their purchasing power, which had been held in abeyance during the impoverished years of the Depression and the regulated era of World War II. Finally, there were no coupons limiting choices, or feelings of guilt associated with expenditures. The American economy increased throughout the postwar years, as thousands of new products appeared in the marketplace.

Many of the new products were made of synthetic materials, such as plastics, molded plywood, fiberglass, and other inexpensive compounds developed during the war. Fabrics such as vinyl, acrylic, nylon, rayon, and polyester were also popular in the 1950s and 1960s. Prior to World War II, artificial materials were considered cheap substitutes for natural substances, but during the war, they became acceptable because

Eero Saarinen, Tulip Chair,
manufactured by Knoll,
1955–57.

they were easy to produce. New synthetics were also versatile, easy to maintain, and durable. Large companies such as Bakelite, Tupperware, and Formica provided colorful products for the modern home. Plastics were used in thousands of applications, including records, radios, telephones, televisions, and car components.

Several well-respected industrial designers developed intriguing products based on synthetic materials utilizing the streamlined concepts of the 1930s. One of the most famous designs of the 1950s was Eero Saarinen's Tulip Chair manufactured by Knoll. It was made of only two materials, aluminum and fiberglass, but its organic shape was painted white and seemed to emanate from a single form. Its elegant streamlining expressed the emerging concept of mid-century modernism.

4.20 The Reaction Against
Standardization

In the nurseries, the Elementary Class Consciousness lesson was over, the voices were adapting future demand to future industrial supply. "I do love flying," they whispered, "I do love flying, I do love having new clothes . . . old clothes are beastly," continued the untiring whisper. "We always throw away old clothes. Ending is better than mending."
—Aldous Huxley *Brave New World*[21]

In 1932, Aldous Huxley published *Brave New World*, a satirical novel that addressed the issues of capitalism and modern industrial systems. Although he recognized the value of efficient production, he was critical of its effect on individual identity. His concern was particularly aimed at assembly lines and standardized systems. For Huxley, the assembly line was not just a method of improving efficiency; it was a dehumanizing concept with broad implications.

The book attacked the ideas of standardization, cultural conditioning, and consumerism through a fictional society set in the future. It also explored the dangers of creating an economy in which, as one of the characters explained, "Every man, woman and child (was) compelled to consume so much a year. In the interests of industry."[22]

In Huxley's dystopia, the assembly line is used to produce people in the same way that cars are manufactured. Embryos are incubated in the factorylike environment of a "hatchery." Each embryo is placed in a dish on a conveyor belt and chemically manipulated to provide a particular type of human being. The process controls the intelligence, appearance, and personal characteristics of the embryo. The system produces alphas, betas, gammas, deltas, and epsilons with the same indifference of a factory generating Chevrolets, Chryslers, or Cadillacs. It ensures a balanced society based on the proportions of a scientific system.

After the children are hatched, they are taught to accept their role in the social hierarchy through a process of sleep conditioning. A handful of slogans are repeated thousands of times while they sleep, establishing patterns in their behavior. Drugs are also used to eliminate any emotional outbursts or undesirable responses to the system.

Huxley was one of several literary Luddites who resisted the trends of mass production, mass communications, and mass culture. His novel attacked the increasing power of corporations to influence public policy, since he felt the marketing techniques used in advertising were a form of cultural conditioning that destroyed freedom of thought.

149

4.21 *A nous la liberté*
(Give us Liberty)

In the 1930s, several filmmakers criticized modern systems and addressed the fundamental problem of maintaining an individual identity in a standardized culture. They also explored the impact of mass production on the worker, the effect of cultural conformity, and the nature of a consumer society, providing classic images of a mechanized culture and life on the assembly line.

The film *A nous la liberté*, produced in 1931, portrays the impact of mechanization on workers in a factory. It was directed by René Clair, who began his career as a surrealist in the 1920s. Clair's early experimental projects, such as *Paris qui dort* and *Entr'acte*, were among the first surrealist films ever made. *Entr'acte* is a short film that was literally shown "between the acts" of a ballet. It contains scenes of Man Ray and Marcel Duchamp playing chess on a rooftop rapidly intercut with objects, to create humorous juxtapositions.[23]

Industrial workers walk past
a modern factory in the film
A nous la liberté, 1931.
Director: Rene Clair.

A nous la liberté has a different quality. It tells the story of an escaped convict who works in a factory and eventually becomes a powerful executive. The buildings are modern structures, designed by the art director Lazare Meerson. He also utilized a machinelike aesthetic in interior environments. His designs emphasize the similarity between factories and prisons, which strengthen the message of the story. The film also portrays the effect of standardized systems on the workers. They dress alike, walk in a procession, and maintain order at all times.

4.22 *Modern Times*

In 1936, Charlie Chaplin's film *Modern Times* showed audiences a dramatic image of a man working on an assembly line. Chaplin had grown up in the working-class neighborhoods of industrial London and was well aware of labor problems. He wrote, directed, and acted in the film and participated in the design of the factory environment in which the story takes place.

The film was shot on a clean, modern set. The major elements were gigantic machines that had a toylike quality suitable to his humor. In one scene, an inventor brings in a new machine that is designed to feed the workers lunch while they continue their jobs on the assembly line. The machine is supposed to increase productivity, but the devious device doesn't work. When it is demonstrated on the worker portrayed by Chaplin, he barely survives the encounter. The satirical scene raises the question, how far should technology go in its quest for efficiency?

Charlie Chaplin and a fellow worker struggle with a giant machine on an assembly line in the film *Modern Times*, 1936. Director: Charlie Chaplin.

M. Hulot searches for his business partner in the film *Playtime*, 1967. Director: Jacques Tati.

Throughout the film, the worker played by Chaplin is inflicted with physical problems as a result of his repetitive job on the assembly line. He is so conditioned by the relentless machine that he eats, walks, and even rests with the same jerking motions of his job on the line. In the film's culminating scenes, he is swallowed by the overpowering mechanism that he serves.

4.23 *Mon oncle* and *Playtime*

In the 1950s, French director Jacques Tati also turned a satirical eye on the subject of mechanization and modern design. Tati began his career as a mime in the 1930s, but by 1932, he was writing, directing, and acting in his own films. In the 1940s, he developed the character of M. Hulot, a self-appointed representative of the premodern world. Tati made two films, *Mon oncle* and *Playtime*, that depict the humorous struggle of M. Hulot to surf the sleek waves of modern life. They were also a direct critique of modern architectural environments.

In both films, this delightful, old-fashioned figure ventures into the modern neighborhoods of Paris and is exposed to the strange experience of a standardized world. In *Mon oncle*, he passes endless prefabricated housing units until he reaches the home of his nephew. The house is in the midst of a huge development. Inside the home, he is confronted with a stark environment of white prefabricated rooms and the intimidating systems of various mechanical devices. He is filled with relief when he returns to his own crooked, medieval house.

His clash with minimalism continues in the film *Playtime*, in which he visits a modern office building. While driving to the office, he navigates through the noise and confusion of a traffic circle, full of honking cars. When he finally arrives, he becomes lost several times while trying to find his way through a floor of offices filled with repetitive cubicles. He is horrified by the boxlike interiors and the machinelike quality of the design.

For this film, Tati created full-scale buildings, as well as portable models of skyscrapers that could be moved to various locations on the lot. Most critics felt his films were aimed at the white box concepts of Le Corbusier and the art deco houses of Robert Mallet-Stevens. Although the avant-garde architects were unhappy with his critical portrayal of modern design, the clever irony of his films could not be denied. *Mon oncle* won the Special Jury prize at the Cannes Film Festival in 1958. A year later, it also won the Oscar for the Best Foreign Film.[24]

4.24 *The Fountainhead*

In 1943, Ayn Rand published *The Fountainhead*, a novel that introduced a heroic image of a modern architect. This dramatic story expressed Rand's philosophical concept of objectivism. Her theories were based on the idea that most major achievements in history were the work of visionary individuals who resisted cultural pressures to conform to the conventions of society. She maintained that capitalism was the only system that supported such strong individuality.

Rand had been raised in communist Russia, and as a child, she was taught to sacrifice her own individual goals for the good of society. She came to detest socialist values. In 1924, she completed her studies at the University of Petrograd and moved to California to develop a career as a screenwriter. She was unsuccessful in this field, but she later wrote novels and philosophical essays that attracted a dedicated following.

The popularity of *The Fountainhead* led to the 1949 production of a film based on the book. The story portrays the struggle of a visionary architect to develop his work in the cynical environment of commercial culture. It contrasts his career with the careers of mediocre designers and critics who are willing to compromise their values for recognition. Although the hero of the story is an architect, the character is based on universal themes.

Unfortunately, the screenplay, written by Rand, was extremely didactic and did not appeal to the public. But the production designs by Edward Carrere were very successful. He created pompous Beaux-Arts structures to represent the work of the mediocre architects, and for the hero's work, he developed slim modern buildings based on the minimal style of Mies van der Rohe.

Journalist Ellsworth Toohey
presents images of modern
buildings to newspaper titan
Gail Wynand in the film
The Fountainhead, 1949.
Director: King Vidor.

Rand's concept of the visionary hero was also based on Frank Lloyd Wright.
Wright was initially pleased with the reference, but he later disassociated himself
from the project. Her portrayal of the visionary architect was compelling, but
her right-wing philosophy conflicted with the humanitarian ideals held by most
artists and intellectuals of the time. She also lost much of her credibility when
she testified against colleagues at the McCarthy hearings.

153

4.25 The Atomic Era

There's only one thing worse than one nation having the atomic bomb . . .
That's two nations having it.
—Harold Urey[25]

In the 1950s and 1960s, the world was held hostage by the fear of another war.
Politicians realized that a third world war would be even more dangerous than the
others, for this time, the conflict would be waged with atomic weapons. The atomic
bomb had been created for World War II as a weapon to end all wars, but instead,
it engendered a whole new era of hostility.

The first atomic bomb was completed in 1945. It was tested in New Mexico before
being dropped on Japan. As scientists watched the smoke rise from the huge explosion, they were shocked by its intensity. Project director Robert Oppenheimer uttered
a quote from the *Bhagavad Gita*, a Hindu scripture: "I am become Death, the shat-
terer of worlds." But his regrets came too late. Pandora's box had been opened. In
1949, Soviet leaders announced that they also had an atomic bomb. This led to an
arms race between the United States and the Soviet Union that would drain the
resources of both countries. The paranoia of the period led to the creation of bomb
shelters, fallout suits, masks, water storage drums, and other emergency products.

The government tried to downplay the danger—school children were taught that the "duck and cover" maneuver would be adequate protection during a nuclear attack—but the public grasped the seriousness of the situation in spite of such absurd propaganda.

During these years, scientists were divided in their attitude toward atomic power. Some were in favor of exploring peacetime applications. Others were opposed to any further atomic research. New applications of the technology continued to appear, however, including atomic-powered ships, airplanes, submarines, and energy plants. The creation of atomic energy systems throughout the world led to a variety of environmental concerns, including contamination, disposal of nuclear wastes, and the danger of a nuclear accident. Years later, when many countries stopped using nuclear power, the sites of their power plants were so contaminated they could not be converted to other uses.

4.26 *Dr. Strangelove or: How I Learned to Stop Worrying and Love the Bomb*

In the late 1950s, production designer Ken Adam was approached by Stanley Kubrick to create sets for the satirical film *Dr. Strangelove or: How I Learned to Stop Worrying and Love the Bomb.* The film presents the story of a paranoid military officer who goes insane during the McCarthy era. His anticommunist conditioning is so powerful that he eventually cracks and orders the unauthorized launching of an atomic bomb. The film ends with the implication that his madness has inadvertently started World War III.

Adam based his dramatic design of the War Room in the film on the real meeting room that was created for the 1957 NATO conference—its dark design seemed to convey the tension surrounding the event. He was inspired by a news photograph depicting the symbolic image of a globe on a black background, placed above a row of diplomats seated at a table. Instead of inspiring confidence, the image expressed the delegates' vulnerability and the atmosphere of secrecy that characterized international negotiations in this era.

Adam's war room has an aura of danger and political intrigue. The walls are dark, except for a few large video screens that show continuous sequences of maps, databases, and technical diagrams. The lighting is shadowy, except for the faces of the actors, which are clearly lit. The strange atmosphere of the space provides a perfect setting for the dark humor of the satirical film.

4.27 The Atomic Car

Unlike scientists and politicians, designers often took a lighthearted approach to the atomic craze. They put forward whimsical concepts based on atomic themes. In 1950, designer George Nelson used the theme of atomic power to create his famous Ball Clock. The wooden balls that radiate from the center of the clock express the idea of atoms circling the nucleus of a molecule.

In the mid-1950s, several French designers developed the Simca Fulgar, an atomic-powered car designed for the year 2000. This two-wheeled vehicle utilized several technologies from the war era. It had its own radar system for navigation, as well as gyroscopes for balance when its speed exceeded 150 miles per hour, although it was designed to cruise at 90 miles per hour.

The war room in the film *Dr. Strangelove or: How I Learned to Stop Worrying and Love the Bomb*, 1964. Director: Stanley Kubrick.

NATO conference room in Paris, December 19, 1957.

The inventors could not have been serious when they created this concept. But if they were, it poses some interesting questions: Did they imagine that atomic fuel would be dispensed at gas stations? Did they consider the disposal of nuclear wastes? What about accidents? Would a car collision have created an atomic explosion? It seems that the atomic car was never developed beyond the design model, but it signified the fact that most new technologies, no matter how inappropriate, were eventually applied to the automobile.

A Fulgar show-model of an atomic powered car, created by the French automobile manufacturer Simca for the year 2000.

4.28 Planners and Antiplanners

The problem that lies behind consideration for pedestrians, as it lies behind all other city traffic difficulties, is how to cut down absolute numbers of surface vehicles and enable those that remain to work harder and more efficiently.
—Jane Jacobs[26]

Obsession with cars culminated in the 1950s and 1960s, when they became the universal form of transportation. But in the late 1960s and 1970s, several leading urbanists began to criticize the impact of automobiles, the most influential being Jane Jacobs, a freelance writer who later became a community activist. Her 1961 book *The Death and Life of Great American Cities* analyzes the effect of automobiles on cities and the failures of the housing policies of the postwar era.

In this seminal work, she attacks standardized housing projects that isolate residents from urban centers and force them to rely on cars. She also criticizes urban highway systems that cut through neighborhoods and destroy communities. As an alternative, she advocates a different planning paradigm, which includes the development of mixed-use neighborhoods and public transportation, as well as the protection of parks and historic communities.

Similar views were expressed by Lewis Mumford and other cultural and architectural critics. They attacked the policies of Le Corbusier, Robert Moses, and Henry Ford, which had created the commuter culture. Their well-constructed arguments inspired many architects and planners to change their own attitudes toward automobiles. Over time, a nationwide effort developed to restore decayed downtown areas of cities and introduce public transportation systems.

In response to this criticism, the automobile industry formed several organizations that continued to advocate cars. In 1974, they established the Antiplanner, an agency that critiqued the work of urban planners who were opposed to automobiles. They also developed the American Dream Coalition, an association that provided

Aerial view of downtown parking blocks in Houston, Texas, where approximately 70 percent of the land is reserved for automobiles, 1978.

propaganda in support of cars. This inventive group wrote reports that showed how automobiles had contributed to the lifestyle of Americans. They claimed that prior to the introduction of private cars, average Americans traveled only about 1,000 miles per year. But by the late twentieth century, many Americans were traveling over 16,000 miles per year. They also asserted that cars created more opportunities for families to own their own homes, because private vehicles made it possible for people to live farther away from their jobs. They also stated that over time, cars increased individual earning power seven times.

The American Dream Coalition also reported that cars reduced the price of consumer goods by 100 times or more, by providing transportation to a variety of stores. They even claimed that automobiles were responsible for "reforesting 80 million acres of deforested horse-pasture lands and the transformation of 40 million acres of other pastures to higher-value croplands."[27]

But those who opposed automobiles had much stronger arguments. By the 1960s and 1970s, approximately one-third of the land in most major cities was dedicated to the use of automobiles. In some cities, like Houston, as much as 70 percent of the urban center was absorbed by cars. The wastelands created by parking lots and service areas were dead zones that ruined the quality of the community. The huge amount of traffic also caused air pollution, increased water runoff, and raised the temperature of the city, which placed a greater strain on resources.[28]

Those issues were just part of the equation. It was later learned that automobiles consumed most of the nonrenewable fossil fuels that were a major factor in global warming. The damage caused by cars was not just limited to active vehicles; it was also a result of manufacturing. Historian Mark Foster, who examined these issues, explained, "one third of the total environmental damage caused by automobiles occurred before they were sold and driven." He also claimed that the creation of one car caused "29 tons of waste and 1,207 million cubic yards of polluted air."[29]

Other studies indicated that cars consumed an inordinate proportion of natural materials. Each year, American cars used about 20 percent of all the steel consumed in the United States and over 65 percent of all the rubber available. Large quantities of lead, gas, coal, aluminum, and platinum were also needed for their fabrication.

Sociologists examined the impact of automobiles on culture and discovered that many commuters spent as much as 25 percent of their waking hours in cars, and, as a result, neglected their families. Some blamed high crime rates and increased divorces on the commuter lifestyle. Doctors also attacked automobile transportation. The number of injuries caused by cars was staggering. In an average year, over 250,000 deaths occurred as a result of car accidents. There were also health problems related to smog, toxic chemicals, and reduced ozone levels.

Despite these negative statistics, the number of cars continued to increase in the late twentieth century. By 1990, over 630 million vehicles were on the road, of which two-thirds were private cars. According to Greenpeace, a new car was manufactured every second, which meant that 35 million cars were manufactured each year, more than even Henry Ford could have ever imagined. Many of these vehicles were being sold in emerging countries, where the romance with the automobile was just beginning, and the same group of problems were beginning to develop.[30]

Notes

1. Aldous Huxley, *Brave New World* (New York: Harper & Brothers, 1932), 25.

2. Richard Guy Wilson, Dianne H., Pilgrim, and Dickran Tashjian, *The Machine Age in America: 1918–1941* (New York: Harry N. Abrams, Inc. in association with The Brooklyn Museum, New York, 1986), 26.

3. Godfrey Hodgson, *People's Century* (New York: Random House, Inc., 1998), 100.

4. Charles E. Sorenson, *My Forty Years with Ford* (New York: Collier Books, 1956), 132.

5. http://en.wikipedia.org/wiki/Great_American_Streetcar_Scandal

6. Robert A. Caro, *The Power Broker* (New York: Random House, Inc., 1975), 895-96.

7. Caro, 518, 715, 897.

8. Le Corbusier, *The City of To-morrow and Its Planning* (New York: Dover Publications, Inc., 1987), 170.

9. Frank Lloyd Wright, *When Democracy Builds* (Chicago: University of Chicago Press, 1945), quoted in John Ormsbee Simonds, *Earthscape* (New York: McGraw Hill Publishing, 1978), 231.

10. Frank Lloyd Wright, "The Passing of the Cornice," in *The Future of Architecture* (New York: New American Library, 1953), 141.

11. Frank Lloyd Wright, quoted in Howard Mansfield *Cosmopolis*, (Center for Urban Policy Research, 1990, 50.

12. Franklin D. Roosevelt, "United States and the Second World War" in *The World's Great Speeches*, edited by Lewis Copeland, Lawrence W. Lamm, and Stephen J. McKenna (Mineola, NY: Dover Publications, Inc., 1999), 541.

13. "Avro York," Wikipedia, http://en.wikipedia.org/wiki/Avro_York.

14. Radio commentator, quoted in Godfrey Hodgson, 243.

15. The estimated cost of World War II was over $2 trillion dollars, based on 1990 adjusted value adjusted dollars. Source: http://www.threeworldwars.com/ overview.htm. The same estimate in 2008 value adjusted dollars is over $5 trillion. Source: http://www.sfgate.com/cgi-bin/article.cgi?f=/c/a2008/03/17/MNBVVL9GK.DTL

16. Martin Pawley, *Architecture Versus Housing* (New York: Praeger Publishers, 1971), 45.

17. Pawley, 75.

18. William Levitt, quoted in David Halberstam, "How William Levitt Helped to Fulfill the American Dream," *New York Times*, Feb. 6, 1994, New York and Region section.

19. Pawley, 57.

20. Pawley, 61.

21. Huxley, 48-49.

22. Huxley, 49.

23. Dietrich Neumann, *Film Architecture: Set Designs from Metropolis to Blade Runner* (Munich/New York: Prestel Verlag, 1999), 139.

24. Neumann, 136.

25. Harold Urey's 1949 comment on the atomic bomb was quoted in *The Seattle Times*, July 21, 1996, in "The atomic era dawns," by Sharon Boswell and Lorraine McConaghy, http://seattletimes.nwsource.com/special/centennial/July/atomic.html

26. Jane Jacobs, *The Death and Life of Great American Cities* (New York: Random House, Inc., 1961), 349.

27. Thomas Angotti, *Metropolis 2000* (London: Routledge, 1993), 12.

28. Greenpeace, quoted in Herbert Girardet, *The Gaia Atlas of Cities* (New York: Anchor Books, Doubleday, 1992), 105.

THE SPACE AGE

We are in pursuit of the new idea and vernacular language that could coexist with the
space capsules, the computers, and the throwaway packages of an atomic/electronic era.
—Warren Chalk, *Archigram*[1]

In the late nineteenth century, science fiction writers Jules Verne and H.G. Wells
introduced the new genre of space fiction. Their novels were not just tales of
adventures in space; they were also explorations of philosophical issues, pondering
such questions as the beginning of the universe, the concept of time, and the origin
of life. As the genre evolved, science fiction stories would include imaginative
ideas for the design of space technology and zero-gravity environments.

In 1903, Konstantin Tsiolkovsky, a Russian schoolteacher, published a series of conceptual designs for space technology. He proposed the idea of a rocket ship using
liquid propellants and designed a rotating space habitat with a "space greenhouse"
as part of an enclosed ecological system. These and subsequent concepts for space
stations, multistage rockets, astronauts' suits, and tethered attachments inspired
later Russian scientists to embark on real space research.

Dr. Robert Goddard, the first American to engage in serious rocket experiments,
began to study liquid propellants in 1909, and he developed the idea of combining
liquid hydrogen and oxygen. With funds from the Smithsonian Institution, he constructed a rocket fueled by liquid propellants that was successfully launched in 1926.

A year later, German physics professor Hermann Oberth established the Society
for Space Travel, a group that included Johannes Winkler, Rudolf Nebel, Wernher
von Braun, and other pioneering figures in space research. Members launched experimental rockets in the 1920s and 1930s and worked on government projects during
World War II, but in 1945, as the war ended, many surrendered to the Allied forces.
Some became part of the Russian scientific community; others were brought to
the United States.

The space age officially began in 1957 when Russia launched the satellite Sputnik I,
followed by Sputnik II, which carried a small dog. The launch of the American
satellite Explorer I in 1958 introduced competition between the two nations. That
year, the United States formally established the National Aeronautics and Space
Administration.[2] In 1961, President John F. Kennedy increased NASA funding with
the goal of achieving a moon landing. Wernher von Braun became the director of
the Apollo program, a division of NASA. The space agency engendered a patriotic

Astronaut James B. Irwin, lunar module pilot, salutes the deployed U.S. flag during the Apollo 15 lunar surface extravehicular activity (EVA) at the Hadley-Apennine landing site.

response from many Americans, but some questioned the priorities of a culture that allocated billions of dollars on space research without attending to the needs of the homeless and unemployed. They also felt that the program was a thinly veiled expansion of the military-industrial complex.

Over time, the space program spawned technological advances, known as "NASA spinoffs," that included diagnostic tools such as ultrasound, MRI, mammography, and portable X-ray machines, as well as more efficient computers, robots, tethered vehicles, and solar collectors. The most obvious innovation of space technology was the development of satellite systems and remote sensing technologies. Satellite maps helped to predict the weather by measuring wind patterns and atmospheric pressures. They also made it possible to conduct environmental research, such as monitoring pollution levels and ozone density. Satellites revolutionized the transmission of messages by eliminating the issue of distance in telecommunications systems.[3]

Space age technology inspired high-tech design. Some buildings were based on machine aesthetics, employing exposed steel structures, colorful ductwork, and industrial lighting. Others were made of lightweight concrete, and featured the smooth curving forms of an airplane or a rocket ship. Prefabrication introduced the concept of "plug-in" housing units, which were premanufactured, then inserted into a building core or a master grid. Inside the housing units, there were also prefabricated bathrooms and kitchens, as well as furniture, based on a "kit-of-parts"

Three Satellites Image from Nimbus 7's TOMS (Total Ozone Mapping Spectrometer), combined and processed in false colors to show the condition of the ozone layer in 1978. Black and red represent low total ozone values; blue and white symbolize high values; yellow and green show a mid-scale range in the total ozone amount.

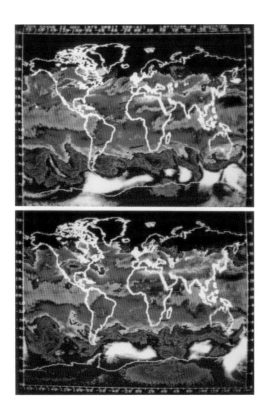

system. Flexible structures, such as tents, geodesic domes, and inflatable designs, made of lightweight materials and portable systems, were based on kit-of-parts concepts. They ranged in size from small houses to megastructures that could be quickly erected for public use, providing instant environments for rock concerts, happenings, and political events.

The children of this era were the first generation to live in high-tech environments. Prefabricated homes had air conditioners, refrigerators, and televisions, and garages contained cars, motorcycles, and power tools. Toy chests were filled with rocket ships, record players, and robots. This generation rejected traditional values. Their music was rock 'n' roll, and their clothing was "mod," or modern. Their cultural icons were the Jetsons and James Bond, an elegant Cold War spy, who could slip a wetsuit over a tuxedo and go deep-sea diving or don a rocket belt and fly away from a hostile encounter. The Bond films implied that any problem could be solved by space age technology and expressed the international vision of the postwar era.

163

5.1   The Concept of Flight

I would say that modern architecture is trying to provide and shape the environment for 20th century man.
—Eero Saarinen[4]

Early notions of flight had a romantic quality, which emerged during World War I when fighter pilots achieved heroic status. The bold image of flyers expanded in the 1920s, when pilots like Charles Lindbergh and Amelia Earhart flew across the oceans for the first time, and the fascination with flight grew in the 1930s with the advent of new vehicles, such as helicopters and seaplanes.

Harley Earl, designer,
Firebird III, Experimental
car built by General Motors,
1958.

The experience of combat was completely transformed by flight during World War II. As planes became a strategic necessity, American factories increased production of air vehicles from about 6,000 to 108,000 per year. The war produced seasoned pilots, established routes and basic facilities for airports, and led to improvements in engines and air traffic systems, which laid the foundations for long-distance airlines. After the war, commercial airlines began to grow, symbolizing a new era of global trade.

During the 1950s, thousands of new products appeared in the marketplace, and millions of new businesses were created worldwide. Planes began to replace ships and railroads as the primary mode of long-distance transportation. They provided systems for global trade, airmail, and passenger travel and made possible systems for overnight delivery of millions of products.

The industrial expansion of this era led to the development of new airports and commercial airlines in cities around the world. The notion of flight became a symbol of the emerging international culture which inspired many designers.

5.2   Experimental Cars

In the 1950s, several manufacturers embarked on experiments to develop the "car of the future." One of the most promising projects was the General Motors Firebird series created by Harley Earl, who was one of the first industrial designers to work in the automobile industry. Thirty years earlier Earl had single-handedly transformed car manufacturing by convincing General Motors to produce cars in a variety of styles and colors. In the 1950s, Earl faced the challenge of reshaping automobiles to suit the emerging generation, which now revolved around cars. In designing the Firebird, Earl applied the bulletlike shape of an airplane to the body of a car.

Firebird I was designed for a single passenger, sitting in a cockpit. It was a dangerous vehicle because the engine was based on the turbine system of a jet airplane. The fumes from the exhaust were hot enough to ignite a major fire, and the tires did not perform safely at high speeds.

Firebird II, designed for four passengers, was a wider, safer vehicle, with a fully independent suspension system. It also contained a guidance system that could communicate with signals, to be implanted in future highways. The concept of highway guidance systems was later analyzed by other engineers, who felt remote-controlled cars might provide a more efficient way of moving traffic and reduce the number of accidents on the road, but the idea was never implemented on a large scale.

Both Firebird II and Firebird III had titanium bodies. Firebird III contained all of the innovations of the second model, with a few new features added. Its steering system was a joystick, instead of a wheel, which was similar to the steering system of an airplane. It was designed to hold two passengers to provide the feel of a sports car. It was also safer than the other designs. The exhaust from the engine was cooler than previous models.

None of the Firebird prototypes was practical for mass production, but they influenced the styling of other cars. The fins of the Cadillac and the streamlined form of the Corvette both hearken back to the Firebirds. The guidance systems that now provide satellite communications in cars had their origins in the experimental vehicles of this period as well.

5.3   Eero Saarinen

Saarinen, who had grown up in Finland, was inspired by the minimal style of Ludwig Mies van der Rohe and the streamlined forms of Norman Bel Geddes, with whom he briefly worked. In developing his own elegant style, Saarinen combined aspects of both vocabularies. His buildings had a sculptural quality, as well as the formality of minimal corporate structures. His most sculptural project was the TWA Terminal at JFK airport in New York. Its continuous curving forms convey

Eero Saarinen, TWA terminal
at JFK Airport, New York,
1956–62.

165

Eero Saarinen, TWA
Terminal at JFK Airport in
New York, 1956–62.

a sense of constant motion. The whole structure has the appearance of an airplane or a bird in flight. The central entry is flanked by two winglike extensions that lead to waiting areas for the gates. The interior space is an intriguing environment of curved walls, floating stairways, and open balconies.

Saarinen later said the symbolism was unintended: "The fact that to some people it looked like a bird in flight was really coincidental . . . that was the last thing we thought about. Now, that doesn't mean that one doesn't have the right to see it that way or to explain it to laymen in those terms, especially because laymen are usually more literally than visually inclined."[5]

Whether or not the analogy to flight was consciously developed, the streamlined form became a symbol of the new era. The dramatic building inspired the creation of other lightweight concrete structures and helped introduce an organic style, known as 1950s futurism.

5.4   Lucio Costa and
       Oscar Niemeyer

Costa and Niemeyer worked together to establish modern architecture in Brazil. As a symbol of Brazil's emerging strength, the government commissioned several large building projects, including the new capital city of Brasilia. Most of the structures were developed in the International Style to express a modern, future-driven outlook.

In 1957, Costa won the competition to create the master plan for Brasilia, an isolated site in the interior of the country. Since the new city was supposed to symbolize the future outlook of Brazil, Costa decided to base the master plan on the shape of an airplane. A strong central axis leads to the main government buildings flanked by wings, or outer neighborhoods on both sides with smaller streets arranged in grids. A few outlying neighborhoods provide additional housing.

Lucio Costa, plan of the city
of Brasilia, 1956.

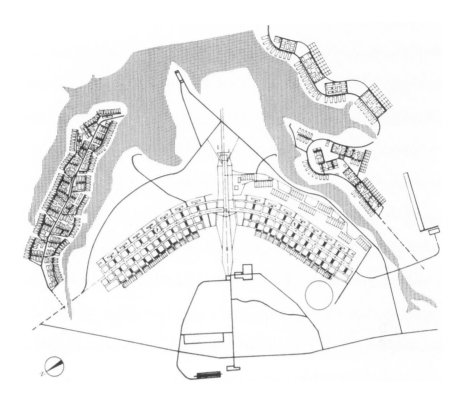

Oscar Niemeyer, Plaza
of the Three Powers,
Brasilia, 1958.

167

This low-density master plan was widely criticized. Not only would residents
be forced to use cars or buses to traverse the city, but the single main street would
create constant traffic problems. The design of the street itself was flawed by
insufficient lighting and lack of amenities for pedestrians.

Costa chose Niemeyer, his former assistant and an enthusiastic modernist, to design
the major buildings of Brasilia, which were developed as reinforced concrete
buildings inspired by Le Corbusier's principles. The most famous structure is the
National Congress Building, which is a striking composition of modern forms.

The main area of the building is a low horizontal structure approached on a central ramp. It contains two tall slim buildings on an axis with the ramp. The facility houses several major government departments with the tall buildings being the seat of the administrative departments. Next to each tower are large curving forms with the assembly halls for the legislature. One of the curving forms, the Chamber of Deputies, faces upward like a bowl. The Brazilian Senate faces downward like a dome. The dramatic shapes form a strong symbolic structure. Tall concrete-slab apartment buildings were sited on the side streets that formed the two "wings" of the plan, arranged in a linear fashion. The repetitive designs are somewhat reminiscent of Ludwig Hilberseimer's projects in the 1920s.

Despite the modern imagery, Niemeyer's buildings were a disappointment to the residents of Brasilia who complained that the monumental concrete structures were sterile, modern superblocks that had no soul or humanity. Although Costa and Niemeyer successfully established modern architecture in Brazil, their design of Brasilia illustrated many of the problems inherent in modern architecture and planning.

5.5 Pop Architecture: Mobile, Flexible, and Plug-in Concepts

In the early 1960s, art collectors Robert and Ethel Scull asked Andy Warhol to create a portrait of Ethel. They wanted the portrait immediately so Warhol took her to a photomat and made thirty-six photographs of Ethel in rapid succession. He later immortalized the images by using them as the basis of a photo-silkscreen portrait, which he called *Ethel Scull 36 Times*. He arranged the portrait as a grid of images and added a layer of color to each.

Warhol brought a quality of motion, almost a cinematic concept to a still image. He also redefined the idea of a portrait; instead of limiting the composition to a single image, he demonstrated the richness of a series of spontaneous poses that reflected different aspects of Ethel Scull's personality.

Some critcs dismissed Warhol's work, feeling it lacked traditional artistic judgment or the choice of one view, but others understood his intention. Although the process was casual, it contained several layers of meaning. His use of the grid gave the images a modern, machinelike quality, and his color added information to the prefabricated material.

American artists who worked with pop art concepts that focused on ordinary culture included Roy Lichtenstein, whose work is based on comic books, and Claes Oldenburg, whose sculptures celebrate common art forms, like a well-built hamburger. Their irreverent attitude toward tradition influenced architects and designers worldwide.

During the 1950s and 1960s, architects and planners investigated ways that design could respond to the new cultural and technological era and tried to develop new urban visions that provided more freedom and greater opportunity for individual expression. In 1956, the French-Hungarian architect Yona Friedman presented a manifesto entitled *L'Architecture mobile*. It introduced a concept of creating lightweight, flexible structures in the design of cities.

In 1963, the British architect Cedric Price created Fun Palace, a single building that could be used to house exhibits, media events, and theatrical performances. The

Yona Friedman, Hudson River Development, project for a spatial city in Manhattan, 1964.

design contains a crane and movable interior elements, such as stairs and platforms. Price intended it as a temporary structure that could be easily disassembled when it was no longer useful since he believed the culture was changing so quickly that buildings should be taken down when they became obsolete.[6]

5.6   Yona Friedman

Friedman developed a series of drawings that led to a second manifesto called *La Ville spatiale*, or *The Spatial City*. His drawings featured large structural grids, or space frames, suspended over cities to provide a new type of environment, a neutral infrastructure that could be defined by individual users, who could "plug-in" their own units. His flexible megastructure was designed to serve an evolving culture, one that was in constant flux. Friedman described his idea as a "spatial infrastructure," a multilevel space frame grid held up by pillars that in turn supported large spans. This infrastructure would represent the fixed part of the city, the mobile part consisting of walls, floors, and partitions for individual spaces. He believed that the best designers of the individual spaces were not the architects, but rather, the people who would ultimately occupy them.[7]

Friedman's concepts were part of the work of megastructuralists, who, collectively, formed a broader movement. His specific group was called GEAM, or Group for the Study of Mobile Architecture. Its members included Frei Otto, who worked with structural fabrics, and Masato Otaka, who was a member of the metabolist group.

5.7   Archigram

In 1961, an energetic group of six architects published the first of nine issues of *Archigram*, a phantasmagoria of architectural designs for the new generation. They also called their group Archigram, a word drawn from combining the terms "architecture" and "telegram." This remarkable association of talented artists/ architects introduced a new way of thinking about environment, combining the high-tech systems of space age technology with new media and prefabricated design. It also expressed the ironic attitude of the pop artists, the Beatles, and the Monty Python group.

169

Peter Cook/Archigram,
Plug-in City, Maximum
Pressure Area Section,
1964.

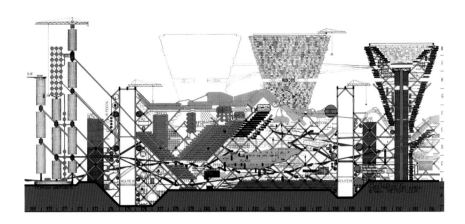

170

The older members of Archigram were Ron Herron, Dennis Crompton, and
Warren Chalk, who had worked together in an architectural practice for several
years. Their projects were associated with the new brutalist movement, developed
by Alison and Peter Smithson and the critic Reyner Banham. The younger members were Peter Cook, David Greene, and Michael Webb, who emerged from a
variety of architectural practices and university programs. Their images were
bright and action-packed, combining the zest of comic books and mod collages
with futuristic technology and clever designs.

Each member developed his own projects. The basic concepts of their work
included high-tech, prefabrication, and movable structures, but unlike most architects, they were in no way hampered by the realistic issues of design, as most of
their projects were imaginative explorations of fantasy environments. Webb's
provocative concept of the Cushicle, a movable house, was based on the idea of
an automobile. The design was an anthropomorphic form of a housing structure
that provided heat, food, shelter, music, and television. Unlike most houses, it
could travel to a remote location and plug-in to another infrastructure. It could
also change shape as it operated in various modes.[8] Greene introduced the idea
of a house as a "movable feast," a reference to Ernest Hemmingway. He called his
design a "living pod," which fused space age technology with an organic form.
His pods could also be stacked on the vertical core of larger structures.[9]

Herron's design for a Walking City is an unforgettable merging of animal and mineral. The huge rotund form of the city has the forceful look of a mechanical ele-
phant, sans trunk, striding across the landscape on short sturdy legs. The drawing
implies that the people of Walking City live an adventurous, nomadic existence
inside the playful plump structure.

Cook's elegant collages include a variety of engaging images that explored various
combinations of high-tech art and mobile environments. The designs emphasize
the ability of modern technology to merge the experiences of town and country
through temporary installations of new structural forms and explore the idea of
humanizing urban environments through the addition of lively textures, colors,
graphics, media, vehicles, and animated systems. Instant City is composed of drawings that introduce a traveling airship that transforms a rural village or an urban
environment into a magical experience. It included images of airships and balloons

Cover of *Archigram*, 1970.

mixed with the experience of a media event, such as an aerial cinema or a colorful tensile structure. In another series of drawings, he developed Plug-in City, a high-tech concept of an urban environment based on prefabrication. The design consists of an extensive infrastructure with shafts, or building cores, that could be developed by plugging-in prefabricated units. The result is a complex multilevel city that reassembles a giant network of machinery. The building systems, movement systems, and infrastructure are all flexible, kit-of-parts designs.

The general concept introduced a new version of postwar housing. It included transferable technology, which allowed urban residents to relocate their housing unit to another building site with the help of gigantic cranes. This intriguing idea influenced an innovative group of architects in Japan, who were also interested in prefabricated design.

5.8 The Transition in Japanese Design

After 300 years of virtual isolation under the Tokugawa Shogunate, Japan embarked on a remarkable process of modernization... This process not only transformed the visible aspects of the country, but wrought a profound change in the Japanese psyche. Until then, a sense of the past had always been implicit in the Japanese notion of the present. The acceptance of modernization added a new temporal dimension. The here and now came to be colored by the anticipation of tomorrow.
—Fumihiko Maki[10]

After World War II, Japan embarked on a major period of reconstruction. Cities that had been damaged by bombing raids lacked housing, infrastructure, and basic urban services. An estimated 4.2 million housing units were required to satisfy the needs of the Japanese people. Transportation networks had been disrupted and required major repairs. American troops remained in Japan for about six years. During the occupation, weapons factories were converted into peacetime industries. Tanks were broken down and recycled into materials for housing, cars, and other products. In addition, the Japanese government made large loans to private industry to encourage growth, mainly focusing on housing and automobiles to develop low-cost prefabricated units and small, efficient cars to address transportation needs. This growth stimulated other key industries, such as steel, wood, and household products, and in turn led to the construction of basic infrastructure for water and power. The Japanese government also established protectionist policies to support recovery.

In 1951, the Treaty of San Francisco officially ended the war and the American occupation. It forced Japan to give up its Asian territories and make reparations to those entities that were damaged by the war. Though their financial burdens were considerable, Japanese leaders were determined to launch a new economic era. Prime Minister Hayato Ikeda invested heavily in highways, airports, subways, and dams. Shipyards and port facilities were also rebuilt. His government supported the development of new import/export businesses to establish international trade.

Japanese leaders introduced new policies for architecture and urban planning that encouraged the development of sophisticated engineering and construction systems that could resist earthquakes and tidal waves and fostered the creation of a new architectural style.

Five large companies dominated Japanese construction. The Big Five had evolved from the leading families whose master craftsmen had been prominent designers, engineers, and contractors for several generations. In the twentieth century, the Big Five excelled in engineering and construction, but they collaborated with architects for the designs. Most were Japanese, and some, including Kuni Maekawa, had traveled abroad to study or work as apprentices, returning with knowledge of the International Style and the determination to launch a modern movement in Japan.[11] Frank Lloyd Wright and his assistant Antonin Raymond were particularly admired because Wright's Imperial Palace Hotel had survived a major earthquake in 1923. The Bauhaus and Le Corbusier were also well respected.

5.9   The Metabolists

Kenzo Tange, who trained with Maekawa, experimented with some of Le Corbusier's urban planning principles and explored the idea of a house as "a machine for living in." In 1950, Tange developed a proposal for rebuilding Hiroshima. His concept won a competition and established his career. He presented his design at a CIAM conference the following year, where he met Walter Gropius, Le Corbusier, and Sigfried Giedion, an experience he described as a "thrill that I shall find difficult to forget." He also visited Le Corbusier's Unité d'Habitation and was deeply impressed.[12]

In 1960, Tange presented a conceptual master plan for expanding the city of Tokyo across Tokyo Bay. He introduced a logical system for urban growth based on the study of Le Corbusier's urban planning principles. The central element was a linear spine of information and communications networks to support a secondary system of streets containing urban structures.

Tange's dramatic proposal introduced three new ideas: insertion of a "communications space," or a gathering space, similar to a European public square but unknown in Japan; expansion of the city across the bay through a series of artificial islands made of landfill; and development of a planning grid to link the existing city with new urban areas through a logical infrastructure system. The proposal also supported the idea of creating infrastructure for plug-in buildings or flexible ele-

Arata Isozaki, Clusters in
the Air, 1960–62.

ments. The concept of building a stable system of infrastructure in combination
with the plug-in architecture was very influential, inspiring a group of emerging
architects who later became known as the metabolists. Other influences on the
metabolists were Yona Friedman's urban proposals and R. Buckminster Fuller's
minimalist structures.

This group included the architects Fumihiko Maki, Kisho Kurokawa, and Kiyonori
Kikutake, as well as the emerging critic Masato Otaka and designers Kenji Ekuan
and Kiyoshi Awazu. In 1960, each of the metabolist architects created a megastructure concept, which included infrastructure for a large housing project and
individual units that could be plugged into the whole. The housing units are based
on the technology of kit-of-parts, and the number of units could be increased or
decreased, based on demand. These proposals were published in *Metabolism 1960*,
booklet that was presented at the World Design Conference.

Architect Arata Isozaki was not officially a member of the metabolist group, but in
1960–62, while working in Tange's office, he developed Clusters in the Air. This
project features tall central cores, or vertical stems, which could support a cluster
of individual housing units. The design leaves the street level more open and raises
most of the building bulk high above the ground. Its treelike concept provides a
powerful vision of an urban landscape.

Kurokawa, who also worked with Tange, developed a design based on the concept
of a helix. His rich organic form has a quality of motion that expresses the under-
lying theme of change central in metabolist thinking. In 1972 he designed the
Nakagin Capsule Tower, containing a central core of structural and mechanical
systems that served plug-in units arranged in a sculptural composition.

Kikutake's design, Ocean City, is an organic composition of podlike platforms.
Each pod was composed of vertical shafts of various heights with plug-in housing

175

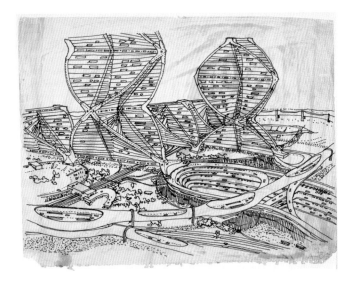

Kisho Kurokawa, Helical
City, 1961.

Kiyonori Kikutake,
Ocean City, 1963.

174

units. The pods would be connected by pedestrian bridges or accessed using water
transportation. The result was an elegant organic vision of an offshore community.

Only a few metabolist projects were built, but the concepts had a major impact on
Japanese architecture. Plug-ins led to the capsulelike hotel rooms in airports and
their planning grids became an integral part of urban projects. Their industrial style
also influenced avant-garde designers. More important, their innovative projects
broke the strict rules of traditional Japanese buildings and inspired future generations of designers.

5.10 Brutalism

The conceptual work of Archigram and the metabolists inspired many architects
in Europe and America, but the work of the early modernists still dominated the
design dialogue in many offices, and several new interpretations of modernism
emerged in the 1960s and 1970s.

In 1954, architectural critic Reyner Banham wrote a book called *The New Brutalism*,
which focused on the work of Alison and Peter Smithson, a British husband-and-
wife team who were creating massive concrete buildings inspired by the powerful
quality of Le Corbusier's postwar structures. They were also intrigued with the
utopian concepts of the International Style, which were related to working-class
values and minimal aesthetics.

The word "brutalism" came from the term, *béton brut* which was introduced
by Le Corbusier to describe the quality of the raw concrete material serving as a

Moshe Safdie and Associates,
Habitat, Montreal, Canada.

basis for his work. The term also expressed the aesthetic idea of heavy walls and fortresslike structures and a rejection of ornament, nature, and contextual issues.

Though the concrete buildings of this era were sometimes considered inhuman, they had a timeless, monumental quality that appealed to many institutional clients. In addition to the Smithsons, other architects, including Niemeyer, James Stirling, Louis I. Kahn, Marcel Breuer, and Paul Rudolf, utilized a similar language.

Moshe Safdie's Habitat '67 at the Montreal Expo was based on several building technologies, the most important being prefabrication. Unlike most prefabricated systems, which were constructed in rigid repetitive structures, Safdie's individual units could be arranged in a rich assemblage of seemingly random forms. It introduced an abstract approach to architectural compositions, which broke the monotony of traditional structures.

Other Brutalist buildings were severely criticized. Paul Rudolf's design for the Yale Art and Architecture Building caused a student protest. The Prince Lucien Campbell Hall at the University of Oregon also incited an uproar. The massive concrete building was considered a "monolith" or a "nine-story dungeon," by many students. It led to a new policy at the University of Oregon, which included the development of a new design process that focused on the creation of humane architecture and planning concepts.[13]

5.11   Centre Georges
        Pompidou

High-tech architecture emerged in the 1960s. The movement was inspired by nineteenth-century iron and glass structures, such as the Crystal Palace and the Eiffel Tower, as well as the steel and glass vocabulary of Mies van der Rohe, and incorporated technology of space structures. The high-tech designers were extremely inventive; they celebrated the idea of a building as a "machine for living in," in ways that Le Corbusier never imagined. They redefined the formal quality of early

175

Renzo Piano and Richard
Rogers, Centre Georges
Pompidou, Paris, 1971–78.

modern buildings into a lively vocabulary of mechanical elements in a rich expression of the industrial aesthetic of exposed steel structures, tubelike mechanical systems, and anthropomorphic details. They even introduced humor and color in their buildings.

In the late 1960s, the French government sponsored a competition for the design of a new arts center in Paris. The winning concept, submitted by a team that included Renzo Piano, Richard and Sue Rogers, Edmund Happold, and Peter Rice, proposed turning the building inside out. The structural and mechanical elements would be placed on the facade of the building with each system color-coded, so visitors could identify its function. The water pipes were painted green; electrical lines were painted yellow; and air conditioning ducts were blue. The ventilation shafts were white. Vertical circulation systems, such as stairs, elevators, and escalators, were red, which provided an accent color. The steel structure was left unpainted, to clarify the form of the prefabricated structural system.

The building itself would have a flexible plan, based on Cedric Price's Fun Palace, featuring undivided space that could be developed using plug-in walls, platforms, stairs, and interior elements for changing exhibitions as well as several dramatic indoor/outdoor spaces. A restaurant on top of the museum would offer a magnificent view of the city. At ground level, an open area in front of the center would provide a gathering space for the public and an impromptu stage for holding spontaneous performances by street artists, musicians, and other performers.

The Pompidou Centre, also known as the Beaubourg, opened in 1977. It was the ultimate illustration of the concept of a building as a machine. It was also associated

Frei Otto and Günter
Behnisch, Olympic Stadium,
Munich, 1972.

with the Brutalist movement. Many Parisians disliked the structure, and referred to it as an "oil rig" or used other names that were less polite. Nevertheless it was a culmination of the 1960s high-tech style and the ultimate expression of flexible space.

5.12   Tensile Structures

In the 1950s and 1960s, industrial fabrics developed by NASA to make parachutes, sails, inflatable rafts, tents, and even space suits for astronauts provided materials that could also be applied in a variety of ways in the public sector. One of the leading pioneers in the field of tensile structures was German architect Frei Otto, founder of the Institute for Lightweight Structures at the University of Stuttgart.[14]

177

In 1967, he and his partner Günter Behnisch built their first major tensile structure, the West German Pavilion at Expo '67. This handsome design provided an innovative concept for the creation of a large, temporary structure, of which a major example was the 1972 Munich Olympic Stadium. The entire complex was conceived as a series of tents curving along the site in the form of a half ellipse. The buildings were covered by a thick acrylic material, strengthened with a grid of steel cables. Larger cables, hung from huge steel columns, supported the major spans. The tensile concept also preserved the natural environment, since the site work involved only the footings for the major columns. The Munich Olympic Stadium was an intriguing indoor/outdoor space, reminiscent of the Crystal Palace. The acrylic material used was translucent, allowing daylight to enter the space but not distract the viewers from the athletic events. When the Games ended, the German government decided to preserve the popular structure and convert it into a permanent health club and swimming pool for the public.

Otto's projects led to a new genre of lightweight structures, which were used for concerts, expositions, and other Olympic events. In the year 2000, Otto served as a consultant to Shigeru Ban on the design of a lightweight structure for the Japanese Pavilion at Expo 2000.

5.13 Space Colonies

A space colony would be an Earthlike habitat, outside Earth's shadow, growing its own food and deriving all its energy from the sun . . . space colonies are still on the drawing board . . . Yet, I believe they will transform society during the twenty-first century as much as the automobile, airplane, and radio . . .
—Gerard O'Neill[15]

After the Apollo moon landing, engineers and scientists began to discuss the possibilities of creating space industry, space tourism, and even colonies in space. Princeton professor Gerard O'Neill, a specialist in particle physics, became the leading spokesman for space colonization. In 1977, he founded the Space Studies Institute at Princeton, a research group that focused on creating technology for space industries and habitation. He also wrote *The High Frontier: Human Colonies in Space*, a book that increased popular enthusiasm for space research.

O'Neill's promotion of space colonization was based on the idea that space could provide a wealth of new resources. He discussed the possibility of developing mining industries on the moon or on asteroids. Research indicated that lunar soil contained titanium, iron, and aluminum, as well as the glasslike crystals used in fiber-optic systems. There were also indications that the moon might have materials that were unavailable on earth, one example being Helium-3, which, some scientists believed, could support the clean nuclear fusion being studied in the 1970s.

He also explained that some manufacturing systems, such as the production of solar crystals, semiconductors, and medicines like Interferon, would be more precise in a low-gravity space environment. New products could also be created, such as foam metal, a product that would be difficult to make in the Earth's gravitational system.

O'Neill believed that space colonization offered an opportunity to introduce a new utopian culture, free of war and economic competition. The challenge of living in space might serve as an incentive to foster new values, such as environmental preservation, minimal consumption, and international cooperation.

Some of his most interesting comments were on the technology of space colonies, which, he believed, were within reach. He felt that earthlike environments could be constructed in space. Air could be produced by microorganisms, similar to the blue-green algae that originally produced Earth's atmosphere. Water could be transported, and then preserved, through a closed cycle. Agriculture could be automated. Solar power could provide an abundant supply of energy. Building materials could be mined on the moon and made into structures in lunar factories.[16]

Through a NASA-sponsored study, O'Neill developed the design of a cylindrical space colony of 10,000 people. The cylinder would be surrounded by several rings of structure, each about a mile in circumference to contain indoor farms and habitable areas of the colony. They would also rotate at a slow pace to simulate Earth-normal gravity. Large arrays of solar panels would be placed at both ends of the cylinder to collect energy for the community, and the two ends of the structure would also contain communications antennas to provide constant contact with Earth.

Dr. Peter Glaser, Satellite
Solar Power Station, conceptual project, 1968.

5.14 Solar Power
      Satellites

One of the most promising areas of research in the early 1980s was the idea of solar
power satellites (SPS). This intriguing proposal involved the construction of
millions of miles of solar collectors in space designed to travel in geosynchronous
orbit and beam energy down to Earth via microwaves. Geosynchronous orbit
means each one would remain over the same location above the Earth, at a distance
of about 25,000 miles from the surface. The energy would be received by collection
antennas in the ocean and plugged into the urban grid.

Solar power satellites were invented in the late 1960s by Dr. Peter Glaser, an engineer   *179*
and environmentalist who worked for the Arthur D. Little Company. His concept
inspired a variety of research projects as scientists throughout the world developed
designs for various components of the system. Some worked on space systems for
supporting the construction of solar power satellites. Others developed better solar
crystals, conversion systems, or antenna receivers.

In the 1970s, Glaser received a $20 million grant to develop patents and ascertain
the practicality of the idea. Though numerous studies were made at NASA and
other centers for space research, many issues remained unresolved, such as the
impact of microwaves on the Earth's atmosphere. There were also questions about
the efficiency of the system and the entropy inevitable in the process of transport
and conversion. The energy would begin as direct current, then it would be transformed into microwaves and sent to Earth. The microwaves would be received by
collection antennas, converted into alternating current, and plugged into the
urban grid.[17]

By 1993, there was general consensus that the project was too expensive, but scientists at NASA and other space programs felt that it might be feasible in the future
and that the system would provide a clean source of energy able to satisfy a large
proportion of the global demand for power.

Howard Wolf, conceptual design of tourist complex in space, begun in 1999.

5.15 Conceptual Structures and Vehicles

In 1967, Baron Hilton, founder of Hilton hotels, told the American Astronautical Society, "we are going to have Hiltons in outer space, perhaps even soon enough for me to officiate at the formal opening of the first . . ." Two years later, Pan American Airlines took reservations for commercial flights into space. Ronald Reagan, then governor of California, was on the list.

However, realistic plans for space hotels were not developed until 1990, when the Shimizu Corporation, one of the largest construction companies in the world, designed Tokyo Orbital International with plans to launch the facility in 2020. Shimizu envisioned a six-day experience in space for sixty-four guests at a time, at a cost of $45,000 per person.[18] The design of the hotel was based on a wheel, like O'Neill's colony, and would rotate about three times per minute to simulate gravity. Guest rooms on the outer ring would provide views of space; the spokes would lead to the public facilities placed in the center of the wheel. Solar panels constructed at the top of the structure would provide energy for the resort community. Several architects, including Howard Wolf, also explored this possibility, but as of 2008, no real projects have been built since the cost is prohibitive.[19]

NASA also conducted numerous studies on space structures. A few innovative architects, such as Michael Kahlil, participated in design studies for the interiors of space vehicles, but the final designs of actual spaceships were always minimal concepts that fulfilled the necessary functions, while eliminating any unnecessary details. One practical design was a lunar outpost published by NASA in 1990. The facility is limited to a few inflatable domes, held down by coiled bags of lunar soil, which also provide protection from radiation. Survey vehicles, research equipment, communications antennas, and a field of solar panels to supply power are also included.[20]

Despite the limitations, several researchers worked on conceptual projects. Jerome Pearson created a sophisticated concept for a "space elevator," to provide a less expensive means of lifting a vehicle out of the earth's atmosphere. It consists of a stream of demagnetized particles, which act in an opposite manner from magnets to propel vehicles into higher orbit. Once in space, the ships would be weightless and could continue to their destinations without the drag caused by heavy fuels.

The concept of a space elevator was first discussed by the Russian schoolteacher Konstantin Tsiolkovsky in 1895. Tsiolkovsky also explored another exotic concept for space travel: he discovered that when the sun shines on an object in space, it sends a stream of solar photons through space, which behave like a light wind and could be used to power a sail.

In the 1970s, NASA examined the possibility of using solar sails for long-distance trips. The designs involved the use of structural fabrics that could unfold to a size large enough to propel a space vehicle. The movement would be slow, but continuous. The British company Cambridge Consultants Ltd. created an elegant design for a solar sail inspired by origami. The sail began as a small cylindrical structure and unfolded in space to a full dimension of 72,000 square yards. Though the design was never fully resolved, it remains an interesting possibility.[21]

5.16 Mir Research Center

In the late twentieth century, a variety of satellite vehicles were launched to conduct meteorological and environmental research. In addition to the daily scanning of atmospheric changes for routine weather reports, these remote sensing devices provided advance warnings of storms, earthquakes, and tsunamis. They could also measure environmental conditions on earth. Unmanned satellites were used to map healthy areas of vegetation, locate mineral and oil deposits, and track pollution levels. As early as 1977, the satellite Landsat detected melting polar icecaps near the Antarctic coast. In 1978, Nimbus 7 provided clear knowledge of the hole in the ozone layer.

Mir Docking System.

In the 1980s, the importance of satellite research led to the idea of creating a permanent manned space station, which became a goal of both the American and Russian space agencies. In 1986, the Soviet Union launched Mir, the first long-term research center in space. The name was based on a Russian word meaning "peace" or "world."

The design of the space station was the ultimate expression of a kit-of-parts system. The parts were launched in a series of modules over a ten-year period, and the modules were assembled in space. Individual components, such as docking stations, solar panel arrays, airlocks, antennas, and living quarters could be disconnected and replaced if they failed to operate.

Many elegant designs were developed to provide comfortable quarters for the rotating crews, but the final form of the interior was a crowded maze of cables and instruments, mixed with books and personal items of visiting astronauts. Food was delivered by monthly visits from a supply ship, which also brought the visiting cosmonauts, who stayed about a week. Long-term crews, such as the two Russian astronauts Musa Munarov and Vladimir Titov, spent an entire year in space.

Mir normally housed a crew of three, but could also support a few visitors. In its last years, Mir was made available to tourists who could pay ten million dollars for the training and experience of traveling in space. The station contained a small gymnasium to fight the bone and muscular decay that would normally occur in a zero-gravity environment. The ship also provided televised linkage with friends on Earth, videotapes, and other forms of entertainment.

In the 1980s, when the government of the USSR collapsed, a cooperative relationship was created among the American, European, and Russian programs to support Mir. The unified governments also tried to bring commercial projects to Mir, and in the last years of its fifteen-year life span a poster hung on the wall of the spacecraft, reading "For Rent . . . The Mir station is now available for your research." Though several commercial visitors took advantage of the chance to travel in space, the resort venture did not succeed. In 2001, the participating space agencies decided to deorbit Mir, and it was sent back into the Earth's atmosphere where its 250-ton mass broke into pieces.[22]

5.17   Cinematic Concepts
       of Space Travel

In 1966, the American astronomer Carl Sagan collaborated with the Russian astronomer I.S. Shklovskii on a book called *Intelligent Life in the Universe*. Their unusual partnership produced a fairly convincing argument for the likelihood of the existence of other living species and speculation about the possibility of making contact with such life-forms. The book inspired articles, dialogues, and projects on this intriguing question and fueled the imagination of writers and filmmakers.

The notion of extraterrestrial societies also inspired the popular series *Star Trek*, which used various forms of fictional space communities to portray some of the political issues of the 1960s. As the crew of the *U.S.S. Enterprise* travels through the galaxy, they encounter a variety of cultures, troubled by racism, sexism, and cultural prejudices, resolve unnecessary conflict, and address environmental issues. This satirical approach to science fiction provided a means of presenting political views.

A stewardess in the gravity-free environment of a space-ship in the film *2001*, 1968. Director: Stanley Kubrick.

Over time, the genre of space fiction began to critique the real problems of space research through stories that addressed the controversial issues of space exploration. They dramatized the politics of space programs, the dangers of space travel, and the environmental impact of space age development, all presented with extraordinary designs of the new technologies. But like *Metropolis* and other important science fiction films from earlier eras, they also expressed ambivalent attitudes toward the human efforts, in this case, to conquer space.

5.18   *2001: A Space Odyssey*

In the late 1960s, there was one film on space travel that transcended all the others: *2001: A Space Odyssey*, created by director Stanley Kubrick and science fiction writer Arthur C. Clarke. The film explored several myths about the source of life in the universe and provides the public with a glimpse of real space technology.

In this epic story, several astronauts are sent into space to investigate the discovery of a monolith, which, officials believe, has been sent millions of years earlier from another planet. They think it might contain information on the source of intelligent life on Earth, but the epic voyage is interrupted by a malfunctioning computer, which shuts down the life support systems on the ship. All of the astronauts are killed, except one, who discovers the danger in time and manages to turn off the computer. He is then forced to continue the trip without companions, communications, or computerized environmental support.

His trip is a spellbinding existential odyssey through space with spectacular special effects, such as abstract light shows, dramatic images of his encounter with natural forces, and introspective scenes of the weary traveler alone in space. The final scenes show the astronaut as an old man, locked in a memory. He dies in a Louis XVI style bedroom, a surprising set for the final scene in a high-tech film. This elegant design is not an ordinary historical set, however, since it also contains high-tech elements anticipating the postmodern movement.

The death of the astronaut is followed by images of a baby, born with its eyes open, which left the audience with many questions about the philosophical message of the film. But the visual experience was not ambiguous. This film, more than any news broadcast or NASA documentary, provided a clear portrait of what space travel could become.

Clarke was not only a novelist, he was also an active contributor to the NASA space program. To assure authenticity, he brought technicians from real space agencies into the project as consultants. As a result, Kubrick and his team of designers produced an extraordinary film, which included a variety of realistic space environments.[23]

The giant space station in the early scenes is portrayed as a rotating wheel that simulates gravity through centrifugal force, but the small lunar shuttle, in which the scientist travels, is presented as a zero-gravity environment. The stewardesses wear minimal uniforms, based on the style of clothing designer Pierre Cardin. They also wear helmets to hold down their hair and magnetic shoes to allow them to walk on walls unobstructed. The film also contains elegant sequences of plug-in docking facilities, solar panel arrays, and tethered vehicles along with scenes of future technology, such as teleconference facilities, hibernation pods for resting astronauts, and food service systems. The interior designs are sophisticated high-tech concepts that combine minimal design with modular forms.

The slow movement of the vehicle, the rich lighting, and the elegant music and sound effects create a hypnotic depiction of space travel. The film received mixed reviews because of its ambiguity and slow pace, but it set new standards for science fiction design. Since the making of *2001*, other serious films about space travel have been designed in consultation with space agencies for the accurate detailing of the environment.

184

The film also raised several important philosophical questions. Do we really want to depend on computers and machines to sustain the quality of our environments? Do we belong in space? The human quest for knowledge seemed to lead inevitably into space, but the lonely odyssey and the astronaut's isolated death appears like a journey into a cultural black hole.

Other images yielded positive interpretations. The death of the astronaut seemed to represent the end of the old way of thinking. The child, born with its eyes open, appears to imply a new era in human existence. Like a new phoenix rising from the ashes of the old bird, it seemed to symbolize the next generation, born with scientific knowledge and self-awareness. Whether or not this interpretation was intended, it was a reasonable speculation on the meaning of the film.

5.19 *You Only Live Twice* Ken Adam, the designer of the Kubrick film, *Dr. Strangelove or: How I Learned to Stop Worrying and Love the Bomb*, later developed the breathtaking environments of several James Bond films.

The series is based on the exploits of James Bond, a heroic spy, armed with a variety of weapons and gadgets. Although he is constantly sidetracked by beautiful women, he always returns to his mission. His superior technology, physical prowess, and

Scene of rocket launching
facility inside a volcano, from
the film *You Only Live Twice*,
1967. Director: Lewis Gilbert.

sharp intelligence make it possible for him to succeed in virtually all of the challenges that confront him.

The films also provide old-fashioned adventure stories of heroic deeds enlivened by sexual innuendo and antifeminist attitudes, which were typical of that era, but the humor is so clearly tongue-in-cheek that it is impossible to regard it as anything but camp entertainment.

The Bond films also express the notion that democracy could be saved through military technology. In the film *You Only Live Twice*, several scenes take place at a rocket-launching site hidden inside a dormant volcano. This unusual facility has been developed by an eccentric billionaire, who threatens to destroy the international balance of power.

These fascinating scenes combine high-tech systems with organic forms in designs exploiting the 1960s love of vehicles, machines, and minimal environments. The design elements bring a stylish elegance to the film by combining inventive weapons, sleek costumes, and dramatic natural forms. The extraordinary set cost a million dollars to construct, which was unprecedented at the time, but the ultimate success of the film probably justified the expense.[24]

5.20 The Reaction Against Space Age Design

By the end of the space age, many designers and architects were beginning to grow weary of high-tech design. They were dissatisfied with the concept of mass culture and the mass housing projects of the postwar era. They were also frustrated with the limitations of minimalism. Their opposition to the machine aesthetic was strengthened by the protest movements of the 1960s, which emphasized the importance of individuality in the era of standardization.

In the mid-1950s, existential philosopher Jean-Paul Sartre published *Being and Nothingness*, an epic plea for individual identity in the age of mass culture. In this powerful essay, he challenges the notion of *être pour les autres*, or "living for others," which was cultivated in most modern societies. He also describes the danger of allowing oneself to be controlled by cultural expectations. Instead, he proposed the idea of *être pour soi*, or "living for oneself."

Sartre believed that if the individual claimed responsibility for his or her own actions, a new era of self-definition would emerge and the old patterns of mass acceptance would diminish. Though Sartre never analyzed the impact of architecture on consciousness, he wrote about the limiting aspects of cultural structures and organizations. He also described the experience of self-discovery as dependent on active enterprise, or being "in situation." His work inspired other philosophers, who expressed similar views and did include commentaries on the urban form.[25]

Sartre's work influenced Guy Debord, a writer and filmmaker who founded the Situationist International (SI) movement in 1957. His group objected to the demoralizing environments of the postwar era and the spiritual debilitation caused by modern capitalism. He also wrote about the alienation of the artist and the loss of individuality as a result of the economic pressures of the mercantile system. Debord criticized the existing city and introduced a new vision of the urban form as a place of movement, an open stage to contain spontaneous events, or "situations," rather than a rigid, impregnable structure.

His concepts were inspired by Sartre's existentialism and surrealism. He later created diagrams that illustrated the idea of "unitary town planning," which arranged urban spaces in a manner that invited movement, chance encounters, and random structures. In a few projects, he collaborated with the artist Constant Nieuwenhuys, who later launched the New Babylon movement.

In 1967, Debord wrote *Society of the Spectacle*, which reached a broad audience of political activists. It expressed objections to the values of postwar society and encouraged instead the development of a postindustrial culture based on leftist systems. He also claimed that a new approach to architecture would promote the creation of a new culture. Debord's political views helped instigate the 1968 student uprisings in Paris.

In the late 1960s, several other architects and designers protested against the cities of the postwar era. Some introduced alternative concepts. Others developed visual images that were critical of traditional culture. Many of these images attacked megastructure and prefabrication, which continued to characterize the conceptual designs of that era.

5.21 *Einstein on the Beach*

Two American artists addressed the theme of individual consciousness and cultural limitations through the powerful opera *Einstein on the Beach*. This experimental production was created by composer Philip Glass in collaboration with designer Robert Wilson. It celebrates the idea of science through visual themes that explore Einstein's vision of general relativity or the relationship between time and space. But it also portrays the 1960s cultural experience of living in an era of minimal environments, high-tech systems, and atomic bombs.

Wilson's most memorable image is a large two-story grid that occupies the entire width of the stage. The grid represents a section of a modern housing project, and

Spaceship IV Scene 3,
Einstein on the Beach, 1976.
Designer and Director:
Robert Wilson.

the structure contains individual actors in various areas of the grid. This disturbing design expresses the sense of isolation incurred by the structured forms of modern environments.

The set also portrays the boxlike limitations of massive standardized structures. The silhouetted figures trapped in the master grid are limited to small rhythmic motions accompanied by the repetitious chanted themes of Glass. Any architect viewing this powerful operatic set could not help but recognize the reference to the boxlike housing of the modern era and the prisonlike quality of postwar designs.

187

5.22 Superstudio and
      Archizoom

In the mid-1960s, several radical design groups emerged in Italy, including UFO, Archizoom Associati, and Superstudio, as well as individual designers like Gaetano Pesce and Ettore Sottsass. They expressed opposition to the extreme functionalism of modern design, preached individuality rather than standardization, and claimed that the one-off, or the single product of a designer, could exist simultaneously with mass-produced items.

These rebellious designers also advocated chaos, sensuality, and emotion, rather than the controlled polemical style of minimalism. They introduced dramatic color, zany humor, and pop consciousness into their work. In 1969, Archizoom published *No-Stop City*, a book of texts and drawings that contained a disturbing image of the future. It acknowledged the growing power of consumer culture and postulated that architecture could become a minor aspect of urban life. It suggested that the supermarket could serve as the emerging model of urbanization.[26]

Another Italian architectural group, Superstudio, was founded by Adolfo Natalini and Cristiano Toraldo di Francia, but it later grew to include other designers. Superstudio created a series of collages and photomontages called *Continuous*

Superstudio, *Motorway*, collage, 1969.

Monument. Their dramatic images also attack the principles of industrialization and express opposition to the destruction of the landscape, caused by consumerism, automobiles, and unbridled urban expansion. The 1969 collage entitled *Motorway* is a clear statement against modern planning systems and the imposition of the automobile on the environment. In addition to their montages, they created smaller, more personal images of alternative structures.

5.23 *Reversible Destiny*

In the 1960s, the artist Arakawa and the poet Madeline Gins began a collaboration that would continue into the twenty-first century. Their early projects led to a series of images, which they called *The Mechanism of Meaning*. This enormous presentation included eighty-three panels containing images of thought experiments and interactive exercises. The focus of the project was an exploration of themes on subjects like time, space, perception, and behavior. Their work emphasizes the idea that meaning is not a matter of cultural acceptance, but rather, the result of individual interpretation. They later began to explore the relationship between mind and body, leading to a project, which they called *Reversible Destiny*.

The basic concept of this study is that human life could be extended indefinitely through the establishment of a creative environment that fosters a different life-style. They rejected the modernist commitment to the grid and claimed they could improve the mental and physical health of a community by building abstract structures. They also denied the value of the twentieth-century emphasis on function, efficiency, and order, and the rigid geometry of the right angle.

They proposed instead the creation of an unpredictable environment to challenge the user. Their experimental drawings and models led to a large traveling exhibition, which appeared at the Guggenheim Museum Soho. They later found support for the development of a real structure to express their views. From 1993 to 1995,

Arakawa and Madeline Gins, *Site of Reversible Destiny*, located on a mountain site at Yoro in the Gifu Prefecture in Japan, 1993–95.

they built the *Site of Reversible Destiny*, a full-scale installation of their concepts. It features an intriguing group of structures on a mountain site at Yoro in the Gifu Prefecture in Japan. This facility attracts a wide variety of visitors interested in experiencing their unique concept.

189

5.24 The Lessons of the
        Space Age

I propose that the architectural departments of all universities around the world be encouraged . . . to invest the next ten years in a continuing problem of how to make the world's resources serve 100% of humanity through competent design.
—R. Buckminster Fuller[27]

Throughout this era, one visionary engineer/environmentalist questioned the broader issues of culture and environment. In 1963, R. Buckminster Fuller published the book *Operating Manual for Spaceship Earth*, containing a compelling series of essays that introduce an intelligent strategy for planning the use of global resources. His vision is based on the metaphor of a spaceship, in which every environmental issue must be resolved in a rational manner.

He began the book with a positive statement about the evolution of technology and human potential. He believed that most of the problems of mankind could be solved through an efficient use of technology and resources. With proper planning and engineering, all nations could be provided with adequate food, water, and shelter, but the achievement of this goal would require a new cultural attitude and a better method of managing resources. The book also contains a critique of the capitalist system with historical examples of how it has damaged the natural environment by encouraging unnecessary consumption and draining precious resources.

R. Buckminster Fuller, *The American Pavilion* at the 1967 World Fair in Montreal.

R. Buckminster Fuller, *Dome over Manhattan*, conceptual project, designed to reduce energy consumption.

Fuller also discussed the weaknesses of educational systems that teach specialization, rather than synergistic thinking. He believed that future generations should be trained to understand the broad issues of society and to work in a more cohesive manner. He considered Leonardo da Vinci to be an outstanding example of a "comprehensively anticipatory design scientist."

He came to the conclusion that if the resources of the earth were utilized as carefully as the resources of a spaceship, all the nations of the world could sustain a decent standard of living, but this could only be achieved if private interests were superseded by a sense of global responsibility and if wasteful systems were reformed by conservation policies.

These statements reflected Fuller's own approach to design. He had discussed these issues for forty years, but finally, people were beginning to listen. His entire career had been devoted to the creation of structures and vehicles that minimized the use of both materials and resources. In the 1920s, he had designed the Dymaxion House, a lightweight structure utilizing minimal materials and the Dymaxion Car, a three-wheeled electric vehicle. In the 1940s and 1950s, he created the Wichita House and the geodesic dome.

The geodesic dome became a symbol of the new era in engineering. The design provides a method for enclosing the most volume of space with the least amount of material. It is also easy to construct. The structure is made of prefabricated struts and joints, which can be easily packaged, transported, and constructed by untrained workers. Its assembly system would require only a few hours of connecting into triangles the pieces that form the dome.

The dome is also much less expensive than other types of structures and could be used for a variety of purposes, including housing, commercial, and public facilities. It became the preferred structure of the hippie culture and the Drop City movement, because of the ease of construction and portability of the structure, but it also appealed to more conservative clients.

Fuller later developed a large geodesic dome for the U.S. pavilion at the 1967 World's Fair in Montreal. His design illustrated the elegant simplicity of the concept and provided a dramatic interior exhibition space. Throughout the 1960s and 1970s, Fuller also developed books, lectures, and exhibits on innovative designs. His university lectures were very popular, though they sometimes lasted six or eight hours, as he tried to make students aware of the full scope of the issues.

In the 1960s, Fuller also created a proposal for the construction of an enormous dome over Manhattan that would reduce energy demand. It could be heated or air-conditioned, as needed. Although the huge dome was never built, the dramatic image of Manhattan under glass lingered in the minds of architects as a symbol of a more efficient society. The dome also seemed appropriate for structures in space, such as a city on the moon, which would require an artificial environment.

Fuller's metaphorical essay on the Earth as a spaceship also influenced several visionary thinkers. In 1965 futurist Kenneth E. Boulding delivered a speech entitled "Earth as a Spaceship." In this inspiring statement, he also urged the integration of social, economic, and technological resources to build a better society. The theme was repeated in 1982, when Disney built a facility called Spaceship Earth, its geodesic structure becoming a main attraction at Epcot Center.

Fuller's work was very controversial. He was one of the first designers to aggressively attack wasteful industrial systems and advocate global planning and conservation of resources. Some of his ideas were thought impractical, or too far ahead of convention to be appreciated. As a result, some people considered him a genius; others questioned his approach. But no one could deny that he inspired numerous architects and left a legacy of important environmental concepts.

A laboratory technician examines the power cables of the Livermore Labs Particle Accelerator.

5.25   The Star Wars
       Project

In the 1980s, the American space program lost much of its credibility when the Reagan administration announced its intention of building weapons in space. This proposal caused an international uproar, for it instigated discussions of a new generation of weapons and an arms race, which was even more dangerous than the Cold War struggle of the past forty years.

It also violated the UN Outer Space Treaty, which was signed by over ninety countries in 1967. The treaty banned the placement of nuclear warheads in space and stated that space should be developed in a manner that benefited all countries of the world.

Reagan's program, the Strategic Defense Initiative (SDI), had already spent billions of dollars exploring the possibility of establishing ballistic missiles in space. Work was underway to develop an Advanced Test Accelerator, which was capable of firing a high-intensity beam of electrons that could guide missiles. The project also included plans to build an antiballistic missile system that would shield the United States from a nuclear attack.

Though space exploration provided enormous benefit to the world, this concept caused it to lose much of its popularity. The misuse of space technology, combined with the expansion of nuclear weapons, presented serious dangers. According to Tom Z. Collina, director of the global security program in the Union of Concerned Scientists, "Even developing and testing these space-based technologies is danger-ous, because it forces our adversaries to do the same thing."[28]

The Star Wars concept was not approved, and further funds for space research were jeopardized by the reaction against it. Some of its leading proponents, such as Donald Rumsfeld, later became part of the George W. Bush administration and tried to revive the program. They evidently forgot the lessons of the 1980s and felt there would be no opposition to the project.

But in July 2001, Stephen I. Schwartz, publisher of *The Bulletin of the Atomic Scientists*, wrote, "It's clearly their intention to put weapons in space to both defend U.S. assets as well as attack enemy missiles and enemy satellites," but the program was not revived, as several months later, the terrorist attacks of 9/11 interfered with such plans.[29]

Notes

1. Warren Chalk, *Archigram 3*, quoted in Ruth Eaton, *Ideal Cities* (New York: Thames and Hudson, Inc., 2002), 220.

2. Kenneth Gatland, *The Illustrated Encyclopedia of Space Technology*, 2nd ed. (New York: Salamander Books Limited, 1989), 10-14.

3. Gatland, 104.

4. Eero Saarinen, quoted in Pierluigi Serraino, *Eero Saarinen* (Koln: Taschen Gmbh, 2005), 12.

5. Eero Saarinen, quoted in Oliver Herwig, *Featherweights* (Munich: Prestel Verlag, 2003), 32.

6. Charles Jencks, *Architecture 2000* (New York: Prager Publishers, 1971), 84-85.

7. Ruth Eaton, *Ideal Cities* (New York: Thames and Hudson Inc., 2002), 221.

8. Eaton, 231.

9. Crompton, 110.

10. Fumihako Maki (speech on the occasion of Kenzo Tange's Pritzker Prize), www.pritzker prize.com/tange.htm.

11. Michael Franklin Ross, *Beyond Metabolism: The New Japanese Architecture* (New York: McGraw-Hill, 1978), 13-18.

12. Ross, 19-20.

13. en.wikipedia.org/wiki/Brutalist_architecture

14. Oliver Herwig, *Featherweights* (Munich: Prestel Verlag, 2003), 70.

15. Gerard K. O'Neill, *2081: A Hopeful View of the Human Future* (New York: Simon & Schuster, Inc., 1981), 61-62.

16. O'Neill, 66.

17. Gatland, 239.

18. Nicholas Booth, *Space: The Next 100 Years* (New York: Orion Books, 1990), 84.

19. Herwig, 151.

20. Booth, 90-91.

21. Booth, 100-01.

22. Booth, 54-61.

23. Piers Bizony, *2001: Filming the Future* (London: Aurum Press Limited, 2000), 12-13.

24. Peter Ettedgui, *Production Design & Art Direction* (Woburn, MA: Focal Press, 1998), 31.

25. Jean-Paul Sartre, *Being and Nothingness* (New York: Washington Square Press, Inc., 1966), 77.

26. Jocelyn de Noblet, *Industrial Design Reflections of a Century* (Paris: Flammarion/ADAGP, 1993), 256.

27. Buckminster Fuller, quoted in Ulrich Conrads, ed., *Programs and Manifestoes on 20th-Century Architecture* (Cambridge, MA: The MIT Press, 1964), 179-80.

28. Tom Z. Collina, quoted in James Glanz, "Cast of Star Wars Makes Comeback in Bush Plan," *The New York Times*, July 22, 2001.

29. Stephen I. Schwartz, quoted in Glanz.

THE MEDIA AND INFORMATION AGE

'The medium is the message' means, in terms of the electronic age, that a totally new environment has been created. The content of this environment is the old mechanized environment of the industrial age. The new environment reprocesses the old one as radically as TV is reprocessing the film.
—Marshall McLuhan[1]

In the late twentieth century, television ushered in a revolution in media and information systems. When the medium first appeared, many doubted that it would succeed, but David Sarnoff, a self-made media mogul, supported it throughout his career. Sarnoff became president of Radio Company of America (RCA) and created the National Broadcasting Channel (NBC), which aired the first public television broadcast at the 1939 World's Fair. He was initially told it would cost $100,000 to develop the technology for television: it actually cost over $50 million.

During World War II, all work on television was halted as media companies concentrated on providing radio systems for the Allied forces. After the war, cable antennas were installed in cities, and many new programs were added, which expanded the reach and popularity of the medium. As television became more established, critics claimed that it lowered the academic performances of children, increased the rate of violent crimes, and expanded the desire for material products. These accusations were undoubtedly true, but it also introduced beneficial changes. In 1964, Marshall McLuhan wrote the landmark book *Understanding Media*, which explored both views.

McLuhan argued that television transformed society from a verbal to a visual culture, which had a profound effect on behavior. Each night, the public witnessed such horrors as the Vietnam War, the high crime rate in cities, and the desolate character of urban slums. The visual experience increased an individual's self-awareness and sense of connection to the larger world, thereby also creating a critical attitude toward society and environment that sometimes led to action.

McLuhan also presented the work of sociologists who felt that television helped inspire the protests against racism and the Vietnam War and influenced other political issues. According to analysts, television coverage of the 1960 American presidential election debate between John F. Kennedy and Richard Nixon had a major impact on citizens' responses to the candidates. Those who listened to the debate on radio were more impressed with Nixon; those who watched it on television overwhelmingly favored Kennedy.

Minoru Yamasaki, Pruitt-Igoe public housing, St. Louis, Missouri, built 1952–55. Protests from residents forced demolition in 1972.

Media audiences not only watched news broadcasts, but also had daily exposure to dramas and comedies performed in contrived environments. The popularity of fictional material stimulated the creation of buildings and communities based on montage, theme parks, and storied environments. Over time, the language of media became absorbed in the language of environment.

In the late 1970s, computers provided designers with better systems for producing construction documents and engineering studies. In the 1990s, as the Internet was emerging, computers started to play an even greater role. In addition to providing a valuable research tool, the Internet fostered another McLuhan idea: the concept of the global village. The Internet gave unlimited access to information and international markets with products from around the world, redefining the idea of community through reduced barriers between nations and improved communications. Design professionals began to rely on constant access to media and information. In the late twentieth century, architectural theory was again transformed, this time to reflect the electronic interdependence of the new global society.

6.1   The Rejection of Modernism

The 1960s and 1970s were decades of political unrest in the United States. The Civil Rights movement engendered protests against segregation in schools, businesses, and government institutions; the New Left was critical of middle-class values, the military/industrial establishment, and the Vietnam War. Both were concerned with the troubled environments of inner cities, and architects soon became involved in the struggle to rebuild blighted urban areas.

Bernard Schneider, *The Reintroduction of the Column*, Photo collage, 1980.

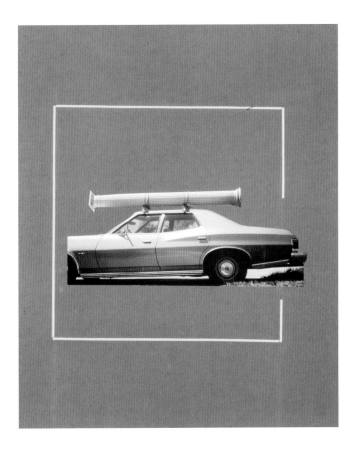

These architects rejected modernist principles and introduced a new set of values in design based on the alternative proposals of Jane Jacobs, R. Buckminster Fuller, and Archigram. Their critique of the minimal structures of the postwar era was not lightly made, since, at the time, the work of modernists like Le Corbusier and Mies van der Rohe still dominated architectural discourse. Avant-garde designers created dramatic collages that introduced charismatic concepts for the 1960s generation. Instead of the Brutalist buildings of mid-century modernism, their designs expressed an iconoclastic attitude with humor, color, social commentary, and ironic historical references. They also helped to reestablish "paper architecture" as an important medium for the emerging era.

6.2 De-Architecture

In the late 1960s, American sculptor James Wines formed a design group called SITE in partnership with poet/artist Alison Sky and photographer/writer Michelle Stone. Wines felt that the modernist focus on form and function failed to produce environments that engaged the community. Architecture, according to Wines, would be more relevant if it included color, humor, and philosophical content. He coined the term "de-architecture" to express the idea that design could include cultural commentary and could relate directly to the context, or the time and place, in which it exists.

The firm's principal client was Best Products Co., a retail firm with a successful catalog business that decided to build new showrooms. SITE developed structures in various stages of decomposition whose bold designs caught the attention of both

197

SITE, Model of Best
Products Indeterminate
Facade, Houston, Texas,
1974.

the public and the architectural community. Some critics compared their projects to the work of Marcel Duchamp while others saw their buildings as existential commentary on social conditions.

The first building in this series was called Indeterminate Facade, an uncanny design that combined existential pessimism and humor. The crumbling walls of the facade are a clear reference to ancient Roman ruins, but they also express the decay of current culture. The haunting structure is an ironic comment on the failures of modern architecture.

Wines later expanded the platform of SITE to focus on environmental design, but he never lost track of his original goal of adding humor and cultural content to his work.

6.3   Postmodernism

I like elements which are hybrid rather than 'pure,' compromising rather than 'clean,' distorted rather than 'straightforward,' ambiguous rather than 'articulated,' perverse as well as impersonal, boring as well as 'interesting,' conventional rather than 'designed,' accommodating rather than excluding, redundant rather than simple, vestigial as well as innovating, inconsistent and equivocal rather than direct and clear. I am for messy vitality over obvious unity.
—Robert Venturi[2]

Postmodernism, which emerged in the late 1960s, recognized that society did not just exist in the present. Most communities were a culmination of varied cultural and historical influences. Twentieth-century society was, by definition, an eclectic concept, in which many styles existed simultaneously. The postmodernists endorsed non-elitist concepts, such as cultural diversity, which the modernists rejected. Some postmodernist attitudes toward high culture were similar to the pop artists—freely mixing high art with commercial references and symbols.

Robert Venturi, Vanna
Venturi House, Chestnut Hill,
Philadelphia, Pennsylvania,
1964.

6.4   Robert Venturi

In 1966, architect Robert Venturi published *Complexity and Contradiction in Architecture*, a polite, but firm, rejection of modernist principles. He called it a "gentle manifesto," although its impact on the design world was far from gentle. He began by stating, "Architects can no longer afford to be intimidated by the puritanically moral language of orthodox Modern architecture."

Venturi argued that the workable patterns of ordinary towns were more successful than the self-conscious plans of modern architects. He encouraged the idea of bringing back vernacular color, texture, and historical symbols in design, praising the picturesque houses of Edwin Lutyens, the vitality of Times Square, and the complexity of the choir at Notre Dame. He noted that the interiors of these structures do not always match the facades of the buildings, thus negating the need for the modernist relationship between function and form.[3]

Venturi's next book, *Learning from Las Vegas*, published in 1972, studied the famous Las Vegas Strip, which he felt was "almost all right." The book lauds the idea of "decorated sheds," or structures that have no architectural concept, but are adorned with symbolic images or shaped like familiar forms. These include 1920s fast-food restaurants, such as the Hoot Hoot I Scream stand, which is shaped like an owl. Venturi calls these cartoon-like buildings "ducks," because his favorite roadside icon is The Big Duck on the south shore of Long Island. Venturi felt the term "decorated shed" also applied to historical buildings, like the Chartres Cathedral and Palazzo Farnese, whose facades use symbolic language. The concept of the decorated shed was further expanded to include other kinds of icons, and the general principles of *Learning from Las Vegas* influenced urban restoration throughout the postmodern era.[4]

In his own buildings, Venturi focused on the idea of context, creating buildings that fit into the existing character of the neighborhood. His designs did not simply reproduce the historical style of the area, however: they included elements of

199

Michael Graves, Clos
Pegase Winery, Napa Valley,
California, 1984–87.

exaggeration, playful references to a more traditional period. The house he built
for his mother, Vanna Venturi, exemplifies this approach. Venturi describes this
house as "both complex and simple, open and closed, big and little; some of its
elements are good on one level and bad on another; its order accommodates the
generic elements of the house in general, and the circumstantial elements of a
house in particular."[5]

6.5   Michael Graves

In the 1980s, when postmodernism became popular, Michael Graves was one of the
first architects to embark on the new path. The Portland Public Service Building,
which was completed in 1982, was his first major structure in the postmodern style.
This controversial design includes humorous references to the Renaissance, exaggerated details, and muted colors. The use of secondary colors would become
part of his personal approach.

Most of Graves's buildings—created for both public and private functions—
combine historical references with ironic or playful elements. In the 1980s and
1990s, Disney commissioned several projects from Graves. His playful approach to
design was very compatible with its theme parks. His first buildings for Disney,
built near the Orlando theme park, were the Swan and Dolphin Hotels, "decorated
sheds," that contain iconic images of their themes. He later designed the Team
Disney Building in Burbank and decorated the facade with statues of the seven
dwarfs. His design for the Clos Pegase Winery was based on a Roman villa but
featured monumental columns rendered in bold colors.

Philip Johnson, holding a model of the AT&T building. Cover of *Time* magazine, January 9, 1979.

6.6 Philip Johnson

In 1978, Philip Johnson began designing the AT&T building, which was a significant departure from his earlier modernist work. At ground level, he introduced classical elements. The entry level of the building is based on the scale and formality of a Roman public structure. He crowned the building with a carved broken pediment, an element from eighteenth-century case furniture loosely referred to as "Chippendale." The notoriety of the design—considered a quintessential expression of postmodernism—stimulated his architectural career. Corporate clients were amused by the idea of owning a building that combined a conservative image with a sophisticated touch of humor.

6.7 The New Urbanists

In the late 1970s, British architect Léon Krier began to openly oppose modernism. He disagreed with Le Corbusier's vision of a vertical garden city and rejected the Athens Charter, a document created by the International Congress of Modern Architecture (CIAM), which many professionals respected. He was against its position on zoning, which he felt destroyed the flexibility and multiuse character of traditional cities.

Krier also attacked the high-tech, plug-in concepts of Archigram and the metabolists. He believed urban planning required serious solutions, rather than trendy, superficial images. He disliked the eclectic quality of postmodernist designs for lacking the conviction of a unified vision. Instead, he advocated the classical model of a European city.

201

Elizabeth Plater-Zyberk
and Andres Duany, Seaside,
Florida, Tupelo Circle,
1981.

He claimed that a city should be planned in neighborhoods, or "quarters." It should not be zoned into separate-use areas, but rather, should contain a healthy mix of local artisan industries and shopping areas, as well as housing and community facilities. The "quarters" should be no larger than a half mile square, a distance that could be traversed on foot in about ten minutes.

He believed institutions, like a church or a courthouse, should contain columns, porticos, and recognizable symbols and that housing should be low-rise structures based on traditional row house forms.

Although Krier considered his approach to be authentic, his projects created artificial environments. The decision to build a twenty-first century town based on a classical city was even more self-conscious than modern planning techniques. Krier's theories resonated with American architects Andrés Duany, Elizabeth Plater-Zyberk, and Peter Calthorpe, who started the New Urbanist movement in the United States. The New Urbanists focused on the idea of creating small suburban communities based on traditional values with the goal of reintroducing early-twentieth-century planning concepts that had been successful in the past.

The first goal was to create a walkable city, discouraging the use of automobiles. Each neighborhood had to have a well-defined urban center within walking distance of stores and public transportation. They wanted to build a safe, close-knit community where residents could meet casually while shopping or running errands with enough activity to maintain surveillance of the streets.

The New Urbanists claimed to be committed to the design of "green" cities: their streets are lined with trees and designed to encourage bicycle and pedestrian traffic. Their communities contain parks or waterfront areas, each house has a lawn or a garden, and parking is hidden behind buildings.

Criticism came from architects who disliked their obsession with traditional design and their nostalgic view of the past. Some green designers felt they were contributing to urban sprawl by creating communities of single-family houses, rather than multiple-use dwellings, which could be served by public transportation.[6] They were also accused of being political reactionaries with a desire to control public space and community behavior. Some considered their strategies to be elitist for driving away the poor from urban areas to create gentrified middle-class neighborhoods and cultivating the traditional values of the far right. Nevertheless, the movement was popular among conservative developers since the designs had a safe, reassuring quality .

6.5 The Theme Park: The Architecture of Reassurance

Walt Disney, the pioneering media mogul, inspired architects and planners throughout the postmodern era, having introduced two important principles: the theme park and the concept of the architecture of reassurance.

As Disney's company grew, he thought about building an "ideal" community. His studio in Burbank became his first large-scale planning effort. The fifty-one-acre site hosted twenty-five landscaped buildings, designed for assembly line film production, but it was also a theme park. Each road was based on a cartoon theme and was given a name like Dopey Drive or Mickey Avenue. Several statues of his cartoon icons were placed around the lot.[7]

Disney also wanted to create a park for his employees' children. The company park was never built, but the discussions for the project led to a much more ambitious public park. For more than a decade, Disney and his employees studied major tourist sites, such as Tivoli Gardens in Copenhagen and the Golden Gate International Exposition in San Francisco, to prepare for the creation of Disneyland. The Chicago Railroad Fair of 1948 and the 1939–40 New York World's Fair were also interesting to Disney. The latter contained an entire town that expressed democratic themes. In developing Disneyland, he created a utopian environment of charm, fantasy, and entertainment. His concept of an architecture of reassurance provided a safe, clean, and innocent atmosphere with nostalgic images of the past.

The park is based on a radial plan with four major streets fanning out from the center to Fantasyland, Tomorrowland, Frontierland, and Adventureland. Four minor

203

Disneyland sign, Anaheim, California.

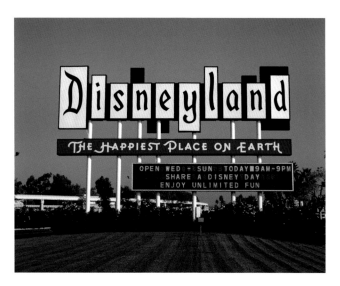

Times Square at night,
New York, New York.

streets led to picturesque parks and outdoor areas. All of the structures are "decorated sheds" adorned with bright colors. Many were built at a reduced scale to seem less threatening. Some facilities were based on narrative film scripts to provide the tourists with a playful interaction with actors dressed like Disney characters.

Disney theme parks inspired a whole new direction in community development. There were many variations on the specific themes, but the basic formula of safe, comfortable environments based on cultural or historical references was consistent.

6.9   Revitalization of
       Times Square

In the 1970s, one of the seediest urban environments in America was New York City's Times Square. Although this historic neighborhood housed the famous Broadway theater district, it also had a high crime rate and a decayed quality; streets were dominated by pornographic movie houses, drug pushers, and sex clubs.

In 1981, the Urban Development Corporation (UDC) mapped out an ambitious plan for the redevelopment of Times Square to provide several new office buildings, a merchandise market, an upscale hotel, and the renovation of nine historical theaters and a major subway station. Government agencies promised to work with UDC to eliminate pornography and crime in the area.

Part of the goal was to bring back tourists and increase the business community and the tax base of Times Square; corporations were offered tax incentives to relocate there and theaters were given funding for renovation. X-rated industries were replaced by companies like Disney and Viacom. UDC wrote design guidelines to retain the bright lights and media image of Times Square with a requirement that all major buildings in the area have large electronic signs.

The effort transformed Times Square into a popular theme park. The area was redeveloped for family-type tourists with stores featuring children's products and legitimate movie houses.

The Las Vegas Strip, Las
Vegas, Nevada.

Additional lighting, police, and security devices were installed, which eliminated
most of the crime.

As a result, the tourist industry began to thrive, the tax base increased, and the
neighborhood became an active commercial center. Some cultural critics were
offended by the change, however. Samuel R. Delany, a provocative social commentator, wrote a book called *Times Square Red, Times Square Blue*, which voices an
objection to the loss of the old ambiance of Times Square and its replacement with
a conventional bourgeois environment.[8]

205

6.10 Las Vegas: Theme
Parks Within Theme
Parks

In the early twentieth century, Las Vegas was notorious for gambling and adult
entertainment. Nevada's liberal marriage and divorce laws also attracted visitors
eager to obtain a change in marital status.

As the city grew larger and more diverse, civic leaders introduced a major program
to transform its image from a "sinful city" into a center for family entertainment.
The redevelopment of Las Vegas, which included the renewal of the historical
identity of the area, would be no small feat. The old downtown streets of the city
were restored and Old West shows and other local themes were revived.

Bugsy Siegel's famous Flamingo Hotel, built in 1946, led to the Las Vegas Strip, a
boulevard lined with hotels and gambling facilities. In the 1950s and 1960s, dozens
of resort facilities were added along the Strip. The Mirage, the first megaresort,
opened in 1989.

The Strip ultimately became a relentless line of "decorated sheds." In the typical
design of a Las Vegas hotel, each entrance was a staged experience, based on the
cinematic concept of a montage, a sequence of images forming a larger concept.
In architectural language, montage refers to a series of visual events to establish a

dramatic linear experience, such as the Las Vegas Strip, where each of the major hotels has a different theme.

The Caesars Palace casino features a Roman theme, expressed through models of Roman ruins and statues of ancient soldiers. The arrival sequence for the hotel New York, New York contains models of the Statue of Liberty, the Empire State Building, and other skyscrapers. The entrance to the Paris, Las Vegas resort sports models of the Eiffel Tower and the Louvre.

The hotel themes within the larger theme of a resort community provided a successful marketing concept and a popular tourist attraction. By the 1990s, surveys indicated that most Las Vegas tourists spent more time walking along the Strip and touring the major hotels than they did at the gambling tables.

Development on a monumental scale continues with the MGM City Center, a seventy-six-acre vertical city site on the Strip between the Monte Carlo and the Bellagio, scheduled for completion in 2009.

6.11 The Integration of Computers and Media Systems: The City as a Consumer Information Center

The computer had an important trait that the ordinary television did not: it could interact with the viewer. You could shop through it. You could send instant messages through it, and receive messages back. You could order up local news from anywhere in the world ... This machine could be the conduit for all information into and out of the home.
—Michael Lewis[9]

The first user-friendly computers were developed in the 1970s at Xerox Parc (Palo Alto Research Center) with systems for graphic user interface (GUI), as well as the mouse, movable overlapping windows, local networking, word processing, file servers, and art and drawing programs. Xerox invented this system but did not produce it on a large scale. The first computer that made these systems available to the public came in 1984 with the Macintosh OS GUI.

The computer industry grew rapidly, and by 1990, the interest in information systems fostered a $19-billion industry. By 2007, the industry grew to a $46-billion sector of the global economy. However, this did not lead to the intellectual renaissance that many had expected. The technology was initially used to expand financial markets, which led to a bubble in the stock market, similar to the surge of investments that occurred in the 1920s, when electricity became available.

The Internet emerged in the 1990s from networking systems invented forty years earlier. The early systems linked university researchers together. In 1969, projects at the U.S. Department of Defense and the Rand Corporation led to the design of an expandable system called ARPANET. This system initially linked researchers at UCLA and Stanford, but by 1981, ARPANET was connected to 213 sites and still growing. In the 1980s, NASA created a new network system that linked over 20,000 scientists worldwide. During these years, web pages were being developed, but they could only be accessed through closed systems. The first search engine was built in 1990 at McGill University and led to the basic concept of an open system or a World Wide Web.

Rem Koolhaas, OMA, Model
of CCTV and TVCC, Beijing,
2003–08.

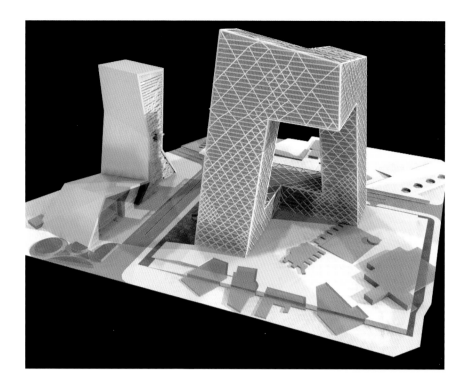

In the 1990s, more extensive database and search engine systems were designed
based on directories with relevancy ranking systems. Google, founded in 1998,
quickly became the most popular system, providing an accessible portal for general
use. This led to numerous online catalogs of commercial applications that stimulated growth in the stock market by providing ordinary investors access to financial
tools. At this stage, media and information systems became an important
aspect of architecture and planning.

The growth of the Internet produced an era of economic prosperity. Although
many designers thought the Internet would reduce the need for real meetings and
detract from urban life, it ultimately stimulated interest in cities. The Internet
increased the size of the economy, which led to new businesses and supported the
revitalization of urban areas. It also led to new architectural concepts that integrated media and computerized systems.

6.12 Rem Koolhaas

Few architects understood the potential relationship between media, computers, and
architecture as well as Dutch theorist and practitioner Rem Koolhaas. Before becoming an architect, he studied screenwriting at the Dutch Film Academy and worked
as a journalist for several years, prior to studying architecture at the London
Architectural Association and Cornell University.

Koolhaas's sophisticated integration of cultural references with futurist designs
led to several major commissions, some of which were media projects, such as Casa
da Música in Portugal, the Netherlands Dance Theatre, and the Seattle Central
Library. In 2002, his firm, Office for Metropolitan Architecture (OMA), won the
competition to plan the headquarters for the television network CCTV in Beijing.
The goal was to create a symbolic building that included an efficient office and

production center, as well as space for public events. The building's design required extensive planning for a wide variety of functions and ultimately housed a workforce of over 10,000 people. OMA's elegant architectural solution includes the image of a continuous loop, which made reference to the film loop as well as the concept of an old Chinese puzzle.

The most memorable aspect of the design is the exterior skin of the building, which includes several layers of information. The walls are made of glass, providing a flood of daylight, but also feature a lattice-like structure. Some areas of the exterior walls contain video images to engage the public and maintain the theme of a media park.

The design of Internet sites had an impact on the design of real cities, where the concept of the street was redefined as a continuous flow of consumer information. At night, the lights of Times Square, Piccadilly Circus, and Tokyo's Shibuya district present huge advertisements of films, fashions, and other products, in video projections and computerized images. Redeveloped using montage techniques as a sequence of projected images, the character of those areas is no longer defined by the architecture of the street but instead by graphic media.

The standard office building of the 1950s, based on Mies van der Rohe's minimal glass skyscraper also changed as architects combined computers and media systems in the development of a new design concept. The quiet dignity of pure glass structures was transformed into walls of light and media, expressing the corporate identities of the owners or simply presenting random advertisements. These dramatic new media structures were sometimes enhanced by special exhibition areas or interactive displays. Collectively, they expressed the idea of a consumer theme park, activated by projected texts and images.

208   6.13 Jean Nouvel

French architect Jean Nouvel developed a variety of buildings based on the themes of media, layering, and transparency. The facade of the train station in Lille, France, is composed of translucent panels that present artistic images of colored lights, screen prints, and holographs, while the Cartier Foundation in Paris contains layers of glazing around an interior garden. The glass panels are arranged in an elegant grid that interacts with reflections of trees.

Nouvel's goal was to minimize the structure, and at the same time, to create an interaction between the permanent elements of a building and transitory events. He explained that the images on the walls were "subject to rapid change," but the environment also emphasized order and logic. Nouvel claimed that architecture should be a "victory over chaos." [10]

In creating an architectural concept for the Galeries Lafayette in Berlin, Nouvel used light as a means of organizing space. The street wall is mostly transparent, revealing the inner activities of the retail marketplace, but the building also contains colored lights, signs, and video images. The interior structure includes several "media cones," or wells of light filled with spiraling images of computerized projections. Despite the many layers of information, the overall effect is subdued, rather than harsh, and provides a harmonious relationship with the street.

Ateliers Jean Nouvel,
Galeries Lafayette, Berlin.
West elevation.

Nouvel believed that new inventions and broad social movements had a greater impact on the planning of cities than the work of individual architects. In an interview, he declared, "History has repeatedly demonstrated that the city lends itself less and less to an overall plan; that, on the contrary, it is the result of economic forces... We [architects] have to face the fundamental truth that modern cities have been invented without us, at times, in spite of us..."[11]

6.14 Diller + Scofidio

Architects Elizabeth Diller and Ricardo Scofidio first collaborated at Cooper Union in the late 1970s. Their New York firm has produced a rich variety of architectural projects, installations, and exhibitions that include layered interpretations of cultural theory, media commentary, and architectural forms.

The Tower of Babel, an installation developed for Times Square, portrayed the loss of cultural diversity. It consisted of a stack of large video screens, each containing the image of a mouth speaking in a different language. The tracks of the eight voices, speaking at once, were modified to create a harmonious mix of sounds and rotated in a programmed sequence to provide a continuous loop of images and voices. The installation alluded to the ancient Babylonian tower described in the Book of Genesis and incorporated references to Pop Art and to the simultaneous poetry of the 1960s.

The Diller + Scofidio renovation of the Brasserie in the Seagram Building in New York, reinterprets the restaurant through transparency, layering, and minimal design—concepts developed in the elegant glass skyscraper by Mies van der Rohe. The architects added a media element to the project, placing monitors at the entrance to videotape each customer arriving. The tape was sent directly to a row of fifteen monitors over the bar so that the other diners could see the new guests. The media elements are combined with a sleek modern environment that includes framed seating areas that also focus attention on the guests. The angled structure around the seating area along one side of the restaurant adds a deconstructivist quality to the design.[12]

209

Diller + Scofidio, The
Brasserie, New York,
1998–99.

In the 1990s, the officers of the New York Stock Exchange wanted to develop a
new database, an Advanced Trading Floor Operation Center for internal use, but
were unable to find a web designer to organize their endless files of information.
They eventually asked Asymptote, a New York design firm, to work on the problem using the same tools they applied to architectural projects.

6.15 Asymptote

Asymptote, a partnership of Hani Rashid and Lise Anne Couture, approached the
problem in an unconventional manner. Rather than create a series of menus based
on traditional computer applications, they arranged data access through interactive
images on a virtual model of a trading floor. The traders could click on an image of
a certain desk or trading facility to obtain related information. The web design kept
the memory of a real trading floor alive to ease the transition to a virtual system.[13]

A year later, Asymptote was asked to develop a command center for controlling
media events. The design for this dramatic interior space utilizes the ingredients of
an urban street, featuring a backlit, curving glass wall of video monitors, carrying
various types of information.

6.16 Deconstructivism

It is the ability to disturb our thinking about form that makes these projects deconstructive.
—Mark Wigley[14]

Although the sudden accumulation of wealth from investments in the stock market
created a conservative culture that supported the traditional architectural styles of
the postmodern era, many architects felt the whimsical humor and cluttered references of postmodernism were inappropriate in the high technology age of computers. Some opposed the decadent quality of the Reagan/Thatcher era, which
produced classical structures and monumental forms. Others were alienated by the

Asymptote, New York Stock
Exchange 3-D Trading Floor
Virtual Reality Environment,
New York, 1997–2000.

Asymptote, New York Stock
Exchange Advanced Trading
Floor, New York, 2001.

kitsch-like vernacular iconography of the postmodernists, which failed to provide
a conception of the future. Others missed the elegant restraint of modernism and
the relationship between design and technology. By the mid-1980s, a new type
of expression had emerged.

The work of architects as diverse as Frank Gehry, Peter Eisenman, Zaha Hadid,
Jørn Utzon, Santiago Calatrava, and the firm Coop Himmelb(l)au is subsumed
under the rubric deconstructivism. Hadid called the term an "intellectual disaster"

Peter Eisenman, Diagram of
design development of House
III, (Mr. and Mrs. Robert
Miller house), Lakeville,
Connecticut, 1969–71.

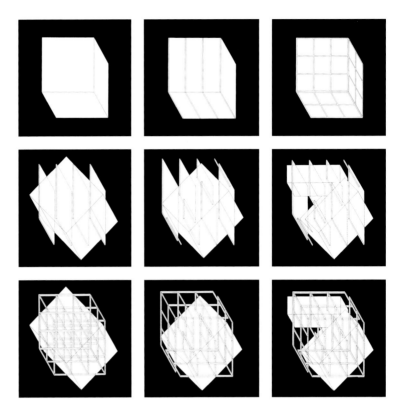

because it has been used to describe a wide variety of unrelated styles. In 1988, the Museum of Modern Art held an exhibition, curated by New Zealand architect Mark Wigley and Philip Johnson, on emerging deconstructivists, which clarified the various concepts of the leading architects.

The deconstructivist movement encompassed a variety of philosophical comments. Some architects expressed the complexity and unpredictability of current culture. Others focused on the existential angst of the emerging era or reacted against cultural traditions. A third group explored purely formal concepts. The dramatic quality of the new structures made them popular with both the public and the architectural establishment.

The development of computer programs and new engineering systems enabled architects to translate complex designs into accurate construction details, and as a result, create precise drawings of the curving walls, leaning columns, and fragmented elements that became the language of the new movement.

6.17 Peter Eisenman

Peter Eisenman's essays in the seminal book *Five Architects* were an early exploration of the theory of deconstructivism. The essay on House I discusses the relationship between form and function. Unlike the classic modernists, Eisenman asserted, "most buildings are burdened by their very description as 'museums' or 'country houses' with a weight of cultural meaning." In describing his project, he adds, "House I was an attempt to conceive of and understand the physical environment in a logically consistent manner, potentially independent of its function and its meaning." Many architects were perplexed by his determination to separate form from function, but he was proclaiming a new era in design, free from the paradigms that had limited

Jørn Utzon, Sydney Opera
House, Sydney, Australia,
1959–73.

architectural experiments in the past. In a second essay on House II, Eisenman
introduces another concept: "modern technology provided architecture with new
means of conceiving space. In a sense, space was no longer necessarily limited or
defined by structure. It was possible to examine such elements as the column and
wall as other than the resolution of functional problems."[15] He pursued the idea
of creating design experiments through a series of projects. In the 1970s and 1980s,
he became a leading voice in the discussion of form and meaning. His essays and
projects challenge traditional definitions and present a cohesive expression of an
alternative approach—many through elegant isometric diagrams.

In creating the diagrams for House III, Eisenman presents a systematic process for
developing the design. The structure begins as a simple cube, which is divided into
smaller cubes. The form is then rotated and spliced by parallel planes, pulled apart,
and then reassembled into another type of diagram. It provides a clear definition of
his process of transforming a traditional cube into a more sophisticated structure.
This project was an early form of deconstructivism. Eisenman's later work would
be inspired by the linguistic analysis of Noam Chomsky and the work of the
deconstructionist philosopher Jacques Derrida, with whom he later collaborated.

6.18 Sydney Opera
House

The first major public building to explore deconstructivism was the Sydney Opera
House designed by Danish architect Jørn Utzon. Construction began in 1959 and
took fourteen years. The delay was partly due to the difficulty of building the precast
concrete forms of the roof structures because his design contained a variety of
curving shapes. Utzon finally suggested that the same shape could be repeated in all
of the shells and arranged in a series. The innovative engineering firm Ove Arup
utilized early computers to complete the structural analysis.

213

Frank Gehry,
Guggenheim Museum,
Bilbao, Spain, 1991–97.

This extraordinary building made Sydney a major tourist destination. The famous curving structures on the roof, which suggest sails or waves, relate to the theaters below, but sophisticated acoustical solutions were needed to make the theaters function properly. Since the form was modern, but did not completely follow the function, some critics described the design as expressionist modernism. The dramatic structure introduced a new era in architecture: its engineering pioneered the use of digital technology in architecture, a powerful new tool that would serve as a basis for the experiments of the deconstructivist era.

6.19 Frank Gehry

Frank Gehry's Guggenheim Museum in Bilbao, Spain, became an immediate icon of deconstructivism when it was completed in 1997. Its cascade of large, curving structures demonstrate the dramatic possibilities of digital design. *New York Times* architecture critic Herbert Muschamp wrote in an article entitled "The Miracle in Bilbao" that Gehry's design was a "shimmering, Looney Toons, post-industrial, post-everything burst of American artistic optimism."

The *Times* received numerous letters in response. Some commentators agreed with his view; one writer described it as "stunningly beautiful." Most of the letters expressed a negative reaction, however. One writer said it looked like a "meltdown of a nuclear power plant." Another called it "a monstrosity." One of the harshest critics was Ethan Kent, who wrote an article for the Project for Public Spaces. He claimed the stairs were dangerous and discouraging, the large scale of the building was oppressive, and the solid walls created isolated outdoor spaces that encouraged

Zaha Hadid, Vitra Fire Station,
Weil am Rhein, Germany,
1990–94.

street crime. Javier Cenicacelaya, an architect from Bilbao, concurred, claiming the building was a vulgar intrusion on the city. Although the museum helped to stimulate the local economy, Cenicacelaya claimed it did not provide a good public space for the city. Gehry later explained that the Bilbao clients, Thomas Krens of the Guggenheim and members of the Basque community, said they needed "a hit there, like the Sydney Opera House."

Gehry gave them what they wanted, while developing a building that expresses the culmination of several decades of experiments.[16] He first explored the idea of using diverse shapes and materials to create a "village of forms" in projects such as the Loyola University Law School and Schnabel house. In the renovation of his own house, he experimented with alternative materials and new spatial relationships. His forms grew more complex and sophisticated with each project. From 1987 to 1995, he developed the Team Disneyland Administration Building, designed around two ideas. The east facade is bright yellow stucco that undulates in a playful manner to express the childlike nature of Disney cartoons, and the west side has a formal facade of stainless steel panels to convey a corporate quality. The Walt Disney Concert Hall in Los Angeles, completed in 2003, is closely related to the Guggehheim Bilbao, and some felt the design was more resolved than Bilbao.

6.20 Zaha Hadid

As a student, Zaha Hadid was inspired by the work of Russian avant-garde designers, such as Kazimir Malevich, Vladimir Tatlin, Yakov Chernikhov, and El Lissitzky, intrigued with the sleek curves and dramatic diagonals in their drawings. She later developed her own style, which critic Germano Celant described as "a process that translates Suprematist and Constructivist iconography, which is Utopian and experimental in character, into a potential instrument for use."[17] The dramatic forms that characterize her conceptual projects were fully realized in the Vitra Fire Station,

215

Santiago Calatrava,
Lyon-Satolas Railway Station,
Lyon, France, 1989–94.

which she completed in 1994. This elegant building portrays the combined concepts of movement and tension inherent in her work. Subsequent larger commissions include the Rosenthal Center for Contemporary Art in Cincinnati, the BMW Central Building in Leipzig, and the high-speed train station in Afragola, Italy.

6.21 Santiago Calatrava

Spanish architect Santiago Calatrava's first projects were a bridge, a warehouse, and a small metro station, but his dramatic structural concepts soon led to larger public projects, including major train stations, cultural centers, and Olympic facilities. His career coincided with the development of the European high-speed train system, which provided him with the opportunity to work on large-scale infrastructure projects.

Some of his designs contain historical influences while others introduce haunting new forms that integrate a sculptural sensibility with sophisticated digital engineering systems. The graceful diagonal lines in the Alamillo Bridge in Seville, built in 1992, evoke the image of a harp. The dramatic shape of the Lyon-Satolas Airport Railway Station, which was completed in 1994, expresses a sense of motion defined by a series of interlocking curves. The elegant streamlined forms provide a powerful demonstration of his engineering capabilities. At the Oriente Station in Lisbon, completed in 1998, the engineering is enhanced by postmodern references, which further demonstrate his versatility as a designer.

Coop Himmelb(l)au,
UFA Cinema Complex,
Dresden, Germany,
1993.

6.22 Coop Himmelb(l)au

In 1996 Wolf Prix and Helmut Swiczinsky, partners in the firm Coop Himmelb(l)au published an essay entitled "A Future of Splendid Desolation." This brief but powerful statement explores some of the basic principles of their work:

217

> The architectures of the future have already been built.
>
> The solitude of its squares, the desolation of its streets . . . characterize the city of the present and will characterize the city of the future as well . . .
>
> Reactionary architecture tends to conceal the problems rather than create the necessary new urban awareness.
>
> Contemporary architecture will be honest and true . . . when the devastation of the city is transformed into fascinating landmarks of desolation.[18]

Prix and Swiczinsky rejected the decorative quality of traditional architecture and thus, developed numerous experimental projects that integrated real issues with dramatic new forms and structures. In 1993, the famous media company UFA, which produced the classic film *Metropolis*, commissioned them to design a cinema complex in Dresden. The site of the project was a difficult triangular tract of land that linked several urban areas, which provided the possibility of creating an important public space. The building is based on a dialogue between a closed structure that houses eight cinemas and an open public space that provides a transparent urban center enhanced by light, color, and cinematic images. It also contains random sculptural elements, such as stairs and bridges, to enliven the form. The general massing of the structure has a jagged quality that is somewhat disturbing, but the rough edges are appropriate to the project. A traditional landmark would not have symbolic meaning for Dresden, a city that was heavily bombed during World War II and required a bold and dramatic structure. Their sophisticated design of jagged forms provides a provocative image as well as a successful urban space.

6.23 Postmodern Films

In the 1980s and 1990s, several dystopian texts were adapted for the screen. The political themes explored in these films were a direct reflection of the turmoil that existed in the real world. Although there were no world wars or major revolutions in this period, the disturbing atmosphere of the Cold War and the constant threat of nuclear weapons created a sense of vulnerability and an undercurrent of fear.

The postmodernist style proved effective in film, with its complex layering of several historical periods. The mixture of various references helped to express the universal nature of the stories. The process of designing these films was different than the process of set design for traditional movies, however. Instead of developing a single vision, designers gathered an array of images from different periods.

New digital effects strengthened the atmosphere of the cinematic environment: films had multiple soundtracks, sophisticated lighting, computer models, and carefully edited scenes, which integrated actors with digital backgrounds. Many of the designs would have been impossible to achieve prior to the advent of computers.

6.24 *1984*

Despite the advantages of new technologies, many writers, social scientists, and cultural critics questioned the impact of media and information systems on culture. George Orwell made one of the most articulate statements in his novel *1984*. He presents the story of a fictional military dictatorship based on the regimes of Nazi Germany, Stalinist Russia, and Maoist China, where media and information systems are used to manipulate society. In this disturbing dystopia, individual ideas are censored by an omniscient "thought police," which monitors citizens to guard against any unconventional behavior. Personal relationships are forbidden as a threat to the autonomy of the State and books that portray a different type of culture are censored.

Winston Smith, the main character in the novel, works as a propaganda writer, rewriting history to suit the interests of the party. Since information is controlled by the State, he has no way of determining the truth. He does not know what year it is or whether his country is at war or not. His ignorance and vulnerability pose a frightening image of a culture in which knowledge is completely suppressed. Orwell's nightmarish vision served as a warning to future generations to avoid the tragic isolation and cultural deprivation of a totalitarian society.

In the year 1984, the film of Orwell's classic novel was released. The screen version paints a tough portrait of a totalitarian society and explores the danger of technology in the wrong hands, an issue that has haunted many science-fiction writers. In this case, the critical technologies are media and information systems, in particular the aspect of teleconferencing. The design of the city is based on urban enviroments in the war era.

The mass rally in the film *1984*, produced in 1984. Director: Michael Radford.

The concept of Big Brother observing private citizens has never been implemented in the way that Orwell imagined, with screens monitoring each person's behavior from their living rooms to the workplace, but giant video screens were later utilized to enhance public events, such as sports, rock concerts, corporate meetings, and political rallies. In May 2001, the *New York Times* published a photograph of a stockholders' meeting that used large televised images of its officers. The image of the meeting bore an eerie resemblance to the mass rally in *1984*.

6.25 *Brazil*

In 1985, director Terry Gilliam created the film *Brazil*, a dark comedy/fantasy set "sometime in the future." Like most of Gilliam's films, it depicts the struggle of an unconventional individual against the cultural pressures to conform. This nightmarish film chronicles an adventure in the life of a nerdy clerk who is determined to avoid upward mobility.

The antihero fights endless battles with massive social systems designed to control individual behavior, including mass housing systems and media and information systems, the most egregious agencies. These powerful systems reduce the individual to a nameless number on a vast cultural grid. As a result, the protagonist dreams of a life of freedom, sensuality, and heroic rebellion, a rich contrast to the compromised realities of his existence.

Actor Jonathan Pryce gets out of a retro-futuristic car in the film *Brazil*, 1985. Director: Terry Gilliam.

Gilliam collaborated with art director John Beard to develop visual satire throughout the film. The designs express the futurist ideas of the 1930s and 1950s, two historical eras dominated by mechanization. However, most of the high-tech environments in this retro-dystopia contain systems that do not work. In one memorable scene, the protagonist returns to his apartment, which is buried in a sea of windows in a housing project. Upon entering his retro-futuristic home, he discovers that the air conditioning system has failed. He calls for repairs and is forced to leave a message on a machine, but an unlicensed engineer, played by Robert De Niro, enters through his window and offers to look at the problem. He gratefully accepts, and the wall is opened to reveal the heaving intestines of the building's mechanical systems.

Gilliam began his career as a counterculture cartoonist and animator. As a member of the Monty Python group, he created the famous Victorian/modern collages used on the show. He later applied the same zany humor to feature-length films. His production designer Beard was also a Monty Python graduate. Beard's concepts for *Brazil* were inspired by the high-tech visions of 1930s magazines and comics. Although it was set in the utopian era of the machine age, this postmodern satire provides a rich commentary on contemporary culture.

6.27 *The Fifth Element*

In the 1980s and 1990s in France, Dan Weil designed sets for several highly regarded films, which helped to reestablish the role of the production designer in European films. That role was downplayed in the postwar era, as most films were shot on-location or with minimal, modern sets.[19]

Weil first attracted attention through his theatrical designs, which led to a collaboration with the acclaimed director Luc Besson, who developed the challenging film

Scene depicting the future of Manhattan in the film *The Fifth Element*, 1997. Director: Luc Besson.

The Fifth Element. The film was not critically successful, but Weil's designs were quite memorable.

The Fifth Element is a science-fiction film that required a concept of a futuristic society. To develop this, Weil assembled a studio of twelve artists and illustrators, some of whom were authors of science-fiction comic books. They discussed various aspects of life, such as housing, food, transportation, and so on, and imagined how each function might change in the future, assuming that the future would be a mixture of existing elements and new ideas. The group provided an intriguing postmodern concept of the urban experience. The most dramatic scene in the film is an image of future New York containing flying cars and landing platforms on the upper stories of buildings. This unforgettable digital collage was created through innovative animation systems with designers inserting flying cars into images of existing New York streets. They also added rich details, such as flashing lights, smoke, and street activities to make the scene believable. The result is a disturbing portrait of the future city.

221

6.28 *Titus*

In 1999, theatrical director Julie Taymor made *Titus*, a film based on Shakespeare's play *Titus Andronicus*. This complex production is a remarkable postmodern exploration of an ironic tragedy. Throughout the film, Taymor introduces sophisticated designs that integrate images from several historical eras to demonstrate the universal themes of the story, but she keeps Shakespeare's basic plot and characters intact.

In collaboration with production designer Dante Ferretti, Taymor created lavish sets that combine scenes of ancient Rome with the iconography of other periods, such as fascist Italy in the 1940s. The rich cultural images portray the timeless

Actor Anthony Hopkins
returns from battle in the film
Titus, 1999.

nature of power-hungry politicians, as well as the decadence and corruption of
ancient Rome. Motorcycle hoodlums interrupt political rallies in a Roman arena.
A modern fascist skyscraper serves as the backdrop for an ancient senator's speech.
Statues come to life in the baths, providing a breathtaking sequence on classical
beauty. As the story unfolds, giant broken sculptures, representing fragments of the
decadent culture, also appear. The costumes reference several historical periods
from ancient to modern times, providing a constant reminder of the similarities
between the corrupt leaders of the past and the manipulative politicians of the
present.

The sophisticated film imagery utilizes postmodern language in a significant manner, and the historical references add provocative images to the theme. The production provides a remarkably artistic demonstration of how real images can be mixed
with imaginary elements to add relevance to the drama.

222

6.28 Cultural Symbols

In the late twentieth century, a number of political systems were transformed. In
1978 Mao Zedong's totalitarian regime in China came to an end. His successor,
Deng Xiaoping, established a new government that turned away from communism
to begin the difficult process of transforming China into a market economy. Over
the next twenty years, the Chinese economy quadrupled, and the lifestyles of the
people began to change.

The communist government of the Soviet Union failed in 1991. For over forty
years, the economy had been burdened with the cost of the Cold War. When
the government finally capitulated, the confederation of fifteen countries formally
dissolved, and each of those nations introduced programs to rebuild their cities
and restore their original culture. Like their Chinese allies, they began to develop
a capitalist system.

In 1993, five European countries took steps toward forming a European Union with
the goal of establishing a political and economic relationship that would stimulate
economic growth and prevent future wars. They also hoped to develop a unified
foreign policy, a shared constitution, a single currency, and other cooperative systems. Although there was much resistance to unification, by the year 2000, fifteen

Christo and Jeanne-Claude,
Wrapped Reichstag, 1971–95,
Berlin.

countries agreed to establish a unified currency. As economic conditions in Europe improved, other nations applied for membership in the European Union.

Collectively, these events established a new era in design and planning. The Chinese government initiated ambitious programs to build new infrastructure and urban facilities. The liberated nations of Eastern Europe began to restore their historical cities and upgrade their physical systems. The members of the European Union also invested in infrastructure to support the new era: they developed high-speed trains, alternative energy, and new communications systems.

6.29 *Wrapped Reichstag*   In Berlin, the artists Christo and Jeanne-Claude developed the *Wrapped Reichstag*, an installation that transformed the identity of a large government building symbolizing the old era. They covered the Reichstag with fabric as a means of deconstructing its historical identity and ceremoniously removing its former meaning. For many Europeans, this symbolized the burial of the past and the beginning of a new era, a ritualistic redefinition of the structure.

Wrapped Reichstag was first conceived in 1971, but it took twenty-four years to obtain the necessary permissions and to establish public support. When it was finally realized in 1995, many Germans were opposed to this expensive installation as a waste of valuable funds, but since Christo and Jeanne-Claude always paid for the projects themselves, accumulating the funds through the sale of images, and preparatory studies of their projects, their concept was ultimately accepted.

The development of *Wrapped Reichstag* was eventually approved through the support of several leading members of the German Parliament, including the parliamentary speaker Rita Süssmuth. On February 25, 1994, Konrad Weiss, a leading member of the Alliance 90/Greens, gave a powerful speech in defense of the idea:

> Art is more than commerce and entertainment. It frees and widens views. It orients and helps us find the reason for our own life . . . The unwrapping in the end is a symbol of the rebirth of democracy, of the awakening of our country that was supposed to have become a new country with reunification.

His speech ended with a powerful statement about the historical relevance of the project:

> I wish for us, ladies and gentlemen, that we find the courage to face the creative provocation of this symbolic wrapping, that we show courage to the ironic distance with ourselves as part of this work of art and at the same time to the responsible integration of our history with all of its highs and lows, with all its good and evil for which this Reichstag stands.[20]

Subsequently, the Reichstag was transformed in a more lasting manner by Sir Norman Foster, who renovated the building and restored its use as a Parliament structure. The work was part of an extensive reconstruction effort in Berlin that began in the 1990s. Foster's design combined ecological and energy-efficient systems with historical symbols.

6.30 The Redevelopment of the World Trade Center Site

Although the political transitions of this era were generally regarded as positive steps, they instigated a negative reaction in some parts of the world. Several Middle Eastern cultures rebelled against the spread of capitalism and the cultural imperialism of western nations. They were deeply opposed to the idea of a global society based on American values and were determined to retain their own cultural traditions.

On September 11, 2001, the United States was attacked by Islamic extremists. Suicide bombers hijacked four airplanes and smashed into strategically chosen buildings that symbolized American power. Two planes crashed into the World Trade Center in New York and demolished the complex; a third plane hit the Pentagon in Arlington, Virginia; the fourth plane crashed in rural Pennsylvania, its mission presumably averted by the brave passengers on that flight. Approximately 3,000 people were killed.

After these tragic events, the citizens of New York engaged in dialogues on rebuilding the city. They not only had to reconstruct the structures and transportation systems of lower Manhattan, they also wanted to create a major memorial site, relocate homes and businesses that had been displaced, address urban security problems, and restore confidence in New York.

Thousands of architects, planners, politicians, and public advocates met to discuss the rebuilding of the World Trade Center site. They hoped to quickly create a new structure that would symbolize the strength of the American system. The Lower Manhattan Development Corporation, a group assembled by the mayor and governor of New York, organized a limited architectural competition for the design of

Daniel Libeskind, design
officially chosen for the
redevelopment of the
World Trade Center site.

225

the new complex. After a lengthy review process, architect Daniel Libeskind was
chosen to develop the master plan of the site.

He created a deconstructivist design, called "Memory Foundations," that combines
a sensitive urban plan emphasizing nature with dramatic new buildings. He also
established symbolic elements to express a memory of the attack on New York:
a "Park of Heroes," on the west side of the site; a seventy-foot-deep "Slurry Wall,"
revealing the original foundations of one of the towers: and a "Wedge of Light"
on the east side of the site.

The Wedge of Light is designed to allow sunlight to enter the memorial space between 8:46 and 10:28 in the morning, marking the moment when the north tower was hit by the first plane and continuing until after the time that both towers collapsed. Libeskind's architectural design would also contribute to the theme of a memorial site. His proposed buildings have a jagged quality that express a memory of the event. The tallest building, Freedom Tower, contains a piercing spire, 1,776 feet high, which would introduce a vertical spike in the skyline.

Many members of the design community were glad that the city chose an avant-garde architect whose design expressed the meaning of the event, but the plan has now been altered to suit the politicians and commercial interest groups that ultimately controlled the site.

In addition to the redevelopment of the World Trade Center site, the events of 9/11 had a deeper effect on the design community. As architects and planners debated the rebuilding of New York, they began to discuss the environmental issues of the city. Although there was pressure to restore the activities of the city quickly, there seemed to be a general consensus that the next era of development should promote the creation of green buildings, parks, and public transportation systems, thus introducing a new era of sustainable design.

Notes

1. Marshall McLuhan, *Understanding Media* (New York: Signet Books, 1964), ix.

2. Robert Venturi, *Complexity and Contradictions in Architecture* (New York: The Museum of Modern Art in association with the Graham Foundation for Advanced Studies in the Fine Arts, Chicago, 1966), 16.

3. Venturi, 64.

4. Robert Venturi, Denise Scott Brown, and Steven Izenour, *Learning from Las Vegas* (Cambridge, MA: The MIT Press, 1977), 88-131.

5. Venturi, *Complexity and Contradictions in Architecture*, 118-19.

6. Andres Duany, Elizabeth Plater-Zyber, and Jeff Speck, *Suburban Nation* (New York: North Point Press, 2000), 15-17.

7. Karal Ann Marling, *Designing Disney's Theme Parks* (Paris: Flammarion/ADAGP in association with Canadian Centre for Architecture, Montreal, 1997), 30.

8. Samuel R. Delany, *Times Square Red, Times Square Blue* (New York: New York University Press, 1999), np.

9. Michael Lewis, *The New New Thing* (New York: W.W. Norton & Company, 2000), 71-72.

10. Jean Nouvel, quoted in Sheila De Vallee, *Architecture for the Future* (Paris: Terrail, 1996), 190.

11. Novel, quoted in De Vallee, 190-191.

12. Philip Jodidio, *Architecture NOW!* (Koln: Taschen GmbH, 2001), 76.

13. John K. Waters, *Blobitecture* (Gloucester, MA: Rockport Publishers, Inc., 2003), 108-11.

14. Mark Wigley, quoted in "Deconstructivist Architecture," in *Deconstructivist Architecture*, ed. Philip Johnson and Mark Wigley (Boston: Little, Brown, 1988), 10-11.

15. Peter Eisenman, "House I" and "House II" in Peter Eisenman, Michael Graves, Charles Gwathmey, John Hejduk, Richard Meier, Colin Rowe, Kenneth Frampton, *Five Architects* (New York, Oxford University Press, 1975), 15, 25.

16. Charles Jencks, *The Iconic Building* (New York: Rizzoli, 2005), 12.

17. Germano Celant, "Zaha Hadid: Adventure in Architecture," in *Zaha Hadid* (New York: Guggenheim Museum Publications, 2006), 18.

18. Sheila De Vallee, *Architecture for the Future* (Paris: Terrail, 1996), 113-14.

19. Peter Ettedgui, *Production Design & Art Direction* (Woburn, MA: Focal Press, 1998), 179.

20. Konrad Weiss, "Wrapping of the Reichstag" (speech at the 211th Session of German Parliament, Bonn, February 25, 1994), www.bln.de/k.weiss/te_wrapp.htm.

THE ENVIRONMENTAL AGE

Only 60 years ago (1930), there were 2 billion of us...a total that had taken 250 million years to attain. Today, there are more than 5 billion (1990); and by 2025, there could be more than 10 billion.

—Norman Myers[1]

In 1962, scientist Rachel Carson published *Silent Spring*. Her research exposed the danger of DDT, a pesticide that was widely used in agriculture at the time, and the book examines both the impact of the poison on human life and the broader concept of ecosystems, or how the loss of one insect could disrupt the entire food chain. Her work was denounced by a few chemical companies and her conclusions denied by the U.S. Department of Agriculture. However, their criticism did not dismantle her thesis.

Time magazine reported, "In their ugly campaign to reduce a brave scientist's protest to a matter of public relations, the chemical interests had only increased public awareness." Carson died two years later, but as a result of her work, DDT was banned in the United States. Many considered *Silent Spring* to be the beginning of the modern environmental movement. Within a few years, other scientists embarked on similar research in related fields.

In 1968, entomologist Paul Ehrlich published *The Population Bomb*, reiterating the Malthus theory that if the population continued to grow at such a rapid pace, there would be insufficient food and resources to meet future needs. He also helped found the organization Zero Population Growth, which promotes family planning systems.

In 1972, a group of scientists from the Club of Rome environmental group published *Limits to Growth*, a controversial report that predicted environmental disaster if the trends in population, industrialization, pollution, and resource depletion continued. It stated that continued use of fossil fuels would reduce the ozone layer, cause the polar ice caps to melt, and induce climate changes. That year, the United Nations established an environmental agency. The new international group proposed legislation to protect diminishing resources, fragile ecosystems, and endangered species, as well as the environments of the ocean, space, and polar regions.[2]

In 1973, the public finally became engaged in the issue of limited resources when Arab nations launched an oil embargo against the United States and Western Europe, threatening to quadruple oil prices if those nations continued to support Israel. As a

Aerial view of Tokyo,
Shinkuju District.

230

result, millions of people paid more for gasoline and weathered the higher costs
of heating in the winter.

The oil embargo caused several governments to fund research on alternative systems,
including a U.S. Department of Energy case study program on solar housing. This
successful program was the beginning of an era of synthesis between technology
and environment and promoted the development of sustainable technologies.

In the next few years, the public grew increasingly aware of environmental issues
through a series of events. In 1978, a court case, called the Love Canal, showed
that children who attended school near a toxic waste site were contracting diseases.
President Jimmy Carter established the Superfund to clean up dump sites, but
the issue of eliminating trash was far from solved. In 1979, the dangers of nuclear
power became known when an accident occurred at Three Mile Island nuclear
power plant. The fear of nuclear power increased in 1986, when there was an explosion at the Chernobyl Nuclear Power Plant. Over 336,000 people were evacuated
to avoid exposure to radioactive fallout. As the public became more aware of the
dangers of certain technologies, new research centers were established to explore
alternative systems. Activists lobbied for legislation to reduce the damage caused
by nuclear power, acid rain, trash incineration, ocean dumping, and air pollution.
They used satellite maps to verify the mounting problems.

In the 1980s, the Reagan and Bush administrations tried to deny these issues, but by
this time, most countries outside the United States were already establishing new
methods to conserve resources, control population growth, and reduce pollution
levels. They also built environmental infrastructure such as hydroelectric systems,
high-speed trains, windmills, and recycling plants to provide for growth.

New concepts were developed in every area of design. Architects utilized solar
panels, lightweight materials, and water conservation systems. Engineers invented
vehicles that reduced reliance on fossil fuels. Industrial designers used recycled

The slums or *favelas* on the hillsides of Rio de Janeiro.

231

materials to conserve resources. Urban planners lobbied for more parks and public transportation systems.

By the 1990s, the world population had reached six billion people with most of the growth occurring in emerging cities with limited resources, such as São Paolo, Mumbai, Shanghai, and Mexico City. *Time* magazine reported that eighteen out of twenty-one of the world's largest cities were in third world nations. According to the World Bank, some African cities were expanding as much as 10 percent a year. The staggering statistics also indicated that 20 percent of the global population had inadequate food, water, and shelter.

Developed cities were also struggling with growth. By the 1990s, the population of Tokyo was approaching 30 million people. The Japanese built more than 100 artificial islands in Tokyo Bay to expand infrastructure and urban systems. Such complex projects led to the creation of new interdisciplinary professions, such as regional planning, macroengineering, and environmental law. Large architectural offices started taking a more interdisciplinary approach, through collaborations with landscape planners and environmental engineers.

In 1992, Rio de Janeiro hosted Earth Summit, the largest environmental conference in history, attended by 100 world leaders and 30,000 other participants. The meetings led to new agreements to protect endangered areas and raise the standards of environmental quality and drew attention to such topics as global warming, the weakened condition of the ozone layer over Australia, and the water shortages in Africa.

James Wines, SITE,
Greening of Manhattan,
project, 1979.

7.1   Green Buildings

By seeing sustainability as both a local and a global event, we can understand that just as it is not viable to poison local water and air with waste, it is equally unacceptable to send it downstream or ship it overseas to other less regulated shores.
—William McDonough[3]

The modern idea of green architecture emerged from the counterculture movements of the 1960s and 1970s. The political activists of that era not only protested against the Vietnam War and fought for civil rights, they also addressed environmental issues and questioned traditional systems of production. Their anti-establishment sentiments led to the creation of communal groups that fostered alternative lifestyles. Some of the communes advocated organic foods; others made handcrafted products, or built alternative structures like the straw bale house.

R. Buckminster Fuller took an active role through his in-depth lectures on global resources and books on alternative structures and industrial systems. His concept of the geodesic dome became a popular symbol of the counterculture movement and was featured in *The Whole Earth Catalogue*, which appeared in 1971 as the unofficial handbook of the movement. Other designers experimented with alternative materials, creating furniture from found objects, discarded products, and recycled materials. Paul Rudolf turned fabric-covered tires into seating systems. Frank Gehry made chairs from corrugated cardboard. Lightweight furniture systems were also developed that could be used in loft spaces or alternative structures.

In 1989, James Wines of SITE presented Greened Manhattan, a concept that portrayed New York City skyscapers immersed in plants. He thought the image would add fun to the dialogue, but some architects were horrified by the idea of covering their pristine glass boxes with vegetation. Others saw the humor in it. Greened Manhattan was followed by other witty environmental images, which also offended conservative designers, but despite the opposition, a green movement slowly emerged.

By the 1990s, environmental research was being done in virtually all areas of design. The United States government established LEED certification, a point system that set standards for green buildings and provided a clear list of recommendations for site planning, orientation, landscaping, and construction. It also encouraged the use of renewable materials, thermal insulation, daylighting, operable windows, shading devices, and efficient lighting and mechanical systems.

Sustainable systems were also introduced in many European structures. In 2007, the UN Environmental Programme (UNEP) presented a report called Buildings and Climate Change, which concluded that European design improvements had lowered energy consumption in buildings by an impressive 20 percent.

7.2   Paolo Soleri

In the 1960s and 1970s, Italian/American architect Paolo Soleri created a series of large-scale concepts for the future city called *arcologies*, which he defined as a combination of architecture and ecology. Soleri envisioned structures that were large enough to house over a million people, and left the surrounding environment undisturbed.

Many architects were skeptical of his conceptual buildings, but in 1970, Soleri began to construct Arcosanti, a small community in Arizona based on the concept of preserving the natural environment. This unique town was to be composed of about 5,000 people who lived in alternative structures. They would rely on solar energy as a major source of power, many years before the technology was ready for such a challenge. Some of the structures in the town were built underground, where Soleri discovered it was possible to retain a temperature of 56 degrees despite the debilitating heat of the Arizona desert. The development of this project was a lifelong struggle, which continued into the twenty-first century.

Paolo Soleri, Foundry Apse and surrounding structures at Arcosanti, near Cordes Junction, Arizona, begun in 1970.

233

Emilio Ambasz & Associates,
Asian Crossroads Over
the Sea (ACROS), Fukuoka,
Japan, 1995.

234

7.3   Emilio Ambasz

In the 1980s, designer Emilio Ambasz became involved with environmental projects, most memorably with the design of the ACROS Building in Fukuoka, Japan. ACROS (Asian Crossroads Over the Sea) planned to create a cultural center with a museum, theaters, shops, and offices on a site adjacent to a park, which inspired Ambasz to develop a design that extended the park into the building.[4] The ziggurat structure has terraces on each level, all planted with rich vegetation so that the exterior wall of the building appears to be a series of gardens stepping down to the level of the park. A large skylit atrium in the center brings natural light into the interior of the building. Its classic expression of environmental principles provides a symbol for the potential integration of nature and man-made structures and an icon of green architecture.

7.4   Hans Hollein

In 1997, Viennese architect Hans Hollein was commissioned to design the European Centre of Vulcanology, a project initiated by President Giscard d'Estaing of France for a site in the northern area of a volcanic region in the Auvergne, France. When Hollein first proposed the idea of constructing a building in a dormant volcano, members of the French Green party were deeply opposed. They attacked the concept in over thirty lawsuits, but it ultimately won approval. The final complex combines a mountainous cone with an extensive underground exhibi-

Hans Hollein, *Vulcania*,
European Volcanism
Centre, St. Ours les Roches,
Auvergne, France, 1994–2001.

tion space carved out of hardened lava. The highly symbolic form of the cone
brought the design instant iconic status, and the project was later accepted by the
environmental community since it also contained an important research center.

7.5   Sir Nicholas
      Grimshaw

In 1995, Tim Smit, a British songwriter and music producer, developed a proposal
for the Eden Project, a park and tourist center that focused on the relationship
between plant life and human activities. He and his collaborators planned to exhibit
several types of landscapes in a series of "covered biomes" designed by Nicholas
Grimshaw & Partners.

Grimshaw based the design of the Eden Project on Fuller's geodesic dome. Then
he collaborated with engineers at Anthony Hunt Associates to create a structure of
several intersecting domes. Instead of using glass and steel, which would have been
too heavy to span the huge space, he chose a lightweight plastic made of ETFE,
or ethylene-tetrafluoroethylene. The material weighed so little that no interior
structure was required. The largest biome encloses 170,000 square feet without any
interior columns or walls. ETFE also provided an excellent environmental solution
since it was a better insulator than glass and required less maintenance. It was also
transparent enough to allow a maximum amount of natural light into the space.
It could even be recycled, if the project ever changed.

The site was a thirty-seven-acre china clay pit in St. Austell, England. The dark
clay on the back wall of the pit served as a natural solar collector, and its shape shel-
tered the facility from heavy winds and collected rainwater that could be used for
the plants. Initially, the complex relied partly on conventional energy sources, but
it was assumed that when the plants matured, they would supply the power needed
for the heating and mechanical systems.[5]

235

Nicholas Grimshaw and
Partners, The Eden Project,
St. Austell, England, 2001.

The Eden Project, which opened in 2001, became a major destination for ecotourists.
In 2005, Grimshaw designed another building for the complex, called The Core.
The new structure added classrooms, exhibition rooms, and multimedia spaces to
the center. The Core is also based on sustainable concepts, which brings another
educational dimension to the project.

236   7.6   Renzo Piano

In 1991, Renzo Piano was selected to design a new cultural center in Noumea,
New Caledonia in honor of Jean-Marie Tjibaou, a leader in the national movement
to gain independence from France. Tjibaou, a Kanak priest who had studied ethnol-
ogy at the Sorbonne, believed that an indigenous culture could not live in the past; it
had to exist in the modern world. However, he wanted his people to remember their
origins. The cultural center was designed to provide information on the Kanak people and other native cultures of the South Pacific. It was to be a gift from President
François Mitterrand of France in an attempt to resolve some of the differences
between the two nations.

The center is composed of ten "Great Houses," which are linked by a covered path
based on the concept of a ceremonial alley through a Kanak village. The shape
and texture of the buildings are a direct reference to the design of Kanak huts, but
Piano's abstract forms bring a modern vision to the center. His haunting concept
reflects the quality of Kanak structures without reproducing the actual forms.

The project is also based on sustainable systems. The woven walls are made of slats
of iroko wood, an indigenous material that is strong enough to resist the fury of
the cyclones that occasionally occur in the region. The curving shape of the walls
captures the prevailing winds from the ocean and provides natural ventilation
throughout the buildings.[6]

Renzo Piano, Jean-Marie
Tjibaou Cultural Center,
Noumea, New Caledonia,
1992–98.

7.7 William McDonough

One of the first prominent advocates of sustainable design was William McDonough, an architect who developed several areas of environmental research. In 1984, McDonough was commissioned by the Environmental Defense Fund to design a green project. According to an article in *Metropolis* magazine, the agency told him that if the building caused any of their employees to become ill, they would sue him. In response, McDonough asked all of his suppliers to provide a list of the chemicals used in their products, but most of the manufacturers refused to divulge that information.

237

As a result, McDonough began conducting research on the toxic content of materials and discovered that many of the products used in traditional architecture contained undesirable substances. He formed a partnership with Michael Braungart, a chemist who worked for Greenpeace. Their new company analyzed the chemical composition of products to determine if they were environmentally safe. McDonough redefined his design practice to focus on building sustainable structures that were free of toxic chemicals.

His clients included major corporations, such as The Gap, Nike, the Ford Motor Company, Designtex, and Herman Miller. Each of his projects led to new research. He persuaded all of these companies not only to invest in the construction of green manufacturing facilities, but to support environmental research on the composition of their own products.

In working with Designtex, a division of Steelcase, McDonough became involved with the Swiss textile manufacturer Rohner, a company that supplied some of Steelcase's fabrics. They had been asked to upgrade their facilities to meet new environmental standards established by the Swiss government, and McDonough

William McDonough +
Partners, renovation of Ford
Rouge Center, Dearborn,
Michigan, begun in 2001.
The original buildings were
designed by Albert Kahn in
1929.

and Braungart's laboratory analyzed the components of the fabric and the chemicals used in the dyes. Their research led to the creation of a toxic-free fabric, which became a valuable asset in Steelcase's product line.

In 2001, McDonough was asked to reengineer the environmental systems of Ford Motor's River Rouge Plant. This 1.1-million-square-foot facility was a symbol of old industrial systems. If the transformation were achieved, it would provide a major demonstration of sustainable systems.

McDonough's plan included the development of a green roof, or what he called a "living roof." The green roof would not only cleanse the air, it would also provide a habitat for local wildlife, reduce the energy requirements of the building by adding extra insulation, and function as a water treatment plant. The roof concept was so successful that it now cleans over 20 billion gallons of rainwater annually, and saved Ford $30 million, or the cost of a new water treatment facility.

McDonough also developed a green environment for a Nike factory. The factory they created was so successful that McDonough also discussed the possibility of redeveloping Nike sneakers as green products. Nike management was intrigued with this concept and decided to explore new ideas for recycling sneakers and using toxic-free materials in their products.

In 2006, McDonough was commissioned to create a plan for a model village in China based on sustainable design. Although their project encountered many difficulties, he and his associates are endeavoring to develop that assignment.

MVRDV, 3D-Garden,
Hengelo NL Design for
32 apartments, Hengelo,
Netherlands, 2001.

7.8 MVRDV

In the 1990s, MVRDV, an innovative architecture firm in the Netherlands, created a series of conceptual drawings of environmental concepts that challenged traditional systems. In *FARMAX* and *Datascape*, two publications they created in the late 1990s, they expressed opposition to the mediocrity of repetitious suburbs and warehouse structures. They advocated contrast, rather than conformity in design, and introduced new strategies to support environmental development.

239

Some were extreme examples of ideas that could be applied in real buildings. The drawing *3D-Garden* is a conceptual image created for a client in the Netherlands, illustrating a proposal for an eleven-story building. The ground floor has commercial spaces; the upper stories contain twenty-nine apartments with cantilevered terraces that project outward like branches on a tree. The metaphor of the tree is further expressed in the fact that each terrace holds several large trees.[7]

The provocative Dutch Pavilion at Expo 2000 in Hanover was based on the idea of "stacked ecosystems." Each floor contained an interior garden with large trees that helped to clean the air and conserve water in the building. The energy system was driven by wind turbines on the roof of the structure.[8]

7.9 Infrastructure and Transportation Systems

In the 1970s, the publication of *Limits to Growth* inspired faculty members at MIT to plan a lecture series on large-scale environmental issues. The lectures introduced a new interdisciplinary area of study called *macroengineering* with the premise that infrastructure and other large-scale projects require input from economists, sociologists, business leaders, politicians, industrialists, environmentalists, artists, architects, planners, scientists, and engineers.[9]

High-speed Train, of the E2
Series, Tokyo train station,
1997.

Frank Davidson, founder of the Channel Tunnel Study Group and a member of
the NASA Exploration Task Force, became director of the MIT Macroengineering
Research Group and helped to create a diverse international organization of large-
scale project developers. As a dedicated environmentalist, he insisted that the
group not only review real proposals, but also discuss visionary designs in energy,
transportation, space studies, and community development.

The group reviewed conceptual designs for environmental infrastructure, such
as Peter Glaser's solar power satellites to provide energy, David Wilson Gordon's
proposal for using computerized cars in urban areas, and Davidson's own idea
of using melting polar ice caps to transform deserts into forests.

240

7.10 High-Speed Trains

In the 1980s, the European community made the decision to revitalize rail transportation. The new technologies available for high-speed trains made them faster
than automobiles, reduced the number of cars in cities, lowered pollution levels,
and provided more efficient systems for most travelers. The new trains also reduced
air travel, which was overbooked in Europe.

Most European countries developed a comprehensive system, not only improving
intercity travel but also upgrading local systems and providing linkage between
commuter and long-distance trains. The sophisticated new systems supported
economic growth and symbolized the concept of unifying the European community. Many cities also built new stations, which were equipped with services for
modern travelers.

There were several definitions of what constituted a high-speed train. Virtually all
high-speed trains were streamlined to reduce friction. The fastest systems required
new tracks, but if there were insufficient funds to build new tracks, a few improvements in the cars enhanced their speed. The new cars were designed to lean, or slide
across the top of the wheelbase when taking a curve, so they did not have to slow
down. The speeds ranged from 125 to 200 miles per hour. The fastest system, mag-

Diagram of the basic
concept of the Eurotunnel.

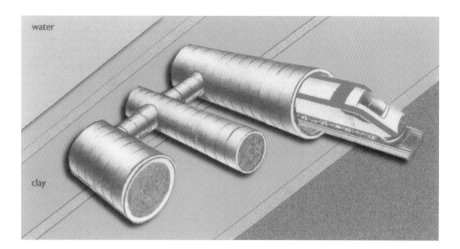

netic levitated trains (maglev), could reach speeds of 350 miles per hour. The
maglev system operates on a magnetic charge, which runs between the train and the
tracks, pulling the cars forward. The cars ride a fraction of an inch above the tracks
to reduce friction. American engineer Tom Stockybrand claimed that if a maglev
train were run through a vacuum tube, it could travel up to 2,000 miles per hour.
His conceptual system is based on the use of a transatlantic vacuum tube built in a
straight line to allow the train to move at maximum speed.

7.11 The Eurotunnel

The development of the European high-speed train system led to the ambitious
project of providing a rail system that linked the British Isles with the rest of the
continent. After reviewing many options, the project was designed as a tunnel system to run underneath the English Channel. The goal of creating a tunnel had a
long history among British engineers and politicians.

The British Isles had been linked to Europe for millions of years. After the Ice Age,
the polar ice caps melted and the sea level rose, submerging most of the land that
connected Britain and mainland Europe. All that remained was a small isthmus,
forming a bridge of land. The isthmus lasted 8,000 years, until it was immersed in
water by a series of floods in the North Sea and Atlantic Ocean. As a result, the
British Isles were separated from Europe by a short distance.

The concept was proposed to Napoleon in 1802 as a way of conquering Britain.
He rejected the idea because the technology for building a gaslit tunnel was uncer-
tain, but the challenge continued to intrigue engineers, who presented other linkage
designs, such as bridges and tubes, throughout the century.

In 1906, a Channel Tunnel bill was proposed in Parliament that also covered a plan
for raising money through an offering of stocks and bonds. The bill was with-
drawn, however, due to lack of support. The concept was proposed again in 1924
and Parliament favored the idea, but Prime Minister Ramsey MacDonald halted
the project after talking to four former prime ministers who opposed the concept.

Finally, in 1986, interest in unifying the European economy overrode all previous qualms. The Eurotunnel was an ideal project to represent the new era. It
became part of the new high-speed train system being developed throughout

241

Europe, providing a ground link between London and Paris in only three hours, and between London and Brussels in two hours and forty-five minutes.

The "Chunnel," as it was dubbed, was a record-breaking project in many areas. It was the longest underwater project ever built, covering a total of 32.2 miles, of which 23.6 miles are beneath the Channel. At a cost of over $15 billion, it was also the largest macroengineering project in history to be financed by private investors.

Dozens of design proposals were submitted. The Channel Tunnel Study Group, an international engineering group, led by Davidson of MIT, created the design that was chosen. Davidson had explored the problem of constructing such a tunnel for nearly forty years. He and his team had compared various kinds of tunnels, immersed tubes, and bridges before choosing the bored-tunnel approach. They proposed building two one-way main tunnels with a third smaller tunnel in the middle of the two branches for maintenance and safety systems.

Most people assumed that the tunnel would contain a highway and cars would be able to drive through the long link. But Davidson's study group convinced the builders to use rail transportation, which would sustain the environmental quality of the project. Though the design was more expensive, they created a ferry train, which would carry cars and buses on a conveyor system.

A substantial investment was also made in the infrastructure connecting the old established routes with the new stations at Sangatte and Westenhanger, which provided the road/rail interface for both freight and passenger services. High-speed train systems were also needed on both sides of the Channel linking the tunnel with the three major destinations of London, Brussels, and Paris. Those segments of the project were funded by the three governments involved.

The Eurotunnel finally opened in 1993. Although the project cost nearly twice its original estimates, the investors believed it would eventually become a financial success. In the first few years, it transported about 20 million passengers and 13 million tons of freight per year.

7.12 Rapid Transit Bus System

In the late 1980s, planners and engineers also explored new concepts for infrastructure and transportation in emerging countries. They looked for ways to reduce the dependence on fossil fuels and encourage the use of public transit systems. They also tried to create innovative planning techniques that integrated transportation with other community development projects.

One of the most dramatic urban transformations occurred in Curitiba, Brazil, which grew from a struggling, third world community of 500,000 people into a sophisticated city of 1.6 million. Its growth was due to the groundbreaking work of Jaime Lerner, an architect and planner, who served three terms as mayor of the city. Through his leadership, Curitiba built a cutting-edge public transportation system, low-income housing, and other public programs. Over time, Curitiba also became a green city with extensive parks, museums, and art installations.

Biarticulated Buses,
used in Curitiba, Brazil.

Lerner was extremely sensitive to the issues of emerging countries. He came from a Polish Jewish family that immigrated to Brazil. After completing his architecture degree, he helped to establish the Institute for Research and Urban Planning of Curitiba. Through this organization, he and his associates developed a master plan that integrated social and economic programs with design and planning proposals to transform the city. Since Curitiba had very low tax revenues, the new concepts also included imaginative ways to finance urban improvements at a lower cost, or if possible, without incurring debt. Curitiba had a large homeless population so Lerner instituted work options that allowed the homeless to trade labor for food. In neighborhoods where the streets were too narrow to be serviced by trash collection vehicles, the program offered food and transportation vouchers to homeless people who cleaned the streets. To increase the landscaped areas of Curitiba, Lerner transformed unused floodplains on the edge of the city into an urban park, using a herd of sheep to "take care" of the grass. He paid homeless people to help keep the park clean and created areas for them to grow vegetables. Lerner instituted low-income housing in middle-class neighborhoods and introduced service jobs for many of the residents. The cross-pollination of income levels improved the lives of both types of citizens.

However, Lerner's most famous accomplishment was the rapid transit bus system, which carried over 2.3 million people daily. There was no budget to develop subways, so he created the concept of the "Speedybus." He convinced Volvo to make long accordion buses, which could carry more people, and these buses made frequent runs along the main streets.[10] Bus shelters made it possible for passengers to pay before the bus arrived, which saved time. The system included six sizes of vehicles with smaller buses being used on minor routes. He later added a zoning plan to increase density along major routes. The buildings on major streets were at least six stories high, which provided enough traffic to support the high-speed system.

243

The MIT Solar Electric Car, built to race in the 2003 World Solar Challenge, a 3,000 km race through the Australian outback.

7.13 Solar Cars

In 1985, sixty owners of solar vehicles met in Switzerland to participate in the first solar car race. Most of the vehicles were motorized bicycles, equipped with a roof or a rear panel containing a solar collector. The race became an annual event, which helped to popularize the concept of alternative vehicles. By the 1990s, car manufacturers and government agencies had awarded grants to several university groups to develop solar-powered automobiles.

The goal was to design cars that expose a large array of photovoltaic cells positioned at the best possible angle to the sun. The solar array established an electric current that flows between the cells. But the system had to be maintained. If a single cell was blocked, it could disrupt the flow and interrupt the power source. The cars were also lightweight and aerodynamically designed. During races, they maintained speeds of 45 to 75 miles per hour.[11]

The MIT solar car Tesseract was built as a high-performance vehicle that could compete in long-distance races. It utilized 2,732 solar cells, which send power to batteries similar to those used in laptop computers. The system powered a 6-horsepower DC motor. The vehicle was structured on a steel space frame, based on a combination of a car/mountain bike suspension system, and weighed only 375 pounds.

The cars used in solar races were not considered heavy enough for normal applications, but the technology led to studies of other types of small solar vehicles like golf carts, motorized wheelchairs, motorcycles, and local delivery cars. Several companies also began research on the concept of solar/electrical hybrid cars, which might lead to broader applications.

7.14 Megastructures

A tall, energy-efficient building in an urban setting where most workers use mass transit may be less energy-intensive than a low, large-floor-plate building in a suburban setting.
—William Browning[12]

In 2003, the National Building Museum in Washington, D. C., held an exhibition on green architecture entitled *Big and Green: Toward Sustainable Architecture in the 21st*

Foster and Partners, Swiss
Re Headquarters, London,
1997–2004.

Century, which confirmed that there was widespread support for green design from
a variety of governments and institutions. The fifty projects demonstrated innovative concepts in site planning, building skins, and mechanical systems, as well as the
overall shape and configuration of structures. Some designs featured exciting new
materials that were lighter and more efficient. Others provided diagrams of new
forms that would enhance air circulation or water conservation systems. Still others
introduced alternative energy systems, such as wind turbines or photovoltaic films.
Collectively, the exhibitors established the fact that virtually all aspects of architecture were being reconsidered.

The exhibition contained several impressive structures developed by Sir Norman
Foster, including the headquarters for the reinsurance company Swiss Re, a sleek
structure shaped like a cigar. As with many iconic buildings, the exterior structure
is so dramatic that it draws attention away from the innovative interior space, but
from an environmental perspective, this building is even more interesting on the
inside. Nine separate gardens were created to improve the air quality of the space.
Spiral light wells provide many employees with access to natural light. The floors
rotate, creating pressure differentials that help to ventilate the space.

The ecological performance is very impressive. The gherkin-shaped tower uses
50 percent less energy than most skyscrapers. Its streamlined shape also helps to

245

Foster and Partners,
Ventiform, model showing
building with integrated wind
turbine, project, 2001.

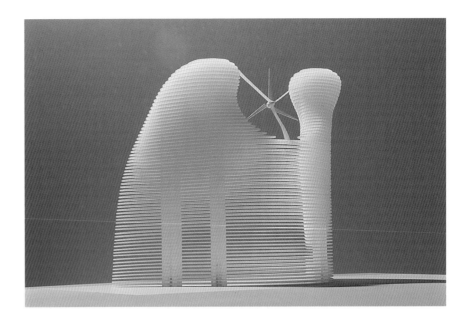

improve the air circulation within the building and reduces the wind pressure at
ground level. The building skin is made of lightweight materials, but the triangular
forms of the curtain wall provide a strong structure, based on the same theory as
the triangular elements of Fuller's geodesic domes.

The exhibition also included Foster and Partners' design for Ventiform, a new
building concept that used wind turbines to generate electricity. Its curving shape
was derived from aerodynamic forms, which enhance the performance of the turbines. The design is a conceptual model, but computer analysis indicates that the
structure might produce enough energy to provide power not only for its own
occupants, but also for an additional 1,500 private homes.[13]

Among the American firms represented were Fox & Fowle Architects (now FX
Fowle); Rafael Vignoli Architects; Cesar Pelli & Associates; Skidmore, Owings &
Merrill; and Kohn Pederson Fox Associates, who were developing green skyscrapers. The Condé Nast Building by Fox & Fowle established new standards for
environmental quality in tall buildings. The developer was the Durst Organization,
an old New York company, which was committed to environmental improvements.
The elegant curtain wall facade of the building contains photovoltaic cells, which
feed directly into the electrical grid. Fuel cells are also integrated in the mechanical
systems of the structure. The building features daylight illumination, water conservation systems, and recycling chutes for all the offices. It even provides 50 percent
more fresh air than required by code.

7.15   Steven Holl

In 1999, Holl was asked to create a new building at MIT. The program for Simmons
Hall included dormitory rooms for 350 students, as well as a lecture hall, performance theater, music rooms, a fitness center, a computer lab, game rooms, a dining
room, and a terrace. The MIT group also wanted the building to have a low-energy
HVAC system.

246

Fox & Fowle, Condé Nast
Building at Four Times Square,
New York, 1999.

Steven Holl, Simmons Hall,
MIT, Cambridge,
Massachusetts, 1999–2004.

Cesar Pelli & Associates,
Solaire, 20 River Terrace,
New York, 2001–2003.

The focus of the design is a massive wall that provides passive solar heating, as well as extensive natural light. It is made of nontoxic materials, including natural concrete and wood and is perforated with numerous small windows based on the idea of a "sponge." It also expresses the theme of a "slice of a city," as it contains an active group of public facilities at street level and a continuous grid of windows on the upper stories as in an urban structure.

Each dormitory room has nine operable windows, which drastically reduce the need for artificial light. The wall is also unusually thick, and the windows are set back, which provides shading from the summer sun, but allows the winter sunlight to enter the room. The massive grid wall is broken in five areas with terraces that bring fresh air and more light into the building. The final result is a powerful urban form that integrates a rich architectural theme with sophisticated environmental systems.

7.16 Solaire

The first major apartment complex with reduced environmental demands was BedZED (Beddington Zero Energy Development), a community in Beddington, England, which opened in 2002. It contains a mixture of eighty-two houses and seventeen apartment units. The buildings were designed to reduce energy demand by 88 percent, lower hot water consumption by more than half, and eliminate about two-thirds of automobile usage by providing public transportation and a fleet of electric cars owned by the community. By 2006, some of these systems had failed, and BedZED was forced to temporarily plug into the public utility systems.

In 2003, the Battery Park City Authority opened Solaire, a large apartment complex designed by Cesar Pelli & Associates in lower Manhattan. The twenty-seven-story building contains 294 housing units and commercial facilities at street level. The complex incorporates two types of alternative energy, a geothermal system and photovoltaic cells, which, in combination, made it 35 percent more efficient than state codes required. It also includes water conservation systems,

Tadao Ando, Rokko
housing development, Kobe,
Japan. Project developed in
three stages from 1981–2003.

which utilized 50 percent less water than most apartment houses, and it has an
advanced HVAC system that is free of ozone-depleting refrigerants. The building
provides community services, including the water used to maintain an adjacent
park. The crowning feature of the complex is a densely planted roof garden and
outdoor area. The Solaire project was the first high-rise residential building to
adopt New York's new environmental codes. It also demonstrates that a tall residential building constructed with government funds could provide humane and
intelligent facilities.

7.17 Rokko Housing

In 1995, a severe earthquake struck the city of Kobe, Japan. Over 5,000 people were
killed, and 300,000 residents were left homeless. After the disaster, the mayor's
office developed a new vision to reconstruct the city. The plan included the building
of Port Island, a large container port facility, the creation of a new convention
center, and the expansion of the highways and airport.

It also featured the development of new housing and cultural facilities. The master plan of the project called for a museum, the Hyogo Prefectural Museum of Modern Art, as well as a large garden and outdoor memorial monument to the earthquake victims. Architect Tadao Ando was chosen to plan and design the entire complex.

In his early years, Ando developed a strong relationship with the city of Kobe. In the 1970s, he built several private houses in the Hyogo Prefecture in Kobe. From 1981 to 2003, he designed a series of three large housing projects, which were built into the hillsides of the Rokko area of Kobe, featuring dramatic roof gardens and public facilities, such as a kindergarten, a swimming pool, and a daycare center for the elderly. In 1986, he added a chapel on Mount Rokko, which became another important meeting place for the community.

In 1995, Ando was awarded the Pritzker Prize, which included a $100,000 grant. He donated the grant to the city of Kobe to help with the earthquake reconstruction. In the next few years, he developed the museum and memorial site, as well as the final phase of his housing project. The dramatic roof terraces of the Rokko housing introduce a green dimension into his work.

7.18 Urban Planting

In 2007, the New York City Department of Parks and Recreation published a report that examined the economic value of planting trees in cities. For two years, over 1,000 volunteers conducted a census of trees in the city. They discovered that New York had nearly 600,000 trees in public areas as well as 4.5 million trees in parks and on private property. Specialists then analyzed the economic benefits of the trees, based on the STRATUM program created by scientists at the U.S. Forest Service and University of California, Davis. The report examined the degree to which trees removed carbon dioxide from the air, saved energy, and increased real estate values in the urban area and concluded that trees provided $122 million of value to New York City each year.

Similar studies were conducted by national research groups in other areas of the country. Some of the studies also measured how much trees reduced stormwater runoff, controlled erosion, eliminated heat island effects, and cleaned the air. According to the U.S. Department of Agriculture, the effect was substantial. The study concluded that one acre of forest absorbs six tons of carbon dioxide and puts out four tons of oxygen.

Several European cities conducted their own landscape experiments. In the 1980s, the industrial city of Stuttgart launched an aggressive program of plantings intended to reduce smog and lower energy demands. The city expanded the program in 1993 by commissioning the design firm Von Gerkan, Marg and Partners to develop a new master plan. The design included the creation of a light rail system and a long linear park to improve air circulation, and by the year 2000, there were measurable improvements in Stuttgart's air quality and reductions in energy demand.

Many cities invested in public parks, transforming abandoned industrial areas, such as depressed waterfront sites or unused railroad yards, into appealing green spaces. Unlike the parks of the nineteenth century, the new urban parks also included museums, cultural centers, marketplaces, and information facilities. They were

Aerial view of housing estate at Brondby, on the outskirts of Copenhagen.

not just considered recreational spaces; they were also seen as tourist attractions that stimulated the economy, provided jobs, improved public health, and enhanced the quality of urban life.

7.19 Brondby Housing Circles

New housing concepts were introduced in European suburban areas as well. Instead of the traditional grid or organic form, architects in Brondby, a suburb of Copenhagen, experimented with a circular plan with twenty-four houses in each circle. A single driveway leads to a circular parking area in the center of each ringed community. The design featured generous lawns and abundant open parkland. Since the planning concept reduced the number of streets and driveways, many of the areas usually occupied by road systems are replaced by planted areas.

Despite these advantages, the project received mixed reviews. Some critics felt the circular plan was ultimately confining, forcing a sense of community on the houses that were grouped together and destroying the sense of privacy. The Brondby suburb had a clear environmental flaw as well. Its low-density plan forced most residents to rely on private cars rather than public transportation.

7.20 Beijing Olympic Site

In 2002, Sasaki Associates, Inc., was selected to create the master plan of the 2008 Beijing Olympic site. Their concept provides not only a dramatic design for an Olympic Green; it also creates a promenade throughout the city. Beijing officials had already decided to establish a linear park along a historical axis of important sites throughout the city leading past Tiananmen Square and the Forbidden City with its Royal Garden to the new Olympic site along the outer ring road. Sasaki Associates, an interdisciplinary firm with landscape designers, civil engineers, planners, and

Aerial view of the Olympic
Green, Beijing. Masterplan
by Sasaki Associates Inc.
National Stadium by Herzog &
de Meuron, 2008.

architects, presented a complete environmental proposal. The plan establishes a canal
or open water-transfer system, which leads to a Forest Park containing wetlands,
forests, and a lake. The Forest Lake provides habitats for a variety of flora and fauna.
The forest will reduce air pollution in the city and increase biodiversity.[14]

The master plan also establishes the dramatic cultural axis linking the ancient
historical sites with the new modern facilities. The Olympic Gate, placed between
the third and fourth ring roads, provides a formal entry to the athletic center.
Proceeding northward, the axis passes the new facilities for the Asian Games, the
National Stadium by Herzog & de Meuron, and the National Swimming Center
built by PTW Architects in collaboration with CSCEC and the Arup Group.

The Olympic National Stadium was conceived as a symbol of a bowl of rice or a
"collective bowl" that could seat 100,000 people. The concept was developed in
collaboration with the China Architecture Design Institute, Beijing Architecture
Design Institute, the Japanese group AXS, and the Tsinghua University Architecture Design Institute. Herzog & de Meuron consulted with Beijing artist Ai Weiwei
on the creation of an innovative building skin. The latticelike system symbolizes
the idea of a tree or a bird's nest—both images rooted in Chinese poetry. The
enormous stadium has no interior columns that could interfere with audience sight-
lines or detract from the spectacle. The lightweight structure is comprised of steel
box girders and a transparent weatherproof membrane composed of inflated cushions. The air-filled cushions provide good insulation without inhibiting the flow of
natural light, and the structure provides a huge span for the indoor/outdoor space.

Millennium Park, Chicago, completed 2004.

7.21 Millennium Park

Millennium Park in Chicago features a music and dance theater designed by Frank Gehry; large sculptures by Anish Kapoor and Jaume Piensa; gardens designed by Kathryn Gustafson; as well as an ice-skating rink, playing fields, fountains, pavilions, and architectural elements. It also features a large plaza with restaurants, galleries, umbrella-covered tables, and an underground parking area.

Opened in 2004, this extraordinary public center is the result of more than a century of planning and discussion to develop the site. Daniel Burnham, Frederick Law Olmsted, and Eliel Saarinen all participated at various stages prior to the master plan by Skidmore, Owings & Merrill. The final form of Millennium Park was developed between 1997 and 2004 through a difficult process of integrating various visions for this important public site. The combination of park and cultural facilities provides a unique green space for Chicago and presents a new direction in park planning, which soon became a model for other cities.

7.22 "Central Park"

In 1998, the Los Angeles firm Clive Wilkinson Architects (CWA) planned the new headquarters for the advertising agency TBWA/Chiat/Day in a warehouse on the outskirts of Los Angeles. The design was based on the concept of an "advertising city," or an urban neighborhood like Greenwich Village, and on the principles of sustainable design. The entire project has an indoor/outdoor quality with treelined interior "streets," a basketball court, snack bars, and a large open area called "Central Park," containing trees, old-fashioned British telephone booths, and picnic tables.

Most of the offices are on a lightweight steel structure, three stories high, which forms a streetlike facade on one side of the park. The structure is painted bright yellow to enliven the space, and most of the walls are made of glass, which provides views into the offices. The layered concept of the design encourages a sense of community

253

Clive Wilkinson Architects (CWA), Offices of the advertising firm, TBWA/Chiat/Day, based on the concept of "Central Park." Los Angeles, 1998.

that appeals to the employees.[15] The lightweight steel structure and exposed mechanical systems are a reference to the early loft renovations of lower Manhattan, but the industrial quality is softened by the use of wood, plants, and environmental materials. The workstations are ergonomic systems, developed in collaboration with Steelcase.

7.23 Lightweight, Portable, and Tensile Structures

Industrial fabrics rarely if ever are designed for aesthetic effect, yet they seem beautiful largely because they share the precision, delicacy, pronounced texture, and exact repetition of detail characteristic of twentieth-century machine art.
—Arthur Drexler[16]

In 1956, Arthur Drexler, a curator at MoMA, developed an exhibition called *Textiles USA* introducing innovative materials, such as plastics, metals, and molded plywood, and fabrics that inspired a variety of lightweight structures, including tensile, pneumatic, and inflatable designs.

Fifty years later, the Cooper-Hewitt National Design Museum presented *Extreme Textiles*, highlighting elegant new materials that were revolutionizing the role of lightweight materials in many fields. The exhibit included industrial fabrics, structural fabrics, and smart fabrics for special applications, such as medical devices or NASA spacesuits. The exhibition also presented new lightweight materials with environmental benefits. Some could resist fire, endure extreme temperature changes, and bear the pressure of intense winds or heavy rain. These materials were composed of several layers of fabric with air spaces between layers for additional insulation. Most required less energy in the manufacturing process and were designed to be reused or recycled.

Also on view were new smart fabrics that featured nanotechnology and electronic textiles that had "intelligent polymers;" for example, some contained sensors for monitoring light and weather conditions. There were also prototypes of thin-film solar collectors, which could reduce the price of solar energy production to a fragment of its usual cost.

Another new direction was the development of plastic carbon fiber, a new material that was being used to reduce the weight of airplanes, bridges, and buildings. Urs Meier of the Swiss Federal Laboratories had spent many years strengthening the strands of resin-impregnated carbon fiber material so that it would be stronger than

Asymptote Architects, A3 module, created for Knoll A3 Furniture Systems.

steel. It was also designed to resist deterioration to last longer and require less maintenance than most materials. This powerful material was being used in Boeing's Dreamliner. Architect Peter Testa and his research group at MIT developed an idea for a conceptual skyscraper made of plastic carbon fiber, which provided environmental efficiencies.

Throughout the twentieth century, architects and designers developed concepts for lightweight, portable furniture that was inexpensive to manufacture. The trend began in the 1920s in the work of designers such as Marcel Breuer, who introduced chairs made of tubular steel. In the 1930s, architect Alvar Aalto designed bent plywood chairs based on similar principles. The 1940s saw Eero Saarinen, Charles Eames, and Harry Bertoia develop a variety of furniture concepts using lightweight materials, such as molded plywood, fiberglass, and wire mesh. In the 1950s, Danish designer Arne Jacobsen's Ant chair also used tubular steel and molded plywood. Postmodernists like Gaetano Pesce found their niche with inflatable chairs in bold colors in the 1960s.

The use of bold colors continued in the 1970s in the work of Joe Colombo and Verner Panton who developed a variety of plastic chairs, and in the 1970s and 1980s, Frank Gehry designed chairs made of corrugated cardboard. In the 1990s, Philippe Starck also developed lightweight furniture using polyurethane and plastics. His Ghost Chair, made of clear plastic, is the ultimate expression of portable furniture because it is almost invisible.

In recent years, designers who were conscious of environmental issues have been exploring lightweight materials. In the spirit of such systems, Lise Ann Couture and Hani Rashid of Asymptote Architects created Knoll A3 Furniture System, a workstation based on movable parts and inspired by the interior elements of airplanes. The most elegant part of the design is the outer shell, which is made of translucent nylon fabric stretched on an aluminum frame.[17]

255

FTL Happold, Pier Six
Concert Pavilions, Baltimore,
Maryland, 1991.

7.24 FTL

In the 1980s, a group of architects who had become interested in tensile structures as students at Cornell reconvened as the FTL group. Unlike most design students of that era, who were absorbed in explorations of the white box, this group was intrigued with the idea of doing more with less. One of their first large public structures was the Pier Six Concert Pavilion, a dramatic performance space on the Baltimore waterfront, built in 1981. The wavy fabric roof structure had an intended life span of only five years, but it was so popular, the city asked them to rebuild the interior walls so it would last at least ten years. In 1991, the Baltimore group returned to FTL and commissioned them to build a new permanent structure.

In 1993, FTL developed a tent for Fashion Week in New York City that was designed to be erected several times a year in Bryant Park. After each event, it could be disassembled and stored for the next occasion. The structure, Seventh on 6th Fashion Village, provides a dramatic interior space, the elegant fabric structure expressing the fashion theme. Its unique design also offers the same advantages as the Crystal Palace, for its construction does not damage the landscape of the park.

In 1996, FTL created a tent for the Atlanta Olympic village composed of a sleek white polyester fabric that could also serve as a movie screen for colorful projections during live events. Inside the tent, they built a flexible structure with movable elevators and floors. The building was designed to travel and was later disassembled and sent to Olympic sites in Nagano, Sydney, and Salt Lake City.

In 2000, FTL developed a concept for a Recyclable, Portable Fabric Skyscraper, a twelve-story office building that could easily be moved. Windows utilize a light-weight fabric membrane stretched elegantly across the facade. Conceived as a structure for disaster relief, it requires only two weeks for construction, and could also be quickly disassembled and moved on trucks to a new location. The construction concept may provide a new direction for the construction of tall buildings in the future.[18]

FTL Happold, Seventh on 6th Fashion Village, New York, 1993.

FTL Design Engineering Studio, Recyclable, Portable Fabric Skyscraper, project, 2000.

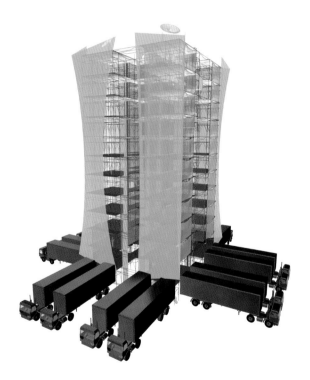

257

7.25 Shigeru Ban

In the 1980s and 1990s, architect Shigeru Ban invented a new type of structure based on cardboard or paper tubes. He chose to use paper as a basic material because the tubes are inexpensive and can easily be replaced or recycled. Ban began using paper tubes in exhibition designs, for a display of Alvar Aalto's work in 1986 and later for that of Emilio Ambasz. In 1989, he built his first paper-tube structure: an outdoor pavilion at a design exposition in Nagoya, Japan. His first permanent structure in this material is the Library of a Poet, 1991.

Shigeru Ban, Japan Pavilion
at Expo 2000, Hannover,
Germany.

In 1995, Ban founded the Voluntary Architects Network (VAN), an organization that introduced inexpensive paper-tube housing in several cities damaged by earthquakes. His experiments were so successful that building authorities in Japan established a new category of construction standards for paper structures.[19]

Ban was later asked to design the Japanese Pavilion at Expo 2000 in Hanover, Germany, whose theme was sustainable design based on Rio de Janiero's Earth Summit. For this pavilion, he created a 3,100-square-foot space, covered by a curved grid structure composed of paper tubes. The structure was reinforced by timber frame ladder arches and intersecting rafters to stiffen the shell. The roof membrane was composed of a fireproof paper, reinforced with fiberglass and polyethylene film. Slim lines of transparent openings were located along the curved ribs of the structure to bring light into the space. This extraordinary design demonstrated that his innovative concepts could be applied to large-scale structures as well.[20]

7.26 Disaster Relief

Though some progress in environmental awareness had been made, it was not until the beginning of the twenty-first century that the public finally realized the extreme dangers posed by global warming. Several severe storms, such as Hurricane Katrina, demonstrated the impact of climate change and made the public aware of the vulnerability of most urban areas worldwide.

The UN Refugee Agency (UNHCR) report, 2005 Global Refugee Trends, examined the living conditions of displaced persons and analyzed the conditions of several types of refugees: those who were seeking asylum from wars or political conflicts, those who were left homeless by environmental disasters, and other displaced people, such as the millions of children left orphaned by the AIDS virus. According to the report, there were 20.8 million people living in refugee-like situations, but other reports, which included broader parameters, suggested that as many 50 million people were displaced.[21]

Refugee Camp, northwest
of Kukes, near Tirana,
Albania.

A large portion of the report covers the subject of environmental refugees who have
lost their homes through droughts, flooding, agricultural disruption, erosion, or
severe storms. The estimates for the future appeared even more disturbing. Members
of the Intergovernmental Panel on Climate Change, an agency that works with the
UN, estimated that by 2050, there might be as many as 150 million environmental
refugees, if the rate of global warming continued.

One of the most important relief organizations is Habitat for Humanity. As of 2007,
this extraordinary organization had built 200,000 houses, which shelter more than
a million people. However, the number of displaced persons worldwide was so
overwhelming that other types of organizations were badly needed. In 2004, the
International Child and Youth Care Network conducted surveys that indicated over
100 million children were living and working on the streets of emerging nations.
They also drew attention to the fact that there were millions of homeless children
living on the streets of Europe and North America, who also needed shelter.

In 1999, writer Kate Stohr and architect Cameron Sinclair established Architecture
for Humanity to develop structures for disaster relief from the war in Yugoslavia, but
they soon realized that a broader effort was needed. Many designs already existed, but
there was no central network that could provide an interface between organizations
like the UNHCR and architectural offices capable of handling emergency situations.

Stohr and Sinclair began by launching two design competitions to help raise funds
and publicize their concept among architects and nonprofit groups. The first competition addressed the problem of creating transitional housing for refugees returning
to Kosovo and the second focused on the issue of designing mobile clinics to combat
HIV/AIDS in Sub-Saharan Africa. From the hundreds of international entries, a
few were viable for development. Shigeru Ban adapted his Paper Log House to
provide some disaster relief in Turkey. His office worked with manufacturers to
develop technologies for waterproofing and strengthening the new buildings and
adapted the designs to suit weather conditions in Turkey, India, and Japan.

259

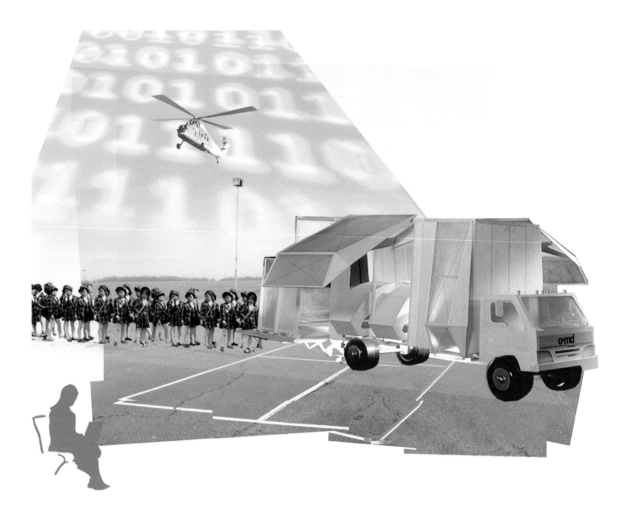

Jennifer Siegal, Office of
Mobile Design, iMobile,
a self-contained vehicle that
unfolds to provide a variety
of functions.

The competition also recognized many portable designs that provided water and
electricity in troubled areas. The Clean Hub System, by John Dwyer of Shelter
Architecture, was a system of small structures that could be brought to campsites
to provide rainwater collection, water filtration, and public bathrooms. Photovoltaic
panels provided enough energy for the various tasks. The facilities he developed
could also be used in cities lacking adequate water systems.[22]

The concept of creating mobile health clinics for remote villages was not a new idea.
Hospital ships were first used in the nineteenth century, during the American Civil
War. AIDS organizations and groups like Doctors Without Borders also traveled in
medical vehicles in the twentieth century. However, this design competition inspired
ideas for lightweight, portable structures and vehicles that could provide either
disaster relief or regular medical services in deprived areas.

Several successful examples were designed by Jennifer Siegal of the Office of Mobile
Design in Los Angeles including Eco Lab, an 8-by-35-foot trailer containing a
multimedia educational facility for teaching children about the environment, and
iMobile, a vehicle that unfolds to provide an expandable structure used for medical
facilities, educational presentations, or refugee services.[23]

7.27 Alternative
Infrastructure

There is no reason, for instance, why Brazil should not develop from the start a com-
pletely smokeless industrialization providing a high standard of living. The smoke char-
acterizing early industrialization of the North is now a mark of unattended inefficiency
to northern engineers—important byproducts are being wasted, environmental frictions
are being increased.
—R. Buckminster Fuller[24]

In 1997, representatives from over 160 countries met in Kyoto, Japan, to develop
an international agreement to reduce global warming, which led to the Kyoto
Protocol, a treaty developed through the United Nations Framework Convention
on Climate Change. Although the treaty had several flaws, it was ratified by the
governments of 169 countries and political entities. They agreed to the goal of
eliminating 55 percent of global greenhouse emissions (GHG). China, Australia,
and the United States were the only major countries that did not sign, but even
those nations acknowledged the need to reduce the utilization of fossil fuels.

The treaty divided the member nations into developed countries and developing
countries. The developed countries agreed to reduce their GHG emissions to about
5 percent below their 1990 levels. In accepting the treaty, the developed nations also
agreed to submit a greenhouse inventory report each year showing their degree of
progress, beginning in 2008. Any country that failed to meet its obligations would
be fined. The developing nations were not restricted, but for each alternative system that they implemented, they were rewarded with "carbon credits," which could
be sold to developed countries.

The Kyoto Protocol was far from a perfect agreement, but it was a first step toward
a solution. Its goal was the "stabilization of greenhouse gas concentrations in the
atmosphere at a level that would prevent dangerous anthropogenic interference
with the climate system."[25]

By 2006, statistics indicated that several alternative systems were being utilized on
a large scale. Some countries had built new dams to produce hydroelectric power.
Others were creating windmills to lower their dependence on fossil fuels. The use
of wind power grew more than 400 percent between 2000 and 2006. It became the
fastest growing source of energy in the world.[26]

7.28 Three Gorges Dam

In 1994, the Chinese government began construction of the Three Gorges Dam
at a critical site on the Yangtze River. Designed to produce 18.3 gigawatts of power,
it would be the largest hydroelectric plant in the world, supplying 11 to 15 percent
of China's energy demand.

This macro-project was probably the most controversial design in modern history.
Environmental groups said it would destroy several endangered species and ruin
the ecosystems of the Yangtze River and eliminate a major geological site, similar
to Niagara Falls in importance. Sociologists and humanitarians argued that the dam
would displace over 1.3 million people and destroy several ancient communities that
housed historical temples, tombs, and cultural sites.

Many technical specialists opposed the dam because it was sited on a seismic fault
that could be compromised by the weight of the structure. They warned that if the
dam ever broke, it would ruin millions of lives and flood numerous communities

Three Gorges Dam on the
Yangtze River in China.

along the Yangtze River. They also claimed that the reservoir would accumulate an enormous amount of silt, which might destroy the effectiveness of the system.[27]

Several environmental groups also objected to the dam project itself. They argued that hydroelectric power was indeed a renewable resource, but it caused some negative effects. The microbiotic activity of the dying vegetation in the area would produce small amounts of greenhouse gases, about 5 percent of a normal power plant. However, most environmentalists were glad that the Chinese had chosen hydroelectric power instead of coal, which was the only other realistic alternative.

Several other designs were considered, including an American proposal for three mini-dams that would have produced the same amount of energy without destroying an important geological site or disrupting so many communities. The Chinese government rejected the proposal in favor of the symbolic image of the massive Three Gorges design.

7.29 Wind Farms

When modern wind power systems were first developed in the 1980s, they were expensive and inefficient in comparison to fossil fuels. However, by the year 2000, the price had dropped by 80 percent, and by 2004, the cost per unit output of wind energy was almost the same as coal or natural gas. And unlike fossil fuels, wind turbines required almost no maintenance.

Banning Pass Wind Farm,
California.

Two types of wind systems were developed: onshore and offshore turbines. Most communities preferred offshore turbines. Although they sometimes caused minor disturbances in port activities and aquatic life, they were less intrusive than the onshore ones. The onshore systems were usually built on wind farms in the mountains or coastal areas, near cities. As a general rule, wind generators become practical in areas that have an average wind speed of at least 10 mph. Before installing turbines, prospective sites were often tested for as long as a year to map the best locations for maximum efficiency.

263

Wind turbines in high altitudes are more effective because of the reduction in drag caused by the Earth's surface. The usual assumption was that if the altitude of the turbine was doubled, the wind speed would increase by about 10 percent, and the energy production would grow by 34 percent.

Local residents and environmentalists opposed the installation of wind farms on some sites, arguing that windmills create noise, destroy the quality of the landscape, affect birds and wildlife, and change the microclimate of the immediate area. Despite the objections, the use of wind power became the fastest growing system in the United States, especially in California. It was even more popular in India, China, and several European countries.

By 2006, wind turbines were supplying 20 percent of the energy requirements of Denmark, 9 percent of Spain's energy demand, and 7 percent of Germany's needs. That year, Denmark announced plans to expand their offshore wind farms to meet half of their energy demands. Large installations were also planned throughout Canada and the United States.

7.30 Indoor Agriculture

Indoor Cattle Farm
near Fukuyama, Japan.

Another great challenge was the development of new techniques for producing food. Based on current systems, whenever the population increases by a billion people, an additional 1.5 million square miles of farmland is needed to provide food. But trends indicated that the global inventory of farmland was decreasing. Each year, several million acres of arable land were converted into housing, industry, or commercial structures. Additional acreage was lost from contamination, decreased water supply, and destructive storms. As a result, agricultural industries were searching for new techniques to compensate for the lack of fertile land. Urban areas, which require daily deliveries of meat, dairy, vegetables, and fruit were especially difficult to service, as Ebenezer Howard had predicted a century ago.

However, it was becoming increasingly hard to find farmland in close proximity to cities. One important new alternative was indoor farming. Some enterprising entrepreneurs in the Honshu area of Japan began experimenting with indoor cattle farms in huge warehouses. Though there were many problems with this concept, the first years of the experiment were successful.

Japanese farmers also built vinyl greenhouses that produced much higher yields of fruits and vegetables than traditional farms. The only requirements for indoor farms were structures that provided warm temperatures, natural light, and adequate water for the crops. They enclosed much less area than outdoor farms, but they could operate twelve months a year, twenty-four hours a day, and thus produce many times the yield of traditional agriculture. For most crops, one indoor acre of farmland was equal to about four to six acres of outdoor fields. Some crops, such as strawberries, produced as much as twenty times more yield in greenhouse facilities.

A flying car from the
film *Blade Runner*, 1982.
Director: Ridley Scott.

In addition to higher yields, there were many other benefits associated with indoor
agriculture. Crops could be organically grown without pesticides or fertilizers.
They were not vulnerable to the destruction caused by inclement weather conditions,
such as droughts or storms. They could even produce their own energy, sometimes
creating more energy than they consumed, which could be returned to the local
power grid.

However, the greatest advantage was the ability to develop a farm in almost any
location. Indoor farms could be built in challenging environments, such as northern
Canada. They could also be constructed near cities, which would reduce the need
for daily transportation from rural areas. As the technology improved, indoor
farms played an increasingly important role in food production.

7.31 The Third Industrial
       Revolution

In 1982, film director Ridley Scott produced *Blade Runner*, a powerful film full of
haunting images of a future city burdened by cultural and environmental problems.
It was based on Philip K. Dick's provocative novel *Do Androids Dream of Electric
Sheep?* and explores the role of machines in society through a story about robots
imitating human behavior.

The robots, or "replicants," are a metaphor for lower-class humans who are
employed in undesirable jobs. Their complex characters inevitably raise the question, what does it mean to be human? The theme is also reminiscent of Mary
Shelley's novel *Frankenstein*, as some of the replicants become killers after mixing
with human society.

The novel offers a vision of a postapocalyptic world that has survived a nuclear war.
Some of the population lives in space colonies to avoid contamination from nuclear
dust. They have replicant servants with human characteristics, which have a life span
of four years. They also have robot pets, such as electric sheep. The plot focuses

A vision of future Los Angeles from the film *Blade Runner*, 1982. Director: Ridley Scott.

on four rebellious replicants who return to Earth hoping to free themselves from their slavish existence. They also hope to find their creator and convince him to extend their lives.

Although *Blade Runner* did not have the landmark status of Fritz Lang's *Metropolis*, the themes are strangely similar. Like *Metropolis*, the film portrays the struggle between a powerful businessman and his exploited laborers. The characters include a cyber-genius, much like the inventor in *Metropolis*. It also features a romance similar to the one in *Metropolis*. The couple includes a replicant (a lower-class robot who thinks she is human) and a policeman, who becomes an intermediary between the two worlds.

The film also portrays a clash of cultures that seems impossible to bridge. It depicts a failing lower-class society, struggling to exist in a polluted, crime-ridden environment. Their lives contrast sharply with the privileges of the wealthy class. The story is enhanced by costumes, special effects, and imaginative sets, and is full of postmodern references ranging from futuristic skyscrapers to refurbished lofts and ethnic neighborhoods.

Much of the action takes place in crumbling urban buildings, which are based on film noir detective stories of the 1950s. Nearly every scene has a decayed, smoky atmosphere, the designs include flying cars that leave a trail of pollution. The costumes are also diverse. The upper-class characters wear elegant 1930s art deco couture, while the rebelling replicants sport offbeat 1980s punk costumes, high-tech spacesuits, or working-class 1950s clothing.

As in *Metropolis*, the creators of *Blade Runner* express both a fascination with technology and a fear of its impact on society and the environment. Although many changes have occurred in the last century, many of the same problems still exist. In the film, the future city is again portrayed as a vast metropolitan region of infinite scale. The limitless sprawl of development and the constant atmospheric pollution is a direct reflection of the problems of real cities.

As the twenty-first century began, architects and planners faced many of the same issues that were present a hundred years ago, but the challenges were occurring on a much larger scale. The global population had tripled and was expected to reach 10 billion people by 2050. If this estimate was correct, the actual population would be 50 percent higher than in the year 2000. Statisticians also predicted the demand for food, housing, and resources would grow at an even faster pace because by 2050, most emerging nations would have a higher standard of living and a greater level of consumption.

Architects, industrialists, and political leaders began to call for a new Industrial Revolution based on sustainable systems. They advocated clean manufacturing systems, new transportation systems, more efficient structures, and better environmental policies. They also insisted on new product concepts that conserved materials and reduced energy demand.

In 2001, William McDonough and Michael Braungart created the documentary film *The Next Industrial Revolution*, presenting several case studies of major corporations that had adopted green systems. They had eliminated the use of toxic chemicals, built water conservation systems, and reduced their energy demand. Although the transformation was a costly process, it was a good investment. Some of the environmental improvements had saved millions of dollars.

In 2004, architect Bruce Mau published *Massive Change*, an optimistic book about the future. It provided interviews with thirty-two experts in new areas of technology and design, including environmentalists, architects, planners, scientists, and engineers who were creating sustainable systems. It begins with the question, "Now that we can do anything, what will we do?"[28]

In 2007, José Manuel Barroso, commission chief of the European Union, announced the beginning of a new Industrial Revolution, based on energy conservation. He listed three goals for a unified energy policy. The first goal was to create more internal energy sources that would free Europe from geopolitical pressures. The second goal was to increase the use of low-carbon systems or renewable resources. The third goal was to reduce energy demand by 20 percent.[29]

Business leaders urged the development of new systems that could reverse environmental damage. Sir Richard Branson of the Virgin Group offered $25 million to anyone who could create a reliable system for removing one billion tons of carbon from the atmosphere each year. His effort to reduce global warming was supported by former American vice president Al Gore. As a result of their campaign, several scientists proposed new kinds of infrastructure to reverse environmental problems.

Engineers offered a concept for changing weather patterns by putting large balloons with mirrored surfaces in orbit. The mirrors would focus sunlight on troubled locations around the world. They could burn off fog at airports, push storms out to the sea, or lower the intensity of hurricanes by creating high pressure systems. They could also illuminate cities with a few extra hours of sunlight at night, which would reduce energy demand.

A physicist at UCLA proposed a plan for rebuilding the ozone layer by sending low-energy electrons into it from a platform in the upper atmosphere. The electrons would collide with chlorine atoms and alter their structure so they could not bind with ozone molecules.

There were also new concepts for removing carbon from the atmosphere. Several scientists proposed the use of magnetized particles to draw the carbon out into space. Others suggested increasing the plant life in the ocean, which would remove more carbon from the air.

All of these ideas were controversial, reflecting the divergent opinions of the environmental community. Some scientists were opposed to tampering with the chemical structure of the atmosphere. Others were against concepts that might disrupt existing ecosystems. However, despite the differences of opinion, the third Industrial Revolution had clearly begun. The new technologies were based on environmental considerations, not just the profit motive. The new industrial processes addressed the complete life cycle of a product, not only its initial concept. The new philosophy endorsed a variety of solutions, not just a single system.

The new architectural approach was also different. Unlike in previous eras, it did not just contain a single aesthetic style. Sustainable designs could be created in many different forms, ranging from passive solar structures with grass roofs to wind-powered skyscrapers. The new transportation concepts were also diverse. Engineers at MIT created a variety of vehicles, such as foldable electronic scooters, stackable cars, and solar-powered delivery vans. Some of the designs were targeted for emerging nations; others were conceived for industrialized countries.

There were also new urban projects, based on environmental planning. In January 2008, Foster + Partners announced plans for constructing a carbon-free city. This ambitious project, now being built in the desert environment of Abu Dhabi, is called Masdar City, a name meaning "the source" in Arabic. It was designed as a city that produced zero waste and utilized carbon free transportation systems— a full-scale model of an urban alternative. It is projected to open in late 2009.

Though the problems of the future are extremely complex, as this book is being published, the outlook is hopeful. Well-established architects are more committed to solving environmental issues than previous generations. Governments and corporations have economic incentives for building better systems. The high price of oil, the rising costs of resources, and the overwhelming losses due to environmental disasters have made it imperative to develop alternatives.

The emerging generation of young people is being educated to institute cultural changes. They are more comfortable with new technology, more open to experiments, and more adaptable than prior generations. According to an article in *The Sun Herald*, it took thirty-eight years for radio to reach 50 million people. Television reached the same number of people in only thirteen years. The Internet needed just four years to acquire 50 million users. Based on this accelerating trend, the prognosis for cultural change is cautiously optimistic.

Notes

1. Norman Myers, *The Gaia Atlas of Future Worlds* (London: Doubleday, 1990), 38.

2. Donella H. Meadows, Dennis L. Meadows, Jorgen Randers, and William W. Behrens III, *Limits to Growth* (New York: Universe Books, 1972), 23.

3. William McDonough and Michael Braungart, *Cradle to Cradle* (New York: North Point Press, 2002), 125.

4. James Wines, *Green Architecture* (Koln: Taschen GmbH, 2000), 73.

5. David Gissen, ed., *Big and Green* (New York: Princeton Architectural Press in association with the National Building Museum, New York, 2002), 100.

6. Francesca Prina and Elena Demartini, *One Thousand Years of World Architecture* (Milan: Mondadori Electa Spa, 2005), 360-61.

7. Marie-Ange Brayer and Beatrice Simonot, eds., *Archilab's Future House* (New York: Thames & Hudson, Inc., 2002), 158.

8. Gissen, 94-96.

9. Frank P. Davidson and Lawrence C. Meador, *Macro-engineering: Global Infrastructure Solutions: Massachusetts Institute of Technology: The Brunel Lectures 1983-1992* (West Sussex, England: Ellis Horwood Limited, 1992), xiii-xvi.

10. Arthur Lubow, "The Road to Curitiba," in *The New York Times Magazine*, May 20, 2007.

11. "Solar Vehicle," Wikipedia, http://en.wikipedia.org/wiki/Solar_car.

12. William Browning in dialogue with Robert F. Fox, Jr. and Bruce S. Fowle, quoted in Nina Rappaport, "It's Not Easy Building Green," in Gissen, 180.

13. Gissen, 20.

14. Layla Dawson, *China's New Dawn* (Munich: Prestel Verlag, 2005), 150-53.

15. Jeremy Myerson and Philip Ross, *The 21st Century Office* (New York: Rizzoli, 2003), 192-97.

16. Matilda McQuaid, *Extreme Textiles: Designing for High Performance* (New York: Princeton Architectural Press, in association with National Design Museum Smithsonian Institution, New York, 2005), 12.

17. John K. Waters, *Blobitecture* (Gloucester, MA: Rockport Publishers, Inc., 2003), 119.

18. Robert Kronenburg, *FTL* (West Sussex, England: Academy Editions, 1997), 8.

19. Matilda McQuaid, *Shigeru Ban* (London: Phaidon Press Limited, 2003), 14, 40.

20. McQuaid, 67.

21. Architecture for Humanity, ed., *Design Like You Give a Damn* (New York: Metropolis Books, 2006), 59-60.

22. *Design Like You Give a Damn*, 289.

23. Jennifer Siegal, ed., *Mobile* (New York: Princeton Architectural Press, 2002), 116-24.

24. R. Buckminster Fuller, *Critical Path* (New York: St. Martin's Press, 1981), 306.

25. "Kyoto Protocol," Wikipedia, http://en.wikipedia.org/wiki/Kyoto_Protocol.

26. "Wind Power," Wikipedia, http://en.wikipedia.org/wiki/Wind_Power.

27. Mau, 70-71.

28. Mau, 15.

29. Jose Manuel Barruso, Commission Chief of the European Union, on BBC News Channel, January 10, 2007, http://news.bbc.co.uk/1/hi/sci/tech/6247199.stm.

Bibliography

Albrecht, Donald. *Designing Dreams*. New York: Harper & Row, Publishers, Inc., in collaboration with The Museum of Modern Art, 1986.

Bush, Donald J. *The Streamlined Decade*. New York: George Braziller, Inc., 1975.

Caro, Robert A. *The Power Broker*. New York: Random House, Inc., 1975.

Conrads, Ulrich, *Programs and Manifestoes on 20th Century Architecture*, Cambridge, MA: MIT Press, 1964.

Copeland, Lewis, Lawrence W. Lamm, and Stephen J. McKenna. *The World's Great Speeches*, Mineola, NY: Dover Publications, Inc., 1991.

Curtis, William J.R. *Modern Architecture since 1900*. Englewood Cliffs, NJ: Prentice-Hall, Inc., 1987.

De Vallee, Sheila. *Architecture for the Future*, Paris: Terrail, 1996.

Dormer, Peter. Introduction to *The Illustrated Dictionary of Twentieth Century Designers*. New York: Mallard Press, 1991.

Eaton, Ruth. *Ideal Cities*. New York: Thames and Hudson Inc., 2002.

Ettedgui, Peter. *Production Design & Art Direction*. Woburn, MA: Focal Press, 1998.

Frampton, Kenneth. *Modern Architecture a Critical History*. London: Thames and Hudson Ltd, 1985.

Fuller, R. Buckminster. *Critical Path*. New York: St. Martin's Press, 1981.

Fuller, R. Buckminster. *Ideas and Integrities*. New York: Collier Books, 1963.

Gorman, Carma, editor. *The Industrial Design Reader*. New York: Allworth Press, New York, 2003.

Hellemans, Alexander, and Bryan Bunch. *The Timetables of Science*, Simon & Schuster, New York, 1998.

Herwig, Oliver. *Featherweights*. Munich: Prestel Verlag, 2003.

Hodgson, Godfrey. *People's Century 1900–1999*. New York: Times Books, Random House, Inc., 1998.

Jencks, Charles. *The Iconic Building*. New York: Rizzoli International Publications, 2005.

Jodidio, Philip. *Architecture NOW!* Cologne: Taschen GMBH, 2001.

Johnson, Paul. *Modern Times*. New York: Harper & Row, Publishers, Inc., 1983.

Koolhaas, Rem. *Delirious New York*. New York: Oxford University Press, 1978.

Le Corbusier. *The City of To-morrow and its Planning*. New York: Dover Publications, Inc., 1987.

Mansfield, Howard. *Cosmopolis: Yesterday's Cities of the Future*. New Brunswick, NJ: Center for Urban Policy Research, 1990.

Mau, Bruce. *Massive Change*. London: Phaidon Press Ltd, 2004.

McCarter, Robert. *Frank Lloyd Wright*, London: Phaidon Press Ltd, 1997.

McQuaid, Matilda. *Extreme Textiles*. New York: Princeton Architectural Press, in association with National Design Museum Smithsonian Institution, 2005.

Myers, Norman. *The Gaia Atlas of Future Worlds*. London: Doubleday, 1990.

Neumann, Dietrich. *Film Architecture: Set Designs from Metropolis to Blade Runner*. Munich: Prestel Verlag, 1999.

Noblet, Jocelyn de. *Industrial Design Reflections of a Century*. Paris: Flammarion/ADAGP, 1993.

Prina, Francesca with Elena Demartini. *One Thousand Years of World Architecture*. Milan: Mondadori Electa spa, 2005.

Raizman, David. *History of Modern Design*. Upper Saddle River, NJ: Prentice Hall Inc., 2004.

Serraino, Pierluigi. *Eero Saarinen*. Cologne: Taschen GMBH, 2005.

John Ormsbee, in *Earthscape*, McGraw Hill, Inc., New York, 1978.

Sorenson, Charles E. *My Forty Years with Ford*. New York: Collier Books, 1956.

Sparke, Penny. *A Century of Design*. Hauppauge, NY: Barron's Educational Series, Inc., 1998.

Thomsen, Christian W. *Visionary Architecture*. Munich and New York: Prestel Verlag, 1994.

Ward, Janet. *Weimar Surfaces, Urban Visual Culture in 1920s Germany*. Berkeley, CA: University of California Press, 2001.

Waters, John K. *Blobitecture*. Gloucester, MA: Rockport Publishers, Inc., 2003.

Wilson, Richard Guy, Dianne H. Pilgrim, and Dikran Tashjian. *The Machine Age in America 1918–1941*. New York: The Brooklyn Museum in association with Harry N. Abrams, Inc., 1986.

Wright, Frank Lloyd. *The Future of Architecture*. New York: New American Library, 1953.

Index

Acknowledgments

I would first like to express my gratitude to Inge Heckel, former president of the New York School of Interior Design, who provided insight, encouragement, and support for this book.

I am grateful for the support of the Graham Foundation, New York State Council of the Arts, and the J.M. Kaplan Fund, which made it possible for me to develop the early research on emerging technologies and planning concepts that served as a basis for this book.

It has been a pleasure to work with the creative team that has given the book its form: Elizabeth White and Andrea Monfried at The Monacelli Press and Susan Evans at Design Per Se. Photo researcher Laura Wyss located and acquired an exceptionally diverse group of images, with assistance from Susan Lovell, director of publications at NYSID. I was also fortunate in having the advice of Janet Fries, who provided valuable information on copyrights and legal issues related to the book.

I would also like to acknowledge those who have broadened my understanding of twentieth-century movements. I first became interested in visionary theories when I was a philosophy student at Smith College and a political activist. Later, while studying architecture at Columbia, I began to see parallel concepts in architecture through Kenneth Frampton's lectures on modernism and his book *Modern Architecture*.

Subsequent work on several documentary films introduced me to the designs of Buckminster Fuller, Yona Friedman, Paolo Soleri, and other conceptual designers. Stefan Sharf, a Russian filmmaker, helped me to understand the vast problems of introducing art and technology in post-revolutionary Russia. John Houseman provided a vivid account of the role of media and information systems during the war years.

Meetings of American Macroengineering Society expanded my knowledge of infrastructure and environmental issues. Discussions with Frank Davidson, founder of the Channel Tunnel Study Group and advisor to NASA, were especially helpful in clarifying the issues of large-scale environmental projects.

The book could not have been compiled without the remarkable projects of the architects and designers included in these pages. Some of them are also longtime friends and colleagues, who not only contributed handsome images of their work but also provided valuable insights. Discussions with James Wines of SITE and Nicholas Goldsmith of FTL were helpful in compiling the last chapters. Texts by Michael Sorkin, Ruth Eaton, Matilda McQuaid, William Curtis, and Charles Jencks served as key references.

Finally, I would also like to thank my parents for their encouragement. My mother located a few rare texts on city planning. My father, who manufactured furniture for several designers in the book, explained postwar assembly methods, as well as the current challenge of adapting green systems into the manufacturing process.

Credits

Chapter 1— *8–9*: UFA/The Kobal Collection, *11*: Art Archive/Kunsthistorisches Museum Vienna, *12*: Archivio Pubbli Aer Foto/Aerocentro Varesino, *14 right*: Réunion des Musées Nationaux/Art Resource, New York, *15*, *18–19*: akg-images, *20*: © Bibliotheque Nationale, Paris, France/Lauros/Giraudon/The Bridgeman Art Library, *22*: © Joe Sohm/The Image Works, *24*: © Bettmann/Corbis, *26*: akg-images, *27*: Courtesy of Unilever from an original in the care of Unilever Archives, *29*: © Bettmann/Corbis, *31*: © Yann Arthus-Bertrand/Corbis, *32*: © Worldscapes/age fotostock, *33*: Hulton Archive/Getty Images, *34*: © LL/Roger-Viollet/The Image Works, *35*: The Art Archive/Culver Pictures, *37*: © Thomas A. Heinz/Corbis, *38*: Scientific American, July 16, 1913, *39*: © PoodlesRock/Corbis, *40*: © Bettmann/Corbis, *42*: Hertfordshire Archives and Local Studies. Document reference: DE/Ho/F4/1, *47*: © Paul Almasy/Corbis, *48*: © Archivo Iconografico, S.A./Corbis, *50*: © Bettmann/Corbis

Chapter 2— *54*: Hulton Archive/Getty Images, *55*: Alinari/Art Resource, New York, © 2008 Artists Rights Society (ARS) New York/Beeldrecht, Amsterdam. *57*: akg-images/Archives CDA/Guillot, *58 top*: Automobilismo Storico Alfa Romeo, Centro Documentazione, Milan, *58 bottom*: akg-images/Electa, *60*: Hulton Archive/Getty Images, *61*: Digital Image © The Museum of Modern Art/Licensed by SCALA/Art Resource, New York, art © V. & G. Stenberg/RAO, Moscow/VAGA, New York, *63*: © Sovfoto, *64*: © Private Collection/The Bridgeman Art Library, *66 bottom*: akg-images/RIA Novosti, *67*: akg-images, *69*: akg-images/Bildarchiv Monheim, *70*, *72*: akg-images/ullstein bild, *73*: akg-images/Erik Bohr, *74 top*: © 2008 Bühnen Archiv Oskar Schlemmer/The Oskar Schlemmer Theatre Estate: 28824 Oggebbio (VB), Italy, *74 bottom*: © Dr. Stephan Consemüller/photo: Bauhaus-Archiv Berlin *76*: © VG Bild-Kunst Bonn, 2007/photo: Bauhaus-Archiv Berlin/Hermann Kiessling, *77*: © VG Bild-Kunst Bonn, 2007/photo: Bauhaus-Archiv Berlin *78 top*: Photography © The Art Institute of Chicago, *78 bottom*: Ezra Stoller © Esto, *80*: ullstein bild/The Granger Collection, New York, *81 left*: Erich Lessing/Art Resource, New York © 2008 Artists Rights Society (ARS) New York, *81 right*: © 2008 Artists Rights Society (ARS) New York/ADAGP, Paris/FLC, *82*: NAI, Rotterdam/EFL Foundation, The Hague archive+inv.nr.: EEST III.250, *83*: Ezra Stoller © Esto, *84*: Photo Rauno Träskelin, *85 right*: © LFC/ARS, *86*: Fabrizio Carraro/artur, *87*: akg-images/L. M. Peter

Chapter 3— *92*: Avery Architectural and Fine Arts Library, Columbia University, *94*: © Lawrence Manning/Corbis, *95–96*: Harry Ransom Humanities Research Center/The University of Texas at Austin, *97*: akg-images, *98*: Henry Dreyfuss Collection, Cooper-Hewitt, National Design Museum, Smithsonian Institution. Gift of Henry Dreyfuss, *100–1*: Department of the Interior, Bureau of Reclamation *102*: Time & Life Pictures/Getty Images, *103*: Horace Abrahams/Getty Images, *104*: Madelon Vriesendorp, 1974, *105*: © Michael S. Yamashita/ Corbis, *106*: The New-York Historical Society, *107:* courtesy Princeton Architectural Press, *109 top*: © 2008 The Frank Lloyd Wright Foundation/Art Resource, New York, © ARS, New York, *109 bottom*: Ezra Stoller © Esto, *110*: © Bettmann/Corbis, *113 top*: Everett Collection, *113 bottom*: Warner Bros./The Kobal Collection, *114*: Fox/Photofest, *115*: © Bettmann/ Corbis, *116*: Library of Congress, *117*: © 2007 GM Corp. Used with permission, GM Media Archive, *118 left*: Henry Dreyfuss Collection, Cooper-Hewitt, National Design Museum, Smithsonian Institution. Gift of Henry Dreyfuss, 1972-88-258-3, *118 right*: © Underwood & Underwood/Corbis, *120*: Digital Image © The Museum of Modern Art/Licensed by SCALA/Art Resource, New York © 2008 Artists Rights Society (ARS) New York/ADAGP, Paris

Chapter 4— *124*: © 2007 GM Corp. Used with permission, GM Media Archive, *126*: © Yann Arthus-Bertrand/Corbis, *127*: © LFC/ARS, *129 bottom*: The Granger Collection, New York, *131*: Palmer/ClassicStock.com, *132*: Fox Photos/Getty Images, *133*: Private Collection/Photo © Bonhams, London, UK/The Bridgeman Art Library, *134*: © Hulton-Deutsch Collection/Corbis, *136*: Photo by Harrison/Getty Images, *137*: © TASS/Sovfoto, *138*: Ezra Stoller © Esto, *140 top*: Getty Images, *140 bottom*: © Christie's Images Limited [1996], *143*: National Archives Administration, *144*: Alan Band/Keystone/Getty Images, *145*: Tim Street-Porter/Esto, *146*: courtesy Estate of R. Buckminster Fuller, *148*: V&A Images/Victoria and Albert Museum, *150*: The Kobal Collection/Tobis, *151 top*: Chaplin/ United Artists/The Kobal Collection, *151 bottom*: photos12/Polaris Images, *153*: Warner Bros. Pictures/Photofest, *155 top*: Columbia Pictures/Photofest, *155 bottom*: Getty Images, *156*: Getty Images, *157*: Alex S. MacLean/Landslides. www.alexmaclean.com

Chapter 5—*162–63*: NASA Photo, *164*: © 2007 GM Corp. Used with permission, GM Media Archive, *165*: © Angelo Hornak/Corbis, *166*: Ezra Stoller © Esto, *167 top*: H. Khan/RWU Studio, *167 bottom*: © Joerg Schoener/artur, *169*: Réunion des Musées Nationaux/Art Resource, New York, *170–71*: Archigram Archives, *173*: © GA Photographers, *174 left*: CNAC/MNAM/Dist. Réunion des Musées Nationaux/Art Resource, New York, *174 right*: Kikutake Architects, *175*: © Jean Francois Pin/AA Travel/Topfoto/The Image Works, *176*: Kord.com/agefotostock, *177*: ILEK Institut für Leichtbau Entwerfen und Konstruieren, Universität Stuttgart, Germany, *179*: NASA Photo, *180*: courtesy WATG, *181*: NASA Photo, *183*: MGM/The Kobal Collection, *185*: DAN-JAQ/EON/UA/ The Kobal Collection, *187*: © 1976 Babette Magolte, All Rights of Reproduction Reserved, *188*: CNAC/MNAM/Dist. Réunion des Musées Nationaux/Art Resource, New York, *189*: Arakawa + Gins, Yoro Park, *190 top, bottom*: courtesy Estate of R. Buckminster Fuller, *192*: © Roger Ressmeyer/Corbis

Chapter 6— *196*: © Bettmann/Corbis, *197*: Foto Marburg/Art Resource, New York, *198*: SITE, New York, *199*: Matt Wargo, Courtesy Venturi, Scott Brown and Associates, Inc., *200*: © Grant Mudford, *201*: Time & Life Pictures/Getty Images, *202*: Scott Jackson/ PhotosFlorida.com, *203*: © Free Agents Limited/Corbis, *204*: © Steve Vidler/SuperStock, *205*: © Richard Cummins/ Corbis, *207*: CCTV/OMA Rem Koolhaas and Ole Scheeren Image, courtesy OMA, *209*: Ateliers Jean Nouvel, *210*: © Michael Moran, *211 top*: Asymptote: Hani Rashid + Lise Anne Couture, *211 bottom*: Arc Photo Eduard Hueber, *212*: © Peter Eisenman, *213*: © Steve Vidler/SuperStock, *214*: akg-images/ Bildarchiv Monheim, *215*: © Dirk Robbers/artur, *216*: ©Jochen Helle/artur, *217*: © Wolfram Janzer/artur, *219*: Umbrella/Rosenblum/Virgin Films/The Kobal Collection, *220*: Universal/Embassy/The Kobal Collection, *221*: Columbia Pictures/Photofest, *222*: © 20th Century Fox Film Corp. All rights reserved. Courtesy: Everett Collection, *223*: Wolfgang Volz/laif/Redux, *225*: Getty Images

Chapter 7— *230–31*: © Yann Arthus-Bertrand/Corbis, *232*: SITE, New York, *233*: Ivan Pintar, *234*: Hirome Watanabe, Photographer/Emilio Ambasz & Associates, *235*: © Bernard Bisson/ Sygma/Corbis, *236*: Charlotte Wood/arcaid.co.uk, *237*: © Tim Griffith/Esto, *238*: William McDonough + Partners, *239*: MVRDV, 1998, *240*: ullstein bild - Wolfram/The Granger Collection, New York, *243*: IPPUC, Curtiba, Brazil, *244*: MIT Solar Electric Vehicle Team, *245*: Grant Smith/ VIEW/Esto, *246*: © Nigel Young/Foster + Partners, *247 top*: Jeff Goldberg/Esto, *247 bottom*: Roland Halbe/Artur/VIEW, *248*: lbert Vecerka/Esto, *249*: Mitsuo Matsuoka, *251*: © Yann Arthus-Bertrand/Corbis, *252*: BOCOG/ Getty Images, *253*: Peter J. Schulz, *254*: Benny Chan/Fotoworks, *255*: Ramak Fazel/Asymptote: Hani Rashid + Lise Anne Couture, *256–257 top, bottom*: FTL Design Engineering Studio, *258*: © Roland Halbe/artur, *259*: © Yann Arthus-Bertrand/Altitude, *260*: Project credit: Jennifer Siegal, Office of Mobile Design, photo credit: Benny Chan/Fotoworks, *262*: © Xiaoyang Liu/Corbis, *263*: © Yann Arthus-Bertrand/Corbis, *264*: © Yann Arthus-Bertrand/Altitude, *265–56*: Ladd Company/Warner Bros/The Kobal Collection

About the Author

Donna Goodman is an architect and educator based in New York City. She studied art and philosphy at Smith College and architecture at Columbia University. In addition to her practice, Ms. Goodman has developed of drawings of a conceptual future city that present new urban and environmental concepts for cities, media and cybernetic systems, infrastructure, and resources. Her projects have been widely published and exhibited.

Digital Center, 2005.

Digital Center introduces a large teleconference center that allows individuals to participate in activities in distant locations without traveling. The space can also accommodate exhibitions of digital art and information systems.

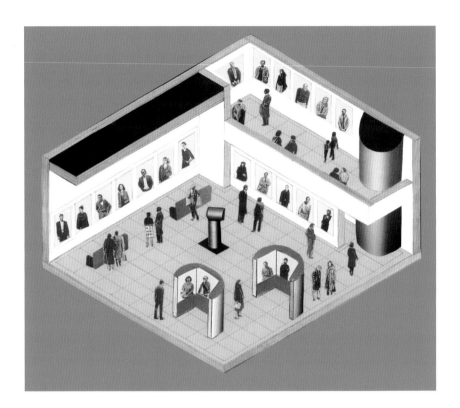

The Urban Underground, 1990–91.

The Urban Underground presents the idea of using subway systems for other services—trash collection, recycling, mail and package deliveries—during off-peak hours. This concept would reduce service traffic on the streets and provide additional revenue for the subway system.